THE
INDONESIAN
TABLE

THE INDONESIAN TABLE

Petty Pandean-Elliott

 Vegetarian

 Vegan

 Dairy-free

Gluten-free

Nut-free

 30 Minutes or Less

5 Ingredients or Fewer

Introduction

INDONESIA, *Ibu Pertiwi*, Mother Earth for over 270 million people and an archipelago of 17,000 islands, is a maritime crossroads between Europe, the Middle East and the Asia-Pacific. In centuries past, it was world-renowned as The Spice Islands, the home of nutmeg, mace and cloves (page 25). Today, it offers a fascinating and diverse cuisine with many flavours, ingredients and surprises. It is the fourth-most populous country in the world, spread over three time zones, with more than 700 local languages. Combine this national diversity in culture, food and beliefs with the outside influences of traders and travellers, and you will begin to appreciate the sheer variety of dishes on the Indonesian table.

This book recollects my culinary journeys through Indonesia, beginning inevitably with my childhood in Manado – a distant north-east corner of Indonesia, the heart of a vast coral triangle and a centre of trade in vanilla, cloves, nutmeg, coconut products and seafood.

The Journey from Manado, North Sulawesi

I can see it all now. My grandfather's verdant coconut plantations set against postcard-worthy volcanic mountains. Pristine beaches skirting coral reefs teeming with marine life. It's a view that triggers memories of the food of my childhood, from mouth-watering candied nutmeg (*manisan pala*) to breakfasts of Banana Fritters (page 61) served alongside slices of soft white bread and chocolate sprinkles (*meises*), fragrant fish stews and Sweetcorn Fritters (page 143).

Tropical seas surround Manado, so naturally one of my favourite foods is fish. We love to barbecue and serve it with *dabu-dabu*, a relish of fresh tomatoes, shallots, chillies, calamansi and mint (page 48). This and many other Manadonese recipes are a world away from the most ubiquitous Indonesian dishes such as Chicken Satay (page 115), Nasi Goreng (page 203) and Beef Rendang (page 134). For instance, in Manado, we have the delightful fish stew with fresh root spices and herbs (*ikan woku blanga*) and a braised chicken dish with turmeric and coconut (*ayam tuturuga*, page 125). We also have the cuisine of the Peranakan, descendants of early Chinese migrants who married locally. National favourites include Sweet Coconut and Pandan Pancakes (page 63) and Pineapple Biscuits (page 235).

Historic Dutch influences are very much part of mealtimes in Manado and especially in my family, as my paternal grandmother was half-Dutch. There's *klapertart*, a pudding made with young coconut, vanilla custard, rum, raisins and almonds and topped with cinnamon dust. We also have Cheese Sticks (page 236) and the heart-warming *brenebon* soup (page 98), which combines kidney beans with nutmeg, cloves, spring onions (scallions) and pork.

And just as Indonesian spices have become a permanent feature in world cookery, Indonesians have adopted and adapted many outside dishes and ingredients. The Indonesian table is rich in history, heritage, colours, texture, taste, aroma and variety. The Minahasan people of North Sulawesi are known for their love of fiery cuisine, blending the heat of chillies and ginger with fragrant lemon basil, lemongrass and lime leaves. (Portuguese and Spanish explorers introduced chillies to Indonesia.) Although Indonesia has the biggest Muslim population globally, a strong following of Protestant and Catholic faiths allows pork to be widely consumed in Manado.

It has been more than four decades since I left the city, yet I still think of Manado as my home. Those precious early food experiences have had a powerful impact not only on the way I cook but also on my whole approach to food – and the catalyst was my maternal grandmother, Oma. How I miss her. My three siblings and I would spend several days a week after school with Oma before our parents came home from work.

Oma had the brightest smile and always wore the traditional dress of a *kebaya*, a tunic-like blouse with a batik sarong. Her large earthen-floored kitchen was a hub of activity, with the constant crackle from her wood-burning stove generating wonderful aromas from bubbling woks. The distinctive fragrance of her home-made coconut cooking oil is never far from my mind.

In a huge garden canopied by coconut palms, she grew root spices, herbs, chillies and vegetables and kept chickens. I would collect eggs, uproot fresh root spices such as galangal and ginger, and pluck chillies and lemon basil *(kemangi)* leaves off plants. The abundance of ingredients from the garden and local market meant little need for other food shopping.

I learned how to slaughter and prepare chicken and gut fish. Such skills sound so out of place in today's world. Oma taught me about taste and smell, to appreciate each fresh root spice and herb and how to develop and evolve the flavour of any dish with a succession of ingredients and timely seasoning during cooking – when and in what order. I was lucky to be taught such skills at an early age, and it has been my pleasure to pass them on to my children, now grown up.

Sundays were always special, with everyone dressed smartly for church. Afterwards, it was straight home for the family lunch. Our Manadonese table was modernly laid, each setting with a spoon and fork (or *leper* and *forok*). No knives were used at mealtimes, and it was not until we had moved to Jakarta that I tried eating with chopsticks.

Food was generally served family-style on the dining table, everyone helping themselves from platters of fish, pork or chicken, stir-fried vegetables and potato fritters *(perkedel kentang)*, all served alongside steamed rice or Sweetcorn Rice (page 201). For a treat, we might eat out in the city centre at a Chinese-Manadonese-style restaurant or a local eatery, enjoying regional dishes such as Makassar Beef Coto, a beef soup with spices and peanuts from South Sulawesi (page 105).

Christmas was the most important time of the year in Manado. Congregations would spill into the churchyard to listen to the service on the loudspeakers. Seasonal feasts were always grand, with my mum, Oma and aunties preparing an endless stream of dishes, replenished throughout the day to ensure any visiting guests could join in whenever they arrived. This included traditional pork and ginger coconut rice as well as a glutinous rice dish with ginger, shallots and coconut milk (page 198), both cooked in bamboo over a wood fire. The tradition of eating with the hands, direct from banana leaves, added something special to the meal's enjoyment – and there was no washing up afterwards!

The Tastes of Java and Beyond

The pleasures of early childhood were interrupted by a move to the capital city of Jakarta, as my father's work responsibilities increased. Also, my mum and dad believed that my siblings and I would gain a better education and broaden our minds from the experience. So, at the age of thirteen, I found myself aboard a large ship sailing through the Makassar Straits and across the Java Sea to Tanjung Priok, Indonesia's busiest seaport. Jakarta was a fast-growing city in the early 1980s, a melting pot of culinary and cultural influences from around the Indonesian archipelago and the outside world. It was a journey into a new life, culture and even language. As I'd been brought up in Manado, with its own language, it took several months at school for me to sharpen my Indonesian as well as the Jakartan dialect and, on top of that, English. I had a modest upbringing – we did not have overseas holidays, nor did we even island-hop around Indonesia – but my parents provided me with a rich and valuable childhood, driven by selflessness, unconditional love and the determination to give us a first-class education at Jakarta's top private school.

My mum was born and raised in Jakarta, so we always had fun visiting her favourite food haunts in and around Chinatown, including her best-loved noodle place in Pasar Baru (Jakarta's oldest market, established in 1884) or Pasar Senen (the famed 'Monday' market). These experiences would often end with a visit to Ragusa, the city's oldest ice cream parlour. Like many Manadonese women, my mum is fiercely independent, outspoken and never one to mince her words. I grew up surrounded by strong women who taught me to be self-confident and assured in my values.

In Jakarta, I discovered new dishes and drinks such as tempeh, *Gado-Gado* (page 86) and *nasi uduk*, the steamed rice dish from the Betawis (an Austronesian ethnic group indigenous to Jakarta and its outskirts). I tasted many different types of noodles, curries and *nasi padang*, a famous West Sumatra-styled rice platter with vegetables, boiled egg balado (an egg dish with sambal) and, on occasion, a meat protein such as chicken curry or Beef Rendang (page 134). Then, there were the Java herbal drinks *(jamu)* and icy drinks with young coconut flesh, avocados and jackfruit (page 242).

The choice of regional street foods seemed endless, from the pushcart vendors (kaki lima) to hawker markets to traditional warung eateries under colourful canvases. There were Indonesian-Chinese and Indonesian-European dishes and dishes with Middle Eastern and Indian influences – together, they created a culinary kaleidoscope of traditions, cultures and histories.

My school friends and I would sit on coloured plastic stools, chatting and laughing over steaming bowls of Jakartan Chicken Noodles (page 214), Siomay dumplings (page 66) or Rice Noodle Soup with Meatballs (page 109). The only problem was the lack of a table. To avoid scalding our hands from the hot noodle bowl, an extra empty bowl was added for insulation and protection. On trips out of the city to Bandung (West Java), Jogjakarta and Solo (both in Central Java), we would dine in warungs, sitting cross-legged on the floor at the traditional low-level tables known as lesehan or spinning the turntables in Chinese restaurants.

Growing up in Indonesia's capital, the centre of culture, economy and politics of thousands of islands provided me with a knowledge of regional Indonesian cuisine and a deeper understanding and appreciation of diversity. Each island and region is defined by its unique cuisine, history, culture, art, language and identity. At the same time, the national motto 'unity in diversity' (page 14) has been paramount to building Indonesia as a nation, living together in peace and harmony yet celebrating the many cultural and ethnic differences within its borders. We are in total unison on one subject: we believe Indonesian food is the best.

I worked at a busy international advertising agency before settling down to a new chapter: married life. This proved a real turning point. Entertaining friends and family at our new home reawakened my interest in cooking. Sadly, Oma was no longer with us, and she had never put her recipes on paper, but I began to reconstruct my culinary past with the help of my mother, aunties and cousins. Gradually, I took cooking more seriously, exploring Indonesia's rich regional cuisines with travels around Java, Bali, Lombok and Sumatra, as well as trips abroad to experience international cuisine during family holidays.

The time spent in Oma's kitchen gave me a strong foundation. She passed on an understanding of how to create basic spice pastes (bumbu, page 43) and ways to combine them with dry spice blends (rempah) and fresh herbs (rempah daun). She had instilled in me valuable culinary knowledge and the building blocks for regional Indonesian cuisine.

Those early culinary influences and experiences proved to be important from another perspective. They were a common denominator: so vital in local conversations during market visits or on volunteering trips where I would feast at long wooden tables in north Bali or sitting cross-legged on the floor of a thatched homestead in the Wae Rebo village of East Nusa Tenggara. I was happy, whether enjoying fried bananas on Friwen in the islands of Raja Ampat, dining at the sultan's palace in Solo, Central Java, or curating menus for a state dinner at the presidential palace in Jakarta. I realized that, across Indonesian cuisine, we share so much in common.

A New Direction

Moving to the United Kingdom, Indonesian food was my key to building friendships. My neighbours and new acquaintances were all keen to try the dishes. Most were experiencing it for the first time, although a few recalled good memories of holidays in Bali. I was shocked to discover that only a handful of Indonesian restaurants existed in the UK, but that is changing. Moreover, Indonesian tempeh (page 152) is gaining real traction with the young and the health-conscious around the world, and an appreciation of Indonesian coffee and coconut products is on the rise.

I have a vision for modern Indonesian cuisine: to preserve the great traditions of classic recipes while exploring exciting, new possibilities. I believe in using fresh, local ingredients wherever possible and applying simple cooking techniques. Flavours must be layered to enliven the palate, and colour is essential on the plate. Food can be simple, but it should never be dull.

I am all too aware of the challenges confronted by home cooks when specific ingredients are difficult to find or prohibitively costly. In the interest of making my national cuisine more accessible, I've included a range of easy recipes that can be re-created with common ingredients available in most supermarkets. This way, newcomers to Indonesian food can quickly grasp the fundamentals and learn to prepare our food with ease, all of which help to make the cooking and dining experience fun and enjoyable.

I am often asked, 'What exactly is Indonesian food?' Yes, we are known for skewered satays, delightful beef rendang and sambal, but there is much more on the Indonesian table. Historically, Indonesian cuisine has been influenced by cultures from around the world, and vice versa. At one point, Indonesia was the centre of nutmeg and clove trade and remains a top producer today. The marriage of Arabic, Indian, European (Dutch, Portuguese and Spanish), Chinese and Peranakan influences with our indigenous ingredients has culminated in a fantastically original culinary tapestry. And this defines our Indonesian food culture.

It has been a magical opportunity to explore the Indonesian archipelago and discover the landscape, the people, history and culture. My experiences and curiosity for food have truly helped me hone my craft, but I must also give credit to the people who set me on this path and fostered my love for Indonesian food: my Oma, my mother, my aunties and the many wonderful people and Indonesian food heroes who have become my friends and my colleagues today.

With this book, I hope readers enjoy discovering the food culture of my homeland through the tastes, aromas and textures of the local cuisine. Indonesian cooking is a celebration of diversity and all about layering flavours to create good food for the body and soul.

Unity in Diversity

Bhinneka Tunggal Ika

Indonesia's distinct yet elegant national motto 'Unity in Diversity' embodies our nation's independence and binds the people of this vast archipelago together.

The diversity is evident: we have 17,000 islands, 1,300 ethnic groups, 700 languages and six main religions. And while Javanese is the most widely spoken 'local' language (40 per cent of the population inhabit Java), everyone must learn Bahasa Indonesian, our official and national language.

The Indonesian term *Bhinneka Tunggal Ika* originates from ancient stories of the Javanese *Prince Sutasoma* by the famous Indonesian poet Mpu Tantular who, during the Majapahit kingdom in the fourteenth century, promoted tolerance of Hinduism and Buddhism. It signifies the importance of living harmoniously among modern Indonesia's many different ethnicities, cultures and beliefs.

This precept is a reminder to strike a balance between the interests of the individual and those of society, to prevent the oppression of the weak by the strong. It has become my guiding principle to embrace and celebrate diversity with those in Indonesia and worldwide. While we may have differences, our shared similarities are even stronger. And we build connections and bonds through food culture.

Regional Cuisine

Much of our regional cuisine has been shaped by the outside cultural influences brought to the archipelago centuries ago, and Indonesians are so proud of those deeply rooted local dishes that define us and connect us to our history. To enjoy the wide variety of Indonesian cuisine, one must understand the background of local culture – from areas where spice is barely used to the regions that revel in it, from east to west.

The food of my birthplace in Sulawesi, for example, is different to that of Java, where I spent my teenage and adult life. And so it goes for the rest of the archipelago. The combinations of spice pastes *(bumbu)* and spice blends *(rempah)* often say more about the history of outside influences of merchants and explorers than the region where they were first used. For example, the humble fishing communities of the Banda Islands use mace in their fish recipes, yet only few of them today understand its importance in the culinary traditions of the Western world.

As *The Indonesian Table* is, first and foremost, an introduction to Indonesian gastronomy, I have chosen to highlight the food traditions of eight key regions – Sulawesi, Java, Bali, Nusa Tenggara, Maluku Islands, Sumatra, Papua and Kalimantan. These regions have had the greatest influence on our gastronomy today, and I've ordered them according to their significance vis-à-vis my own food journey.

Throughout my career as a chef and a food writer, I have travelled the archipelago to experience the many cuisines of my homeland. Living abroad has changed my perception of Indonesia and its regional food culture. I wanted to dig deeper into my Manadonese heritage, create connections with provincial cuisine and discover new local fare.

Visiting traditional markets in remote areas was a great place to start. It reminded me of childhood days accompanying my Oma around fresh seafood and produce stalls, so colourful and vibrant, with the stallholders' cries ringing in my ears. Time spent with indigenous communities was equally valuable – just watching them cook food in bamboo set over wood fires triggered recollections of my own childhood in Oma's kitchen when we would prepare meals together, gathering herbs and vegetables from the garden and witnessing the magic of food in the making.

The Indonesian table is a unique tapestry of culture, history and biodiversity. I have ventured around the archipelago to discover that they always connect me to the same place: my childhood in Manado, North Sulawesi. So here is where I start to share my journey around the largest island nation on Earth.

Sulawesi

A distinctively shaped island of four peninsulas in north-eastern Indonesia, Sulawesi (formerly known as the Celebes) is famed for its scuba diving and snorkelling, pristine natural beauty and fantastic coral reefs. The Minahasans in the north and the Bugis community in the south, descendants of the kingdom of Gowa, are well-known for their customs, ceremonies and food. The ancient burial sites of the Toraja highlands, located in the centre of the island, offer fascinating cultural insights.

Long before European missionaries arrived to spread Christianity, the Minahasan people were uniquely identified by their rituals and craft skills, including a highly distinctive textile tradition. Sadly, much of this has disappeared over time, but thanks to the Manado community in Jakarta, *bentenan* cloth-making has been reintroduced and is now widely available.

North Sulawesi, my birthplace, is a centre of Christianity with considerable European influence and a stark contrast to, say, the Islamic background of Java and southern Sulawesi. My Manadonese upbringing was filled with a variety of food, reflecting a diverse family background and the abundance of fresh ingredients available on the island.

It is here where my grandmother introduced me to cooking. She taught me how to make the basic spice pastes *(bumbu)* and spice blends *(rempah)* that defined Manadonese cooking. These aromas, colours and textures of Manado cuisine provided me with a strong foundation of our food culture and aided my appreciation for other cuisines around the archipelago.

We in Manado favour spiciness and commonly use a fiery Rica-Rica (page 116) to season our dishes. In this coastal region, fish is the protein of choice and, here, skipjack tuna smoked on a bamboo frame *(cakalang fufu)* is featured in many dishes, such as a filling for Spicy Empanadas (page 65). Another signature Manadonese dish is *Bubur Manado* (page 204), a rice porridge with spinach, pumpkin, sweetcorn and sweet potatoes. Pork is widely available in the north and the centre but less so in the south with its predominantly Muslim population. One of my favourite dishes is Sour Fish Soup (page 94), a simple infusion of tomatoes, lemongrass and makrut lime leaves. It is perfect for serving hot or chilled alongside a plate of lightly fried Sweetcorn Fritters (page 143).

As the largest city and capital of South Sulawesi, Makassar is home to the eponymous Makassar Beef Coto (page 105), a traditional beef stew seasoned with garlic, galangal, lemongrass, spices and umami-rich miso sambal – a dish I first experienced dining out with my parents. I also adore the Prawn and Seaweed Salad with Spiced Coconut Dressing of South Sulawesi (page 82) and Steamed Plantain with Strawberry Granita and Coconut Custard (page 226).

Most inhabitants of Sulawesi earn their living from agriculture, trading, forestry and fishing. Seafood is plentiful and coconuts, cloves, coffee and cocoa are essential crops.

Java

Our family moved to Indonesia's capital Jakarta when I was thirteen years old; it is the city where I spent my formative teenage years and most of my adult life. It is where I studied, worked, married and raised my children. Jakarta, my home for over thirty years, has a special place in my heart.

Java has a rich culinary heritage, and the food is next to none. The people of this island province gave us tempeh (page 152), the fermented soy-based superfood; the delicious Sour Tumeric herbal drink (page 246); satisfying bowls of soto and, of course, grilled satay with sweet, spicy and tangy peanut sauce (page 115). In fact, sweet soy sauce and most satays *(sate)* originated in Java. Thanks to its fertile volcanic soils, Java had the perfect conditions for cultivating rice and its practice spread across other major islands.

Taste preferences across the island vary widely. In Central Java, food can be characterized as sweet. In West Java, dishes such as Crudité, Tempeh and Tofu with Shrimp Paste Sambal (page 80) and Vegetables with Kencur and Peanut Sauce (page 88) reveal how vegetables are often served with spicy sauces. And inhabitants on the island's eastern end prefer bolder, spicy, savoury and umami flavours, as seen in ingredients such as *petis,* a fermented prawn paste.

In many ways, Indonesia's food scene has been Java-centric. The magnetism of Java's most significant city Jakarta has brought together different regional cuisines served by those arriving in search of work. Most Betawi (indigenous Jakartans) agree that the city's street food scene is a fair representation of the entire archipelago – a cultural and ethnic melting pot and a great starting point for those seeking to explore regional Indonesian cuisine without having to leave the island. From the famed *Gado-Gado* (page 86) to the coned Turmeric Coconut Rice (page 201) to a delectable Coconut Pudding with Palm Sugar Syrup and Roasted Cashews (page 229), these signature dishes are a taste of regional authenticity.

Bali

As the most popular destination in Indonesia, Bali, along with its neighbouring island of Lombok (see Nusa Tenggara), needs very little introduction. Bali is undeniably beautiful, especially in the tourist areas, where you'll find plenty of five-star resorts and postcard beaches. But beyond this is an unforgettable destination with a vibrant Hindu culture where ritual and ceremony remain a part of daily life. North Bali – from the seventeenth-century port of Singaraja and the farmlands of Kintamani to Nusa Penida and the Nusa Lembongan islands – provides a revelatory experience beyond those in commercial centres.

Bali is home to many dear friends whose lives have intertwined with mine, from a shared attendance at a rare royal burial ceremony to my work over the decades with leading hotels and restaurants on the island.

Some of the island's signature dishes include Seafood Satay (page 112) and a slow-cooked duck wrapped in banana leaves and buried in a coal fire for several hours. Another noteworthy dish from the region is *tipat cantok,* a salad featuring boiled rice cakes, fresh vegetables, fried tempeh, ground peanut dressing and crispy shallots. Omit the boiled eggs and the shrimp paste, and you have yourself a deliciously balanced, plant-based meal.

The basic Balinese spice paste *(base genep)* is an aromatic blend of fresh aromatic roots, garlic, shallots, chillies, lemongrass, makrut lime leaves, candlenuts, nutmeg, coriander seeds, cloves and cinnamon. *Base genep* is often regarded as the mother of *bumbu.*

Nusa Tenggara

To the east of Bali lies the province of Nusa Tenggara, a string of islands which include Lombok, West Nusa Tenggara, Komodo National Park, Sumba and East Nusa Tenggara. These islands are beyond the line drawn over a hundred years ago by naturalist Alfred Wallace to mark biogeographic changes. Unlike the tropical jungles so typical of Bali, here you'll find temperate grasslands and a drier climate more closely associated with northern Australia.

Lombok is known for its popular tourist destination of the Gili Islands and its undeniably delicious and varied cuisine, which includes dishes such as the iconic Roast Chicken (page 183) with sambal and an equally-pleasing vegetable dish of Water Spinach with Shrimp Paste and Tomato Sambal (page 146).

Sumba, one of the closest islands to Australia, exemplifies the sheer diversity of Indonesia's archipelago. Vestiges of the Stone Age are evident in the megalithic tombs seen in every village and town. The indigenous people have preserved and maintained their heritage in tribal dress and traditional stilted houses clustered in hilltop villages. Their beautiful hand-woven ikat textiles are well-known, and ancient subsistence farming methods are still prevalent today. At the annual *Pasola* festival, spear-wielding men on sandalwood ponies joust with vigour, for this is a celebration of rice planting and the hope of a good harvest. Their courage and passion hold a special place in my heart.

North-east of Sumba across the Savu Sea lies the busy seaport of Maumere, on the island of Flores, East Nusa Tenggara, historically known as the 'lesser' Sunda islands. There is nothing 'lesser' about the beauty of the local scenery and the skills of the people. After enjoying the seafood and fresh produce markets in Maumere, we headed inland to spend time with artisans who create stunning handloom woven sarongs and wraps while sharing traditional music and dance with the passing visitor. While I was en route to the multicoloured volcanic lakes of Kelimutu, I met up with a local farmer who encouraged me to choose a pineapple, which he sliced and served with a sprinkling of sea salt and a cup of fresh coconut water. A much longer drive can take you from the southern coastal town of Ende to the charming Wae Rebo village, where I once overnighted before descending to Labuan Bajo, a gateway to Komodo island.

The diet is simple and features little spice. Not surprisingly, the seafood is superb, and local farms offer fresh produce (stunning avocados, pineapples and cashews), poultry and pork. The tasty smoked Aubergine (Eggplant) Sambal (page 50) reminds me of a baba ganoush with cooked chillies, garlic, shallots, basil and coconut. *Se'i* is smoked pork or beef served with a sour and fiery Lemon and Chilli Sambal (page 48) and accompanied by Stir-Fried Leafy Vegetables (page 146). Coffee connoisseurs enjoy top-quality Flores Bajawa coffee with its wonderful aroma and flavour.

Lying just a short 'step' eastward from the popular islands of Bali and Lombok, Sumba, Flores and Labuan Bajo have become new tourist destinations.

Maluku Islands

To the north and further east from Nusa Tenggara lie the Maluku Islands, located in the Banda Sea between Sulawesi and New Guinea. Famously known as The Spice Islands, this is where one will find the highly prized spices, including nutmeg, mace, cloves and cinnamon (page 25).

Mealtime staples include barbecued fish, Seafood and Sago Porridge in Turmeric Broth (page 208) and Raw Tuna in Spicy and Tangy Citrus (page 85). This is also where you might taste a Banda delicacy known as *terong saos kanari*, which combines aubergines with spicy local almonds, or the very popular barbecued seafood with local Tomato and Sweet Soy Sambal (page 176). Rice, a heterochthonous crop to this region, was introduced by the Javanese centuries ago and is now part of everyday diets.

The locals in Ambon, the capital of Maluku province, are famed for their excellent singing voices. Also known as Ambon Manise (meaning sweet Ambon), the city is recognized as a UNESCO City of Music.

Visiting the islands is always a delight, especially Ternate and Tidore in North Maluku. I recently discovered some similarities between their local culinary traditions and those of my birthplace – for instance, the smoked skipjack tuna here *(komu asar)* is not unlike the Manadonese *cakalang fufu*. I suppose many connections and influences from island to island in eastern Indonesia existed even centuries ago.

The local cuisine includes Spiced Tea with Almond Flakes (page 245) and Molucca-Style Smoked Fish and Vegetables with Spiced Coconut (page 156), similar to the Balinese Vegetables with Spiced Coconut (page 156) or the South Sulawesi Prawn and Seaweed Salad with Spiced Coconut Dressing (page 82). The Jailolo Bay Festival in West Halmahera is an unforgettable experience with copious opportunities to sample local dishes and witness ancient tribal rituals. I was surprised to find that they cook not only rice or meat but also vegetables in bamboo.

Sumatra

Sumatra is Indonesia's largest island, located furthest west in the archipelago and more than 5,000 kilometres (3,100 miles) from The Spice Islands. And yet, here, we find some of the nation's richest foods, layered with robust flavours and spices.

The Malacca Strait forms a crucial seaway and historical gateway through which many outside influences have come. This marked the arrival of Islam, the entry of Indian culinary influences and the introduction of chillies by Spanish merchants, as trade grew between Europe, the Middle East and Asia – and, not least, mighty China.

Historically, West Sumatra, with thriving cities such as Padang and Bukittinggi, has been the epicentre for pepper, coffee and gold trade. I have many fond memories of my cooking sessions with the local women, learning to make traditional rendang with fire and a large wok. It is known for its spicy dishes and the well-known *nasi padang*. It is also home to a range of curries *(gulai)* and the famed Beef Rendang (page 134). West Sumatra's dishes are often prepared with local curly red and green chillies, garlic, shallots and dried garcinia fruit *(asam kandis)*, an ingredient regarded for its lip-puckering sourness.

I first visited North Sumatra thirty years ago, travelling around Samosir Island by motorbike and spending time in Batak villages along the shores of Lake Toba, the world's largest volcanic lake. The north of the island gave us the extraordinary Acehnese Noodles (page 217), a spicy fried noodle dish with beef, lamb or seafood and a topping of crispy shallots and cucumber – with its complex flavour profiles of warm curry, sweet soy and tangy lime juice. *Arsik* is a delightful fish stew with fresh Andaliman peppers or Szechuan peppercorns (page 178). This region is well-known for unusual ingredients, such as the sun-dried belimbing *(asam sunti)* and dried garcinia skin *(asam gelugur)*.

Further south, in the city of Palembang, we find the Sumatran classic, Chicken Curry with Pineapple (page 126) and a fish cake *(mpek-mpek)* served with a thin sauce that is, all at once, sour, sweet and spicy.

Papua

This vast, diverse province of rainforests and mountains makes up 22 per cent of Indonesia's total land area. Still, it is home to just over 1.5 per cent of the population, a mix of tribal Papuans living inland, Melanesians on the coasts and, much later in its history, the Malays. Deep in the interior, some people still live in treehouses as they did thousands of years ago.

Locals cultivate sweet potatoes, sago and yams, while the forests provide plantains, wild game, fruits, tubers, mushrooms and insects. As a result, the diet is primarily plant-based, with fish or pork consumed only on special occasions. Papua, being so remote, has very little outside influence. Interestingly, in the largest city Sorong, the food scene has many elements of Manado and Makassar as more and more people have migrated from Sulawesi to this area.

I had the pleasure of working with women in sago-farming communities in the Matemani district in South Sorong. They were keen to share their knowledge of their indigenous ingredients and food culture. Nothing is more authentic than the well-regarded Papuan dish of savoury Seafood and Sago Porridge in Turmeric Broth (page 208).

Sadly, the monoculture of rice, sugar and oil palm crops threatens Papua's natural primary forest habitats. The popularity of imported processed foods, such as instant noodles and biscuits, has also divided the people: some view them as symbols of modern life while others see them as tasteless fare, inferior to nature's larder and the forest food culture.

Kalimantan

Indonesia's Kalimantan comprises over 70 per cent of the enormous island of Borneo, the third largest in the world, with a rich ecology and vast areas of rainforest, coastal peat swamps and extensive river basins. The people are a mix of indigenous tribal Dayaks living inland and Malay Muslims on the coast, with significant Chinese influence, more so than from the various European visitors who have featured in its history.

Not surprisingly, the highly varied diet draws from both wild forest ingredients and local agriculture: tubers, honey, fruits, bushmeat (such as venison and wild boar) and rice. The delicious Grilled Jumbo King Prawns with King's Sambal (page 173) can be enjoyed with vegetables and boiled eggs.

Visiting the district of Benua Anyar within Banjarmasin city, I first sampled authentic Chicken Soto Banjar (page 103), a delicious chicken soup infused with star anise, cloves, cardamom and cinnamon. It reminded me of the home-made Javanese Chicken Soto with Turmeric and Lemongrass (page 103).

The Crispy Pork Belly (page 188) from Ambawang, West Kalimantan, is well-known around the archipelago. The original recipe is traditionally grilled on a barbecue, but I have used a standard oven with excellent results. It is divine when served with *sambal antuha,* a blend of chillies, shrimp paste, calamansi citrus and sugar. This region of the archipelago is likely to become better known when Nusantara in East Kalimantan replaces Jakarta as the national capital.

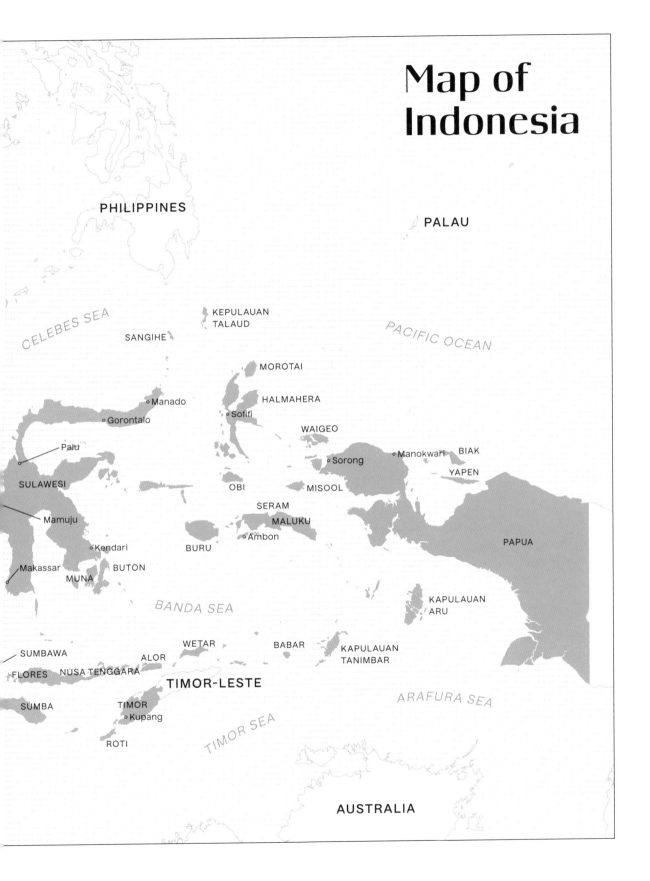

Map of Indonesia

PHILIPPINES

PALAU

CELEBES SEA

KEPULAUAN TALAUD

SANGIHE

PACIFIC OCEAN

MOROTAI

o Manado

HALMAHERA

o Gorontalo

o Sofifi

WAIGEO

Palu

o Sorong

o Manokwari

BIAK

SULAWESI

YAPEN

OBI

MISOOL

Mamuju

SERAM

MALUKU

o Ambon

PAPUA

o Kendari

BURU

Makassar

MUNA

BUTON

BANDA SEA

KAPULAUAN ARU

WETAR

BABAR

SUMBAWA

ALOR

KAPULAUAN TANIMBAR

FLORES

NUSA TENGGARA

TIMOR-LESTE

SUMBA

TIMOR

ARAFURA SEA

o Kupang

ROTI

TIMOR SEA

AUSTRALIA

How We Eat

Food is very personal to Indonesians. There is food at the family table, in restaurants or street-side warungs, for ceremonies and for special occasions. Each is different in the way we approach and enjoy it.

When meeting a friend, work colleague or family member, it is typical to ask, 'Sudah makan belum?' meaning 'Have you eaten?' This is not only a query about whether you have eaten but also, and more importantly, a regard for your welfare and well-being. Depending on the time of day, it becomes an opportunity to enjoy each other's company over a snack, meal or a hot drink. Indonesian meals can be both simple and intricate depending on the occasion – from a bowl of soto or a plate of Gado-Gado (page 86) to as many as twenty dishes at the same time when you dine at a Padang restaurant. In many parts of Indonesia, a wedding party, funeral, birthday or move into a new house is an elaborate affair accompanied by a feast.

Meals at home will be served family-style at the table. Diners will be served a meat, fish or tempeh dish, vegetables, and rice, sago, sweet potatoes or steamed bananas. And, of course, sambal are the condiment of choice and appear on every table, along with fresh tropical fruits.

At home, my mum delighted in cooking Manadonese and Chinese-Indonesian food but never Padang, the food of West Sumatra. Why? Because Indonesians also take pleasure in dining out in restaurants or warungs and she prefers the experience of visiting the best Padang restaurant in her neighbourhood.

Food is always a feature of Indonesian ceremonies, an obvious way for any community to bond. The ritual of makan bersama (literally meaning 'eating together'), a communal meal at a long table, is a feature of many regions. In Manado, during our Thanksgiving (pengucapan syukur), lunch is set out on long tables layered with banana leaves, which seat at least fifty people.

The very distinctive and universally-loved turmeric and coconut rice cone (nasi tumpeng) is placed in the centre of a large serving dish or bamboo tray and surrounded by a wonderful array of vegetables, chicken, tempeh and sambals to feed hungry guests. (Notably, the first plate always goes to the most respected and eldest person in the room.) Mini moulds (tumpeng) are often used to make individual cones of rice or shape mashed cassava with grated coconut and palm sugar. In the Banda Islands and other parts of Maluku province, the cone has the curious name of suami, meaning 'husband'.

Special occasions call for special foods. Whether Christmas, Ramadan, Idul Fitri or Chinese New Year, cakes and cookies are always part of the holiday celebrations. These include the Pineapple Biscuits (page 235), Cheese Sticks (page 236) and Thousand-Layer Cake (page 238).

The Spice Islands

Tucked away in the heart of Indonesia are a scatter of islands collectively known as The Spice Islands, the largest producers of mace, nutmeg and cloves in the world. Ternate Island in North Maluku has been cultivating cloves for hundreds of years. This is where visitors can admire the 400-year-old 'Afo Clove' tree, the oldest living clove tree in the world.

Travel 400 miles (645 km) south to the Banda archipelago in the province of Maluku, and you'll find the home of nutmeg. In fact, on the island of Banda Besar, you can walk under giant canopies of ancient kenari trees, shading the smaller nutmeg trees while yielding local wild almonds, often featured in local coffee, nougat with palm sugar syrup and young coconut tart known as *klapertart*. Mace is more valuable compared to a nut of nutmeg nowadays as a whole nutmeg fruit produces just one thread of mace. Interestingly, the people of Banda use plenty of fresh mace to cook fish soup.

The Spice Islands gained fame after Portuguese traders brought the indigenous spices to their European homeland in the early sixteenth century. Unknown to many, these beautiful islands made significant contributions to shaping the world of modern trading and cuisine. In 1667, the Dutch saw the inordinate value of spices on a global scale. Under the Treaty of Breda with the British, they acquired the island of Run and the nutmeg monopoly, in exchange for Manhattan Island (or New York). This deal meant little, even less today, for the islanders themselves as most continue to live by subsistence farming and fishing in a place barely visible on a map.

These spices were all part of my childhood. I grew up with sweet or spicy candied nutmeg, *manisan pala*, a pork dish with young nutmeg and clove leaves and speculaas cookies, featuring the Manadonese spice blend (page 41). Whether used individually or as part of a blend, these spices have made an indelible mark on global cuisine and played a dominant role in kitchens the world over – from Chinese five-spice and Indian garam masala to North African ras-el-hanout and baharat to the French quatre épices and Dutch speculaas.

How We Cook

Indonesians are very resourceful and versatile when it comes to preparing food. For that reason, traditional Indonesian cooking techniques include steaming, frying (shallow, deep, pan-fry, sauté), grilling, barbecuing, smoking, roasting, boiling, baking and cooking with bamboo segments and many different leaves, including banana leaves.

Remote communities still rely on a single large wok and clay pots with coconut shells used for utensils, ladles from lontar palms, bamboo plates or tamarind wood chopping (cutting) boards. And I adore the fact that Papuan food is still cooked using hot stones. My Oma cooked over a wood fire, resulting in incredible flavours in her food.

Modern cooking equipment and appliances are widely used in contemporary households and restaurants. However, some traditions are simply too good to give up. For example, every home has a basalt pestle and mortar. A distinctive angled handle helps the grinding action needed to break down and crush ingredients into a paste on the classic wide and dish-shaped mortar. Food parcels (packages) are still wrapped with leaves made from banana, palm or teakwood, then steamed or barbecued. After all, why mess with a good thing?

These days, I do all my home-cooking from my kitchen in England. Yes, with some adaptation, especially the cooking of savoury dishes in the oven and new ideas to bring Indonesian flavours to your home without compromising authenticity.

Ingredients and Flexibility

Throughout this book, I have ensured that every recipe can be a stand-alone meal or combined with other recipes. Seasons and special occasions always play a role in enjoying great food at the Indonesian table, beyond daily family meals or dinners at home with friends.

To accommodate the different eating styles, whether as courses or family-style, recipes are generally suited to serve four to six. For fish dishes, I tend to provide recipes for two, which can double up easily. I'm forever mindful of food waste. For this reason, I try to include storage suggestions where possible.

My greatest piece of advice as you cook from this book is to be flexible and use the best local ingredients you can find. (The obvious exception would be ingredients such as spices, coconut products, chocolate, tea and coffee that are simply impossible to grow outside their origins.) I always advocate using beef, chicken, fish and vegetables from local farmers, fishers and producers. It is no secret that fresh, less-travelled ingredients make a meal tastier. And where possible, I have chosen to feature ingredients that tend to be more readily available in the Western world (for example, banana shallots rather than Asian shallots).

If at the time you don't have one of the ingredients specified in the recipe, carry on and do not be deterred. There is an alternative in most cases (check the Glossary, page 28), or you may simply omit the ingredient. A good example is candlenuts, which can be easily replaced by macadamia nuts or omitted entirely with equally satisfying results.

Fresh turmeric and ginger last for roughly two weeks in dry and cool open storage, but both will quickly deteriorate in the refrigerator. You may also store whole galangal, ginger, turmeric, lemongrass, fresh chillies and pandan leaves in the freezer and use them when needed. Unless specified otherwise, do not peel turmeric, ginger and galangal – simply brush them clean before use.

Indonesian food is about spice pastes (*bumbu*) and sambal. Cooked spice pastes and cooked sambals without tomatoes can be refrigerated for up to three weeks as long as you add a touch of oil on top to preserve it. Half of the preparation of most dishes is in the making of your pastes and sambals. Have them readily available.

Always taste your food. It should have a balance of salt, spice, sweetness and, in some dishes, tang and umami. It's important to season curries or stews with enough salt.

Coconut oil solidifies in cooler climates (below 24°C/76°F) – simply melt one heaped tablespoon solid coconut oil in a pan and you will have two tablespoons liquid coconut oil.

When it comes to coconut milk, I use high-quality canned coconut milk that contain only two ingredients: water and coconut. Test out different quality brands to see which best suits your needs. Ultimately, any curry or stew with coconut milk should be well balanced and not too rich. I often dilute it with water to achieve this flavour balance. And if you're feeling ambitious, you could always make your own (page 38).

A Word on Condiments

To fully appreciate Indonesian food, you must understand the role of condiments in our diets. Sambal is a consistent theme and features at every meal (even breakfast), each region often touting distinct variations defined by native ingredients and tastes – a local sambal from Sabang at the northern tip of Sumatra is nothing like the version from Merauke at southeastern Papua.

I want to celebrate sambal not as a condiment but as part of the cooking itself, and its evolving role in modern Indonesian cuisine. At times, I will use them to create dishes and infuse them with desirable flavours.

The type of condiment at the table also varies across the regions. (Sweet soy sauce is generally served as a condiment in Java, but rarely will you see it outside of this region.)

Glossary

My cooking features many familiar Indonesian ingredients, but it also incorporates some new and unexpected ones. While purists may turn their nose up, my approach is practically minded so that Indonesian recipes may be re-created sustainably, with ease and in support of local economies.

asam gelugur
This is the thin, sun-dried product of a fruit resembling mangosteen. Known also as asam keping, it lends sourness to curry dishes, especially those from North Sumatra.

asam kandis
Also known as garcinia fruit, the unripe sour fruit is green, whereas the ripened version is yellow. This important ingredient in West Sumatra cuisine is the dried skin of this fruit, revered for its acidity.

banana leaves
See sidebar on page 35.

calamansi
This sharp yet refreshing citrus fruit is frequently used in Manado and most of eastern Indonesia. It can be added to any sambal and makes a good seafood marinade. Or mix it with water and sugar to make calamansi cordial. Calamansi ranges in colour from green when young to yellow and orange when mature.

candlenuts
This oily nut is often used as a thickening agent and is not recommended to consume raw. I rarely use it and often omit it if not available, but macadamia nuts make a good substitute.

cardamom
Indonesian white cardamom has a fresh and distinct aroma to enliven dishes. It can be substituted with green cardamom, which has a slight peppery note.

chillies
Indonesian chillies range in heat level and colour from vibrant green to orange and yellow to a deep red. As they can be difficult to source outside of Indonesia, I substitute them with bird's eye chillies, which belong to the same family. Indonesians also use large, curly chillies to impart colour, rather than heat, to a condiment or dish. You'll find attractive mounds of curly green and red chillies in markets across West Sumatra. In this book, I use the mild red chilli.

Chinese celery

Known in Indonesia as *seledri,* this ingredient adds flavour and colour to a dish, but it can be challenging to find. When added to a recipe for flavour, you can substitute it with celery leaves. When Chinese celery is added to a dish solely for colour, I replace it with parsley.

chive bulbs

The bulbs *(bawang batak)* are an important ingredient in one particular fish stew *(arsik)* made by the North Sumatran Batak community. The Bogor community in West Java also pickle them. They have a strong garlic flavour when raw but a pleasant aroma when cooked.

coconut oil

This was Indonesia's primary cooking oil until the palm oil boom in the 1980s. I mainly use coconut oil for pan-frying or sautéing dishes, but sunflower and rapeseed (canola) oil can also be used. It's worth noting that coconut oil maintains its liquid state above 24°C/76°F. If your coconut oil solidifies, simply melt it gently in a pan.

coconut sugar

Made from pure nectar of coconut blossom, coconut sugar can be used instead of palm sugar.

fish sauce

This is not a traditional Indonesian ingredient, but I use it in place of shrimp paste. The umami flavour from the fish sauce will yield a slightly different result.

galangal

A member of the ginger family, galangal is harder than ginger when it is mature. Young galangal has a slightly soft texture with small pink tips. It has a pleasing soft fragrance and delicate taste compared with ginger.

garlic

Along with shallots, it is the basis of Indonesian cooking and used in most savoury dishes. One variety *(bawang putih tunggal)* has superior health benefits and comes as one large bulb rather than a head with many cloves.

jackfruit

Known as *nangka,* it is enjoyed both in ripe and unripe form. When unripe, it can be added to curries or *gudeg,* a dried stew from central Java. In its ripened form, we add the fruit to ice drinks or enjoy it as is. The seeds of ripe jackfruit are delicious when boiled with coconut milk and palm sugar, which is the traditional way to make *kolak.*

kencur

Also known as aromatic ginger or sand ginger, kencur is part of the galangal family and used extensively in Bali, West Java and a few Sumatran regions. It has a distinctive fragrance with a pungent and bitter taste, earthy undertones, and less spice than ginger and galangal. We tend to use it unpeeled.

lemongrass

We can attribute the fresh and intense tang in our dishes to this ubiquitous ingredient. To release its oil, crush the light green and white parts of larger stems before cooking. The white part can be thinly sliced and eaten raw.

lime

This fruit needs no introduction. Indonesians love using it for its versatility: in cooked dishes and refreshing beverages.

long pepper

Known as *cabe jawa,* this chilli is indigenous to Java and Bali. It has a mild heat, vibrant red colour and soft texture. Nowadays, ripe long peppers are harvested and sun-dried or dried in a dehydrator for a longer shelf life. The Balinese use long pepper most within the archipelago.

makrut lime leaves

A king among Indonesian citrus fruits, the makrut lime has a fine fragrance (though not much juice) and their aromatic leaves lend a citrus note to Indonesian dishes. Available fresh, frozen or dried, they are often added to sambals, satays and Siomay (page 66). Before adding it to a recipe, you must remove the tough centre stem and vein and thinly slice the leaves. In curries and stews, the leaves are torn slightly to release their flavours and then removed before serving. To prepare dried leaves for a recipe, soak them first in hot water for 3–4 minutes. They are occasionally sold as 'lime leaves' in western supermarkets.

melinjo (emping) crackers

These thin, delicious plant-based crackers are made from the kernel of the native *gnetum gnemon* plants. Sweet, spicy or naturally flavoured, they make a great accompaniment to soto, noodle and rice dishes.

mung beans

These beans are among the most essential pulses (legumes) in Indonesia. We use them in porridge and ice creams and to make glass noodles.

palm sugar

Harvested from a specific palmyra tree, palm sugar is made from the nectar of flowers from palm sugar. (Common Indonesian varieties include arenga, toddy palm and nipa palm.) The sweet, watery sap drips from cut flower buds and, once collected, it is heated until thickened and placed in a coconut shell or small mould to set firm.

Every island boasts of their own, but good-quality palm sugar should be dark, softly textured and naturally sweet with a hint of toffee. Some are even smoky.

You may replace the palm sugar with coconut sugar, which has a slightly different aroma and texture.

pandan leaves

This leaf infuses cakes, drinks and rice with a warm, delicate fragrance and a pale mint green colour. Knot whole leaves first before adding them to recipes.

peanuts

Many Indonesian dishes feature peanuts, from *Gado-Gado* (page 86) to Chicken Satay (page 115). They tend to be deep-fried with the skin on, but I opt to roast peanuts (with or without their skin) in a 170°C/338°F/Gas Mark 3 oven for 18–20 minutes, mixing them halfway, for a healthier option. Combine the peanuts with cashews to add a hint of sweetness and creaminess to a sauce.

peppercorns

Peppercorns come widely available in green, black and white varieties. Fresh green peppercorns are fermented and sun-dried to produce hard black peppercorns. While these are used in our cuisine, many Indonesian dishes call for white pepper's distinctive aroma and spice. In North Sumatra, fresh green Szechuan peppercorns are a must in the fish stew known as *arsik*.

pineapple

This delicious tropical fruit features in everything from sambals to curries to desserts, balancing out heavy or spicy dishes with its sweetness and sharpness. When preparing fresh pineapple, the Indonesians use a very simple technique. First, cut off the top and bottom so the ends are flat, then trim off the skin around the sides. Look carefully and you'll notice that the inedible eyes spiral around the pineapple. Using a paring knife, remove the eyes by cutting away at them, making V-shaped trenches as you rotate the pineapple. This creates a decorative whole pineapple.

salam leaves

These aromatic leaves have a subtle woody flavour, generally functioning similarly to bay leaves. Use bay leaves if salam leaves are not available.

sago flour

This indigenous Indonesian ingredient has been a part of the cuisine for centuries. It is made from the refined extract of a sago palm tree, while cassava or tapioca flour is made of an extract of cassava root. Both flours function as a gluten-free thickening agent, though you could replace it with cornflour (cornstarch) at a pinch.

shallots

Aromatic Asian shallots are an essential Indonesian ingredient. With locality and sustainability always in my mind's eye, the recipes throughout this book are prepared with the more common banana, or echalion, shallots. An average banana shallot weighs approximately 50 g/1¾ oz. If you use Asian shallots, adjust the quantity accordingly. Shallots are always peeled before use.

shrimp paste

Every island boasts its own unique locally produced shrimp paste, which has a pungent, fermented aroma and lends incredible umami to sambals, fried rice dishes and stews. Before adding it to a recipe, dry-roast it for 2–5 minutes. Many Indonesians will barbecue (grill) the shrimp paste over an open flame to mellow out its strong fragrance. If unavailable, replace every teaspoon of shrimp paste with 2–3 tablespoons fish sauce, taking into consideration that fish sauce has a higher sodium content. (See also 'fish sauce'.)

tamarind

The fruit grows everywhere in Indonesia. Unripe green tamarind adds sourness to the Jakartan and West Javanese vegetable dish known as *sayur asem*. Ripe tamarind has a sticky pulp used to make Tamarind Paste or Tamarind Water (both on page 44). In Bali, the best chopping (cutting) boards come from the tamarind tree.

tempeh

See sidebar on page 152.

torch ginger

Known as *kecombrang or rias or honje,* this beautiful pink flower and its buds have a distinctive taste and fragrance, something between lemongrass, lemon and ginger. It is essential in Sumatra and Bali cuisine.

turmeric

Often adds a unique taste and vibrant colour to dishes. While the preference is for fresh whole spices, you can replace every 10 g/¼ oz of fresh turmeric with 1–2 teaspoons ground turmeric, depending on quality and strength.

Banana Leaves

The habit of wrapping food in fresh leaves is as old as cooking itself. Indonesia is spoiled for choice: we use the leaves of young coconut, papaya, guava, bamboo, palm (*woka*) and, of course, banana leaves.

The broad, flexible banana leaf holds a unique place in cooking and serving food. Dried banana leaves are used to wrap ready-made palm sugar. Fresh leaves can wrap meat, fish or seafood and impart their unique flavour to these dishes.

Banana leaves are commonly used as tablecloths and serving plates. In fact, at ceremonies, they make practical yet decorative liners for large bamboo trays of mountain-shaped *rice tumpeng* – often neatly covered with a coned banana leaf topper.

No matter how they're used, banana leaves bring an authentic touch of Indonesia to the dining experience. Here are some tips for usage and storage:

- *Pepes* (page 167) is the most well-known dish to feature banana leaves, which can be folded like a handkerchief or rolled into spring rolls. Each is secured with cocktail sticks, toothpicks or short skewers to prevent them from opening during cooking.
- Soft, young banana leaves are easy to fold and normally used for sweet dishes. You can soften banana leaves by steaming them for 1–2 minutes or gently heating them up with a kitchen torch to help make them easy to fold.
- Wrap left-over banana leaves in plastic and store in the refrigerator for up to a week.
- Banana leaves freeze well – simply thaw out for 30 minutes prior to use. It's worth noting that while frozen banana leaves are perfect for cooking, they're unsuitable for presentations as the frozen leaves tend to look washed out and a bit tired.

The Essentials

Bahan Dasar

While food culture varies greatly around the archipelago, chilli is the one ingredient which connects us Indonesians – we love chillies. Though it is not an indigenous ingredient, it lies at the heart of every sambal. The simple addition of just one ingredient – that's salt – will create our most basic sambal to enliven everything from fresh tropical fruits to a simple tray-baked chicken. You can create countless versions of this ubiquitous chilli paste with this foundation. It can be prepared with aromatics such as garlic and shallots, fresh herbs, vegetables, tempeh, shrimp paste and soy sauce, with varying degrees of complexity.

West Sumatran markets have the most magnificent displays of fresh chillies. Here, chilli vendors freshly grind massive quantities of curly chillies (which are not too spicy) on large, flat stone mortars with rounded ovular pestles so unfamiliar and different from the pestles in Manado or Java.

Many of my friends tell me that I am not a real Manadonese as I have always struggled to handle the spicy level of long-established Manado dishes. Our regional cuisine is renowned across the archipelago for its fiery spice. Rest assured, recipes can always be adjusted to suit your preferred spice levels.

The Basics

Here are store cupboard (pantry) essentials that will bring Indonesia's distinct flavours into your home. Certain ingredients are integral to Indonesian cuisine and play an important role in adding authenticity to our dishes. Some are indigenous to Indonesia, while others have been influenced by world cuisine from centuries past.

Coconut Milk
Santan Cair

When it comes to coconut milk, I like to use high-quality canned coconut milk with only two ingredients: water and coconut extract. However, here is a recipe for fresh coconut milk if you feel inclined; it's balanced and not too rich.

Makes 750 ml/25 fl oz (3 cups)

* 2 (550-g/1 lb 4-oz) mature coconuts

Crack the coconuts open. Using a knife, carefully remove the flesh. (If necessary, remove it in chunks.)

Finely grate the flesh, then put it into a mixing bowl. Add 800 ml/27 fl oz (3½ cups) warm water and mix well. (Alternatively, combine the grated coconut and warm water in a blender and blend well. Transfer the mixture into a bowl.) Using your hands, squeeze the mixture repeatedly. Strain the mixture through a fine-mesh sieve (strainer). Discard the grated coconut. You now have ready-to-use coconut milk.

To make coconut cream, use only 400 ml/14 fl oz (1⅔ cups) water.

Freshly Grated Coconut
Kelapa Parut

While preparing your own freshly grated coconut is certainly possible, it's beyond time-consuming. There are a few alternatives. You can place 275 g/9¾ oz fresh coconut flesh (brown skin removed) into a blender and blend it for 10–15 seconds until it has a grated texture. Or, try the method here by combining desiccated coconut, which is available everywhere, and quality coconut milk. It'll be less fluffy, but it's an acceptable alternative.

Makes 275 g/9¾ oz (1½ cups + 2 tablespoons)

* 50 g/1¾ oz (⅔ cup) unsweetened desiccated coconut
* 100 ml/3½ fl oz (scant ½ cup) coconut milk

Combine the desiccated coconut and coconut milk in a large bowl and soak for 20 minutes. You now have grated coconut with natural flavour.

Sweet Soy Sauce
Kecap Manis

We use two types of fermented soy sauces in Indonesia. Salty soy sauce such as dark and light soy (*kecap asin*) and sweet soy sauce (*kecap manis*). Dark and light soy sauces can be found everywhere, but you may need to go to larger supermarkets to find sweet soy sauce. And if you don't have access to sweet soy, you could always make your own with this recipe.

Makes 150 ml/5 fl oz (⅔ cup)

* 1 star anise
* 1 (2-cm/¾-inch) cinnamon stick
* ½ stalk lemongrass, crushed and tied into a knot
* 100 g/3½ oz palm sugar, thinly sliced, or coconut sugar
* 10 g/¼ oz galangal, cut into 3–4 pieces
* 3½ tablespoons dark or light soy sauce

Combine the ingredients in a saucepan. Add 3½ tablespoons of water and bring to a boil. Reduce the heat to medium-low and simmer for 15 minutes, or until the palm sugar has dissolved and the liquid has reduced by half. Set aside. The sauce will thicken as it cools.

Strain, then pour the sweet soy sauce into a jar or bottle. It can be stored in the refrigerator for 3 months.

Simple Syrup
Sirup Gula

This very handy syrup is a staple in my home. I highly recommend doubling up the recipe and storing it in the refrigerator.

Makes 500 ml/17 fl oz (generous 2 cups)

* 400 g/14 oz (2 cups) sugar

Put the sugar and 200 ml/7 fl oz (scant 1 cup) water into a pan and bring to a simmer. Stir until the sugar has dissolved. Set aside to cool, then refrigerate until needed. It can be stored in the refrigerator for 1 month.

Palm Sugar Syrup
Sirup Gula Aren

A popular Indonesian sweetener for desserts and drinks.

Makes 250 ml/8 fl oz (1 cup)

* 1 pandan leaf, coarsely chopped
* 300 g/10½ oz palm sugar, coarsely chopped
* Pinch of salt

Put all the ingredients in a saucepan, add 100 ml/3½ fl oz (scant ½ cup) of water and bring to a boil. Simmer for 15 minutes, until syrupy. Set aside to cool, then strain. The sauce will thicken as it cools. It can be stored in the refrigerator for 1 month.

Variation:
- **Kolak Sauce (Saos Kolak)**
  To make this coconut and palm sugar sauce, combine 150 ml/5 fl oz (⅔ cup) coconut milk and 100 ml/3½ fl oz (scant ½ cup) palm sugar syrup. (You can adjust the sweetness to your desired taste.) Serve it with Banana Fritters (page 61) and grilled pineapple.

Pandan Extract
Sari Daun Pandan

Used throughout Indonesia, pandan adds natural green colour and a wonderful fragrance to rice, curries or palm sugar syrup.

Makes about 150 ml/5 fl oz (⅔ cup)

* 4 long pandan leaves, thinly sliced
* 150 ml/5 fl oz (⅔ cup) milk or water

Combine the pandan leaves and milk in a blender and blend for 3–4 minutes. Strain the mixture through a fine-mesh sieve (strainer). Use immediately.

Peanut-Cashew Butter
Selai Kacang Tanah dan Kacang Mede

Peanut-cashew butter is easy to make and essential to Indonesian cuisine. It can be added to Mixed Salad with Spicy and Tangy Peanut Sauce (page 86) or Vegetables with Kencur and Peanut Sauce (page 88). Alternatively, you could make pure peanut butter without the cashews or buy a quality store-bought version.

Makes 400 g/14 oz (1½ cups + 3 tablespoons)

* 200 g/7 oz (1⅔ cups) peanuts, with or without skin
* 200 g/7 oz (1½ cups) cashews

Preheat the oven to 170°C/338°F/Gas Mark 3.

Put the nuts on a baking sheet and roast for 15–17 minutes, mixing occasionally until golden brown. Turn the oven off and leave the tray inside for 5 minutes. Set aside to cool.

Combine the roasted nuts in a blender or food processor and blend for 5–7 minutes until smooth.

For crunchy peanut-cashew butter, simply blend 250 g/9 oz (1 cup) of the roasted nuts until smooth. Then add the remaining nuts and blend until a coarse purée. It can be stored in an airtight container in the refrigerator for 2 months.

Seasonings

There are countless ways to add depths of flavour to Indonesian cuisine. From koya to speculaas, spice blends can introduce exciting new elements to savoury and sweet dishes. Also, any conversation about Indonesian seasonings must include *kerupuk*. Although technically a cracker, it provides flavour and texture to dishes.

Speculaas Spice Blend
Rempah Spekulas

The European speculaas spice blend is the foundation for the eponymous biscuits (cookies), but it can be used for so much more. Add speculaas to coffee, pancake or cake batters, Apple Crumble (page 234) or Manado Pork Stew (page 191).

Makes 30 g /1 oz (2 tablespoons)

* 2 whole nutmegs
* 1 (10-g/¼-oz) stick cinnamon, broken into small pieces
* ½ teaspoon whole cloves
* 1 tablespoon ground ginger or 2 tablespoons dried ginger slices

Combine the nutmeg, cinnamon and cloves in a frying pan and dry-roast for 5–6 minutes over medium heat until fragrant, stirring occasionally to prevent them from burning. Combine all the ingredients in a spice grinder or small blender and grind to a fine powder.

The spice mix can be stored in a glass jar for 6 months.

Variation:
- **Ngohiong Spice Blend (Lima Macam Rempah)**
  Popular among Chinese Indonesians, this spice blend is essentially a five-spice powder. Omit the nutmeg and add 3 star anise and 1 tablespoon of fennel seeds when dry-roasting the spices.

Crispy Shallots
Bawang Goreng

This traditional topping adds a layer of flavour to our dishes. Commercially produced versions often include flour to preserve the crunchy texture over a longer shelf life.

Makes 40 g/1½ oz (¾ cup)

* 200 ml/7 fl oz (generous ¾ cup) vegetable oil
* 2 banana shallots, thinly sliced
* ¼ teaspoon salt

Heat the oil in a saucepan over medium heat. The oil is ready when a cube of bread dropped in sizzles on contact and turns golden in 10–15 seconds. (Alternatively, use a thermometer and heat to 180°C/350°F.)

Season the shallots with salt. Add half the shallots to the pan and deep-fry for 3–4 minutes until golden brown. Using a slotted spoon, transfer the shallots to a plate lined with paper towels to absorb the excess oil. Repeat with the remaining shallots. Store in an airtight container for up to 2 days.

Dried Shrimp Powder
Ebi Bubuk

Dried shrimp powder adds a boost of umami to dishes. The key is to start with a quality dried shrimp and dry-roast it to release the flavours.

Makes 50 g/1¾ oz (generous 3 tablespoons)

* 50 g/1¾ oz quality dried shrimp

Dry-roast the dried shrimp in a small frying pan over low heat for 10–15 minutes.

Transfer to a small blender or a pestle and mortar and grind to a fine powder.

Dried shrimp powder can be stored in an airtight container in the refrigerator for 2 weeks.

Koya
Koya

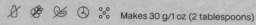

Makes 30 g/1 oz (2 tablespoons)

This delicious topping is made with fried garlic and shrimp crackers, which are then ground into a powder. We use it to flavour Chicken Soto with Turmeric and Lemongrass (page 103). You could also replace the deep-fried garlic with one tablespoon of garlic powder.

* 200 ml/7 fl oz (generous ¾ cup) sunflower oil
* 6 large cloves garlic, thinly sliced
* Salt, to taste
* 4 deep-fried prawn crackers

Heat the oil in a medium saucepan over medium-low heat. The oil is ready when a cube of bread dropped in sizzles on contact and turns golden in 10–15 seconds. (Alternatively, use a thermometer and heat to 170°C/338°F.)

Season the garlic with a pinch of salt. Add the garlic to the hot oil and deep-fry for 2–3 minutes until golden. Using a slotted spoon, transfer the garlic to a plate lined with paper towels to drain.

Transfer the garlic and crackers to a food processor and process to a powder. Koya can be stored in an airtight container for 1 week.

Rice Crackers
Rempeyek

Makes 20

We Indonesians love texture in our food. Don't be surprised by the assortment of flavoured crackers (*kerupuk*), made from ingredients such as rice, cassava, prawn and even pork or beef. We even have a plant-based cracker made with melinjo (*emping*) nuts. (You'll find the most options on Java.)

This recipe is deceptively easy to make at home. The crunchy, paper-thin crackers have been infused with citrus notes from the lime leaves, but they can be prepared with peanuts, soybeans or baby anchovies.

It's best to use a wok rather than a frying pan, as the batter needs to be poured from the rim of the wok and not directly into the oil.

For the paste:
* 2 candlenuts or 3 macadamia nuts
* 1 banana shallot, thinly sliced
* 1 clove garlic, thinly sliced
* 1 teaspoon ground coriander
* 1 teaspoon salt

For the rice crackers:
* 6 makrut lime leaves, centre stem removed and finely chopped
* 1 egg yolk
* 180 g/6 oz (generous 1 cup) rice flour
* 150 ml/5 fl oz (⅔ cup) coconut milk
* 500 ml/17 fl oz (generous 2 cups) sunflower oil, for deep-frying

To make the paste, combine all the ingredients in a small blender and blend into a smooth paste.

To make the rice crackers, combine the lime leaves, egg yolk and rice flour in a medium bowl. Stir in the paste.

Slowly whisk in the coconut milk and 100 ml/3½ fl oz (scant ½ cup) of water. Whisk gently until the batter is smooth.

Heat the oil in a wok over medium heat. Using a spoon, pour a tablespoon of oil, along one side of the pan. Carefully tap a tablespoon of the batter, about 4 cm/1½ inches above the oil, along the side of the wok, so the batter slides into the oil. Deep-fry for 1–2 minutes until golden. Turn it over and cook for another 20 seconds.

Using a slotted spoon, transfer the cracker onto a plate lined with paper towels to drain. Repeat with the remaining batter. The rice crackers can be stored in an airtight container for 2 days.

Pastes

Bumbus are essential spice pastes used to impart flavour and aroma to Indonesian dishes. We use five – white, red, yellow, black and green – mainly to flavour proteins such as fish, meat, tempeh or tofu.

Bumbus are a fragrant combination of garlic, shallots, fresh root spices (ginger, galangal or turmeric) and, except for white paste, chillies. Traditionally, the paste is ground using a pestle and mortar; however, in regions such as Bali and Manado, the ingredients are finely chopped.

I recommend a full quantity of paste for every 1 kg/2 lb 4 oz of protein. You could also double the recipe and store it in an airtight container, topped with oil, in the refrigerator for 2 weeks.

White Spice Paste
Bumbu Putih

p.45

This foundational recipe is the basis for the spice pastes in this book. I also use it in Vegetable Curry (page 123) and Fragrant Chicken Curry (page 130).

Makes about 100 g/3½ oz (½ cup)

- 2 candlenuts or macadamia nuts, coarsely ground (optional)
- 2–3 tablespoons coconut oil or sunflower oil
- 4 cloves garlic, sliced
- 2–3 small banana shallots, sliced
- 20 g/¾ oz fresh root ginger, sliced
- 10 g/¼ oz galangal, thinly sliced

If using the candlenuts, heat a frying pan over medium-low heat. Add the candlenuts and dry-roast for 3–4 minutes. Transfer the candlenuts to a plate.

Combine all the ingredients in a blender and blend into a smooth paste. It is now ready for use in a recipe.

Red Spice Paste
Bumbu Merah

p.45

A red bumbu will always have two types of red chillies: bird's eye chillies impart the fiery kick, while large yet mild red chillies add volume and lend fruitiness. If you prefer a milder paste, seed the chillies or simply reduce the quantity of bird's eye chillies.

Makes 110 g/3¾ oz (generous ½ cup)

- 1 quantity White Spice Paste (page 43)
- 4–6 red bird's eye chillies, coarsely chopped
- 2 large red chillies, coarsely chopped

Combine all the ingredients in a small blender and blend into a smooth paste.

Yellow Spice Paste
Bumbu Kuning

p.45

Turmeric will change the flavour and colour of white and red basic pastes. You can create a mild yellow spice paste by omitting the chillies entirely, but it won't have the same impactful flavour or colour.

Makes 115 g/4 oz (generous ½ cup)

- 1 quantity White Spice Paste (page 43)
- 4–6 red bird's eye chillies, coarsely chopped
- 2 large red chillies, coarsely chopped
- 15 g/½ oz fresh turmeric or 1–2 teaspoons ground turmeric

Combine all the ingredients in a small blender and blend into a smooth paste.

Black Spice Paste
Bumbu Kluwak

This spice paste is made with fermented black (kluwak) nuts, which come from the kepayang tree. Often added to stews and soups, they impart an earthy, nutty flavour with a hint of acidity and deep black colour. They may be substituted with a black olive tapenade.

Makes 135 g/4¾ oz (¾ cup)

- 4 black (kluwak) nuts or 25 g/1 oz black olive tapenade
- 1 quantity White Spice Paste (page 43)
- 4–6 red bird's eye chillies, coarsely chopped
- 2 large red chillies, coarsely chopped
- 15 g/½ oz fresh turmeric or 1–2 teaspoons ground turmeric

Soak the nuts in a bowl of water overnight.

Crack open and remove the flesh. Combine all the ingredients in a small blender and blend into a smooth paste.

Green Spice Paste
Bumbu Hijau

Use this green spice paste for green sambals and fish curry. Green tomatoes and lime juice give it a touch of acidity.

Makes 280 g/10 oz (generous 1 cup)

- 10 large green chillies, coarsely chopped
- 6–8 green bird's eye chillies
- 3 tablespoons coconut oil
- 2 cloves garlic, coarsely chopped
- 2 banana shallots, coarsely chopped
- Juice of ½–1 lime
- Salt, to taste

Bring 500 ml/17 fl oz (generous 2 cups) of water to a boil in a saucepan. Add the chillies and cook for 5–7 minutes until softened. Drain the chillies, then place them into a bowl of cold water for 5 minutes to stop the cooking process and retain the vibrant colour. Coarsely chop, then set aside.

Heat the oil in a frying pan over medium heat. Add the garlic and shallots and sauté for 6–8 minutes, until softened and fragrant. Add the chillies and cook for another 3–4 minutes.

Transfer the mixture to a blender and blend well. Put the paste into a bowl and stir in the lime juice. Season to taste with salt.

Tamarind Paste
Asam Jawa

This spice paste...
Tamarind paste and tamarind water can be found at larger supermarkets, but it is also easy to make at home. The flavour and colours of shop-bought tamarind paste may be convenient, but some products may lack the sharp intensity of a home-made version. All recipes in the book call for home-made tamarind paste; however, if you are using a shop-bought tamarind paste, I encourage you to taste your dish frequently and add more as needed.

Makes 100 ml/3½ fl oz (scant ½ cup)

- 50 g/1¾ oz tamarind pulp, torn into small pieces

Put the tamarind pulp into a bowl and add 200 ml/7 fl oz (generous ¾ cup) of hot water. Soak for 15 minutes. Using your hand, squeeze the pulp. Strain, then discard the solids.

Put the tamarind paste into a small saucepan and bring to a boil. Reduce the heat to medium-low and simmer for 2–3 minutes. Leave to cool. Tamarind paste can be stored in the refrigerator for 2 weeks.

Variation:
- **Tamarind Water (Air Asam Jawa)**
  Simply dilute the tamarind paste in 400 ml/14 fl oz (1⅔ cups) water.

Opposite: 1. Yellow Spice Paste (page 43); 2. Black Spice Paste (see above); 3. Green Spice Paste (see above); 4. White Spice Paste (page 43) and Red Spice Paste (page 43).

Sambals

In Indonesia, sambals are either raw (*sambal mentah*) or cooked (*sambal matang*). The foundation of sambal couldn't be easier – at its most basic, all you need is chilli and salt. You can build the complexity of flavour by adding aromatics such as garlic and shallots, fresh herbs, tempeh, dried fermented shrimp paste, soy sauce, or dried or canned anchovies.

You may prepare cooked sambal by boiling or frying the chillies and introducing umami ingredients such as shrimp paste or salted fish (or anchovies). Lime juice, tamarind and vinegar brighten up sambals with much-needed acidity. We also prepare our cooked sambals with coconut oil, reaping its myriad benefits in both nutrients and taste. However, coconut oil does solidify at a cooler room temperature (anything below 20°C/68°F), so I swap it out for a fat such as sunflower oil here in the UK.

And while sambals generally act as condiments for noodles, satays and rice dishes, some sambal varieties are used to create dishes such as Sambal Tempeh (page 155) and Pan-Seared Duck Breast with Soy Sambal (page 187).

All sambals can be stored in an airtight container in the refrigerator for 1 week, except for any with tomatoes, which can be stored for 2 days.

Chilli and Salt Sambal
Sambal Garam

Makes 10 g/¼ oz (generous 1 tablespoon)

This very basic sambal can be served as a dip with fresh tropical fruits or used as a flavourful rub for roast chicken. Simply rub the inside and outside of the chicken with the chilli salt and juice of 2 limes, then brush with 2 tablespoons of melted coconut oil.

* 2–4 red bird's eye chillies, finely chopped or ground
* 2 teaspoons salt

Combine the ingredients and mix well.

Chilli and Lemongrass Sambal
Sambal Matah

📷 p.49

Fragrant, spicy and tangy, this versatile Balinese sambal can be served with Seafood Satay (page 112) or Bali rice.

Serves 4–6

* ½ teaspoon shrimp paste or 2–3 canned anchovies
* 2 banana shallots, thinly sliced
* Salt, to taste
* 2–3 heaped tablespoons coconut oil or sunflower oil
* 5 makrut lime leaves, centre stem removed and thinly sliced
* 3 stalks lemongrass, white part only, thinly sliced
* 2 cloves garlic, grated
* 1–2 red bird's eye chillies, thinly sliced
* Juice of 2 limes

Dry-roast the shrimp paste in a small frying pan over medium-high heat for 2–3 minutes. Using a pestle and mortar, grind finely and set aside.

Using your fingertips, rub the shallots with ¼ teaspoon of salt for 2–3 minutes to soften.

Heat the oil in the same frying pan over medium heat. Turn off the heat. Add all the ingredients and mix well. Season to taste with more salt or shrimp paste.

Variation:
- Chilli and Lemongrass Sambal with Ginger Flower (Sambal Matah dengan Kecombrang)
  Add 1 small finely chopped ginger flower bud when mixing all the ingredients together.

Chilli and Tomato Sambal
Dabu-Dabu

Serves 4

This spicy sambal is vibrant, refreshing and very versatile. Unripe green tomatoes are traditionally used, but regular tomatoes are an acceptable substitute.

* 3 green or red tomatoes, chopped
* 2–3 red bird's eye chillies, thinly sliced
* 1 banana shallot, finely chopped
* 2 tablespoons coconut oil or extra-virgin olive oil, warmed
* ¼ teaspoon salt
* Pinch of sugar (optional)
* Juice of 2 limes

Put all the ingredients in a bowl and mix well. Serve immediately or transfer to an airtight container, top with oil and store in the refrigerator for 2–3 days.

Variations:
- Chilli and Tomato Sambal with Mint or Basil (Dabu-Dabu Kemangi atau Daun Mint)
  Add a bunch of chopped mint or basil to create a vibrant and herbaceous sambal.
- Chilli, Tomato and Sweet Soy Sambal (Colo-Colo)
  This is a well-known sambal from Ambon in Malaku. Simply omit the oil and add 2–3 tablespoons of Sweet Soy Sauce (page 38).

Mango Sambal
Sambal Mangga

Serves 4–6

This refreshing sambal is ideal for barbecued seafood, chicken or fish dishes.

* 1 small unripe mango, peeled and coarsely grated
* 1 banana shallot, finely chopped
* Salt, to taste
* 2–3 red bird's eye chillies, finely chopped
* 1 large red chilli, finely chopped
* 1 clove garlic, finely chopped
* 1 teaspoon coconut sugar
* 1 teaspoon roasted shrimp paste (optional)

Combine the mango and shallot in a medium bowl. Season with salt. Rub the mixture between your fingers for 1 minute to mix and release some moisture. Add the remaining ingredients and mix well.

Lemon and Chilli Sambal
Sambal Lu'at

Serves 4–6

This unique sambal from Flores has heat, tang, a hint of bitterness and a pleasing fragrance. Large unpeeled makrut limes are typically used in this sambal, but I prepare it here with lemons. If you find it too spicy or tangy, add ½ teaspoon of sugar. Serve it with Crispy Pork Belly (page 188).

* 2 large lemons
* 5 red bird's eye chillies, coarsely chopped
* 2–4 large red chillies, finely chopped
* 2 banana shallots, finely chopped
* Small bunch of basil, coarsely chopped
* ½ teaspoon salt
* ½ teaspoon sugar (optional)

Using a peeler, peel the lemon zest, then coarsely chop. Halve the lemons and juice them into a small bowl. Set aside.

Using a pestle and mortar, grind the chillies finely to release the juices. Combine all the ingredients in a bowl. Season to taste. The flavours will deepen with time.

Opposite: 1. Sriracha (page 54); 2. Tomato, Chilli and Basil Sambal (page 53); 3. Red chillies; 4. Sambal Tempeh (page 155); 5. Tomato and Shrimp Paste Sambal (page 54); 6. Mango Sambal (see above); 7. Soy Sambal (page 187); 8. Green Sambal (page 51); 9. Boiled Sambal (page 53) and 10. Chilli and Lemongrass Sambal (page 47).

Shallot Sambal
Sambal Bawang

This fragrant sambal gives a kick to fried rice dishes, fried noodles and condiments.

Make 1 small jar

* 2–3 tablespoons coconut oil or sunflower oil
* 3 cloves garlic, finely chopped
* 2 banana shallots, finely chopped
* 3–4 red bird's eye chillies, finely chopped
* 1–2 large red chillies, finely chopped
* ¼ teaspoon salt
* Juice of ½–1 lime

Heat the oil in a frying pan over medium heat. Add the garlic, shallots and chillies and sauté for 8–10 minutes, until softened. Season with salt and lime. If storing, be sure to add enough oil to cover the sambal.

Aubergine Sambal
Sambal Terong Sumba

📷 p.45

This is another favourite of mine from Sumba Island. Long, slender, pale purple Asian aubergines (eggplants) are traditionally cooked over an open fire, but I simply grill a large aubergine in a broiler (grill). It won't have the smoky aroma, but the flavour is still wonderfully layered with chillies, garlic and basil. I like to make a big batch of this, with less fire, and have it on-hand as a quick dip.

Makes 300 g/10½ oz (1¼ cups)

* 1 aubergine (eggplant)
* 4 tablespoons coconut oil or sunflower oil
* 4 cloves garlic, finely chopped
* 1 banana shallot, thinly sliced
* 4–6 red bird's eye chillies, finely chopped
* Large bunch of basil, coarsely chopped
* ½ teaspoon salt

Preheat the broiler (grill).

Place the aubergine (eggplant) on a baking sheet. Grill for 20 minutes, turning every 5 minutes, until softened. Leave to cool.

Meanwhile, heat the oil in a frying pan over medium heat. Add the garlic and shallot and sauté for 4–5 minutes. Add the chillies and sauté for another 2–3 minutes. Set aside to cool.

When the aubergine is cool enough to handle, carefully remove the skin and discard. Finely chop the flesh, then add it to the chilli mixture. Add the basil and salt and mix well. Season to taste with more salt.

Green Sambal
Sambal Lado Ijo

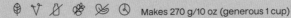

[📷] p.45 & 49

The heaped piles of curly red and green chillies in West Sumatran markets are a sight to behold. This versatile sambal can be served with a variety of dishes. Since finding these chillies outside of Asia can be challenging, use large green chillies to intensify the colour and add body to the sambal without imparting too much heat. It's great with fish, chicken and Indonesian fried rice without sweet soy.

Makes 270 g/10 oz (generous 1 cup)

* 10 large green chillies, coarsely chopped
* 4–5 green bird's eye chillies
* 2 banana shallots, coarsely chopped
* 1 green tomato, coarsely chopped
* ¼ teaspoon salt
* Juice of 1 lime
* 3 tablespoons coconut oil

Put all the ingredients, except the coconut oil, into a blender and pulse until a coarse paste forms.

Heat the oil in a frying pan over medium heat. Add the chilli paste and sauté for 10 minutes until softened and fragrant. Season to taste with salt.

This sambal can be stored in an airtight container in the refrigerator, topped with oil, for 2–3 days.

Variations:
- **Raw Green Sambal (Sambal Ijo Mentah)**
  Use only 1 banana shallot and put all the ingredients into a blender. Add 3 tablespoons water and the juice of another ½–1 lime. Do not cook.
- **Anchovy Sambal (Sambal Ijo Teri)**
  Once the chilli paste has been cooked, stir in 5 thinly sliced canned anchovies or 2 tablespoons deep-fried dried anchovies. As the anchovies are already salted, season lightly to taste.
- **Balado Sambal (Balado Sambal)**
  Use red chillies and tomatoes instead of green.

Miso Sambal
Sambal Tauco

This incredible sambal is a must with Makassar Beef Coto (page 105), but it is equally delicious with grilled fish or roast chicken. Tauco, an Indonesian miso, is coarser than its Japanese counterpart and difficult to find outside of the archipelago. I've replaced it here with light or dark miso.

Serves 8

* 2 tablespoons coconut oil or sunflower oil
* 2 banana shallots, finely chopped
* 2 large red chillies, finely chopped
* 2–4 red bird's eye chillies, coarsely chopped
* 2 tablespoons light or dark miso
* 1 tablespoon honey
* Salt, to taste

Heat the oil in a frying pan over medium heat. Add the shallots and sauté for 3–4 minutes until softened. Add the chillies and sauté for another 1–2 minutes.

Stir in the miso, honey and 3½ tablespoons of water and mix well. Bring to a boil and simmer for 5–7 minutes. Leave to cool.

Transfer the mixture into a blender and blend until smooth. Season to taste with salt.

Peanut Sambal
Sambal Kacang

Peanut sambal and the peanut sauce for *Gado-Gado* (page 86) may sound similar, but do not mistake them as the same. Peanut sambal is prepared with fried garlic and boiled or fried chillies, whereas gado-gado peanut sauce is not.

This delicious sambal has the thick consistency of honey and is tinted red from the chillies. It makes the perfect accompaniment to serve alongside Siomay dumplings (page 66) or Pasty with Vegetables and Rice Noodles (page 70).

Serves 8

* 3 tablespoons coconut oil or sunflower oil
* 150 g/5½ oz (1¼ cups) peanuts, with or without skin
* 2 cloves garlic, thinly sliced
* 1 banana shallot, finely chopped
* 3 large red chillies, finely chopped
* 2 red bird's eye chillies, coarsely chopped
* 2 makrut lime leaves, centre stem removed and thinly sliced
* 2–3 tablespoons coconut sugar or palm sugar
* 1 teaspoon salt
* 1 tablespoon Sweet Soy Sauce (page 38)
* Juice of 1 lime

Heat 2 tablespoons of oil in a frying pan over medium heat. Add the peanuts and sauté for 5–7 minutes until the skin begins to peel or the skinless peanuts turn golden. Transfer the peanuts to a bowl.

Heat the remaining tablespoon of oil in the same frying pan. Add the garlic and shallots and sauté for 3–4 minutes. Add the chillies and lime leaves and sauté for 4–5 minutes. Turn off the heat.

In a blender, combine the chilli mixture, coconut sugar and 200 ml/7 fl oz (generous ¾ cup) water. Blend until smooth.

Transfer the mixture into a bowl, then season with salt, sweet soy sauce and lime juice. If needed, add 1–2 tablespoons of water to loosen the sambal. Leave to cool.

Boiled Sambal
Sambal Rebus

Makes 100 ml/3½ fl oz (scant ½ cup)

This sambal makes a good condiment for soto, meatballs, rice porridge or noodle soups.

- 2–3 red bird's eye chillies
- 1 large red chilli
- 1 clove garlic
- 1 tablespoon sugar
- Salt

Bring a small saucepan of water to a boil. Add the chillies, garlic and sugar and boil for 6–8 minutes, until softened. Reserve 4 tablespoons of the water, then drain. Transfer the mixture to a blender and blend until smooth. If needed, add the reserved water to loosen the mixture to the desired consistency. Season to taste with salt.

Variation:
- **Vinegar Sambal (Sambal Cuka)**
  Replace the 4 tablespoons of water with 4 tablespoons of apple cider or rice vinegar.

Tomato, Chilli and Basil Sambal
Sambal Tomat Sumba

Makes 500 g/1 lb 2 oz (2 cups)

p.45 & 49

A medley of chillies, tomato and basil, this iconic sambal from Sumba Island can accompany fish, chicken, tempeh, tofu and vegetables. I have reduced the chillies to a more comfortable heat, but feel free to adjust the amount to your preference.

- 4 tablespoons coconut oil or sunflower oil
- 2 banana shallots, finely chopped
- 2 large cloves garlic, thinly sliced
- 4–5 red bird's eye chillies, coarsely chopped
- 2 large red chillies, finely chopped
- 3–4 tomatoes, chopped into 1-cm/½-inch cubes (about 2 cups)
- ½ teaspoon salt
- Bunch of basil, coarsely chopped

Heat the oil in a frying pan over medium heat. Add the shallots and garlic and sauté for 4–5 minutes, stirring occasionally. Add the chillies and sauté for another 2–3 minutes. Stir in the tomatoes and bring to a boil. Reduce the heat to medium-low and simmer for 15–20 minutes until reduced by a quarter. Season with salt. Stir in the basil and cook for another 2 minutes. Season to taste.

This sambal can be stored in an airtight container in the refrigerator, topped with oil, for 2–3 days.

Variation:
- **Sweet Soy-Tomato Sambal (Sambal Tomat Kecap)**
  Omit the basil and add 2–3 tablespoons of Sweet Soy Sauce (page 38).

Tomato and Shrimp Paste Sambal
Sambal Terasi Tomat

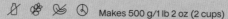

📷 p.45 & 49

Makes 500 g/1 lb 2 oz (2 cups)

This iconic Sundanese sambal combines chillies, tomato, garlic, shallots and shrimp paste for mega umami flavour. Plus, it's super versatile, so it can accompany fish, chicken, tempeh, tofu and vegetables. Makrut lime is occasionally added for a touch of acidity and a delightful fragrance.

* 4 tablespoons coconut oil or sunflower oil
* 2 banana shallots, coarsely chopped
* 2 large cloves garlic, roughly sliced
* 4–5 red bird's eye chillies, coarsely chopped
* 2 large red chillies, finely chopped
* 1–2 teaspoons shrimp paste
* 2 tomatoes, chopped into 1-cm/½-inch cubes (about 1 cup)
* ¼–½ teaspoon salt
* 1–2 tablespoons lime juice

Heat the oil in a frying pan over medium heat. Add the shallots and garlic and sauté for 4–5 minutes, stirring occasionally. Add the chillies and sauté for another 2–3 minutes. Add the shrimp paste and cook for another 2–3 minutes. Stir in the tomatoes and bring to a boil. Reduce the heat to medium-low and simmer for 10 minutes until reduced by a quarter. Put the mixture into a blender and blend until smooth. Transfer the sambal into a bowl. Season with salt and lime juice.

This sambal can be stored in an airtight container in the refrigerator, topped with oil, for 2–3 days.

Sriracha
Saos Sambal

📷 p.49

Makes 1 (150-ml/5-fl oz) jar

This condiment requires no introduction and it's available everywhere across Indonesia. It's called saos (sauce) sambal due to its thick consistency, but it is also known as *sambal botol,* meaning 'bottled chilli sauce'.

Sriracha can be used as a dipping sauce for Spring Rolls (page 70) and Potato and Beef Croquettes (page 69) or added to Rice Noodle Soup with Meatballs (page 109).

* 8 large red chillies, seeded
* 2–4 red bird's eye chillies
* 4 large cloves garlic
* 3½ tablespoons rice or apple cider vinegar
* ½ teaspoon salt
* 3 tablespoons sugar

Bring a large saucepan of water to a boil. Reduce the heat to medium, then add the chillies and garlic. Boil for 10 minutes until the chillies are softened. Drain and let cool.

Combine the chillies, garlic, vinegar and salt in a blender and blend until smooth. Transfer the mixture back to the saucepan.

Add the sugar and gently heat over medium heat for 2–3 minutes until the sugar has dissolved. Season to taste with extra sugar or vinegar. Leave to cool.

Pickles

Some of the pickles in our food culture are a result of Middle Eastern and Chinese influences. These two pickles make easy and delicious accompaniments.

Pickled Pineapple
Pacri Nanas

Delightful and refreshing, this pickle is infused with coconut and spices, making it the perfect condiment for Duck Curry (page 133) or Beef Rendang (paged 134).

Makes 1 kg/2 lb 4 oz (about 4 cups)

* 3½ teaspoons salt
* 1 pineapple, peeled, cored and eyes removed
* 4 large red chillies, seeded and coarsely chopped
* 2 star anise
* 1 (4-cm/1½-inch) stick cinnamon
* 100 g/3½ oz (½ cup) granulated sugar
* 200 ml/7 fl oz (generous ¾ cup) coconut milk
* 3 tablespoons apple cider vinegar

Combine 300 ml/10 fl oz (1¼ cups) water and 3 teaspoons salt in a large bowl. Add the pineapple and soak for 2 minutes. Drain, then cut into 2.5-cm/1-inch chunks.

Combine the chillies, star anise, cinnamon and sugar in a medium saucepan. Add 100 ml/3½ fl oz (scant ½ cup) water and bring to a boil. Boil for 8–10 minutes. Reduce the heat to medium, then add the pineapple, coconut milk, vinegar and the remaining ½ teaspoon of salt. Bring to a boil and simmer for another 8–10 minutes to soften the pineapple.

Transfer the mixture into a bowl and let cool.

Pickled Shallots and Chillies
Acar Bawang Merah dan Cabe Rawit Ijo

This sharp and flavourful pickle is often served with Beef and Egg Martabak (page 64), fried noodles or Nasi Goreng (page 203). While I use banana shallots throughout the book, I've made an exception of using round shallots for this recipe, purely for aesthetics.

Makes 375 g/13 oz

* 20 green or red bird's eye chillies
* 15 small round shallots or pearl onions, peeled
* 200 ml/7 fl oz (scant 1 cup) apple cider vinegar
* 1 teaspoon salt

In a large bowl, combine all the ingredients and 400 ml/14 fl oz (1⅔ cups) of water and mix well. Pour the mixture into a large, sterilized jar. Set aside for at least 24 hours. Pickled shallots and chillies can be refrigerated for a month.

Variation:
- **Mixed Pickles (Acar Campur)**
  Cut 1 carrot and 1 cucumber into 1-cm/½-inch cubes and add with the shallots. Double the vinegar and salt.

Snacks

Jajan Pasar

The Manadonese love their food and love to eat. And food is always part of the conversation. Thanks to a lively and joyful upbringing in a large family, my childhood was filled with gatherings and memories of many varied sweet and savoury snacks served for such occasions. Snacks included European-style cakes, Chinese- and Peranakan-influenced confections, Banana Fritters (page 61) served with spicy smoked garfish sambal (*sambal roa*) and the popular *bak pao* bao buns with red beans and black sesame paste. We'd often have stuffed pasties (page 70) and empanadas filled with smoked tuna, grated young papaya and chillies (page 65) at our table.

On relocating to the capital city of Jakarta in my early teens, there were plenty of new snacks to sample. Some were made with sticky glutinous rice, mung bean flour or agar agar; others were sweetened with palm sugar or grated coconut. This is where I discovered triangular patties of rice filled with palm sugar grated coconut (*lupis*), croquettes and mashed cassava flavoured with chocolate, vanilla or strawberry with freshly grated coconut (*getuk lindri*). However, my go-to was the sweet rice ball rolled in freshly grated coconut known as *klepon* (page 60), which I would often enjoy with a cup of coffee or tea.

The snacks in this chapter are some of my favourites, and I hope you enjoy them as much as I do. It brings to mind the Indonesian word *oleh-oleh*, a term we use when sharing gifts of food with family and friends.

Sweet Moonshine Pancake
Martabak Manis Terang Bulan

This springy pancake with its honeycomb texture originated in Bangka Island, just east of Sumatra. Originally prepared by Hokkien immigrants, it is now available across larger cities around the archipelago. I've always admired the street vendors who've perfected the art of making this snack.

Traditionally, the pancakes were prepared with sugar and sesame seeds. These days, you'll find an expansive variety of pancake flavours, including strawberry, cheese and pandan. The key to perfecting this treat is to ensure an even heat distribution on the pan. I also recommend using a large, heavy non-stick frying pan, about 22 cm/8½ inches in diameter.

Origin: Sumatra

Preparation time: 25 minutes, plus 1 hour chilling time
Cooking time: 15 minutes

Makes 1 large thick pancake

For the pancake:
* 125 g/4¼ oz (1 cup) self-raising flour, sifted
* 1½ tablespoons cornflour (cornstarch) or tapioca flour
* 1 tablespoon sugar, plus extra for sprinkling
* 1 tablespoon vanilla extract
* ¼ teaspoon salt
* 1 egg, lightly beaten
* ½ teaspoon baking powder
* 1 teaspoon bicarbonate of soda (baking soda)
* 1 tablespoon sunflower oil, for frying

For the topping:
* 2 tablespoons butter
* 100 g/3½ oz (scant 1 cup) grated medium or mature Cheddar cheese
* 100 g/3½ oz (scant ½ cup) grated dark (bittersweet) or milk chocolate
* 50 g/1¾ oz (scant ½ cup) roasted cashews or peanuts
* 1 tablespoon sesame seeds, toasted
* 2 tablespoons condensed milk, for drizzling (optional)

To make the pancake, combine the flour, cornflour (cornstarch), sugar, vanilla extract and salt in a stand mixer fitted with the whisk attachment. Add 150 ml/5 fl oz (⅔ cup) water and mix on a medium speed to start with, then increase to high speed and mix for 5 minutes.

Remove the bowl from the stand mixer. With a rubber spatula, fold in the egg and baking powder and take care not to overmix. Transfer the mixture into a large jug (pitcher) and refrigerate, uncovered, for at least 1 hour.

Remove the jug from the refrigerator. Add the bicarbonate of soda (baking soda) and 4–5 tablespoons of water and mix briefly. It should have the thin consistency of crepe batter, which will result in a light and springy pancake.

Put the oil onto a paper towel and grease a frying pan. Heat the frying pan over medium-low heat. Check the heat by splashing a little water in the pan – if it sizzles and evaporates instantly, it's ready.

Pour the batter into the pan and swirl to create a uniform layer. Cook for 8–10 minutes, until surface bubbles start to burst. Reduce the heat to low. Cover the pan for 30 seconds to cook the top of the pancake. Turn off the heat.

Transfer the pancake to a chopping (cutting) board. Sprinkle with sugar, then cut the pancake in half into 2 discs. Spread 2 teaspoons of butter on the cut side of one half, then sprinkle cheese and chocolate on top. Add cashews and sesame seeds and drizzle with condensed milk, if using. Sandwich the pancake together, spread the remaining butter on top of the pancake to create a glossy finish and cut the pancake into 10–12 squares or wedges. Drizzle with condensed milk, if using. Serve hot.

Sweet Coconut-Coated Rice Balls
Klepon

This Javanese and Balinese sweet treat is made with glutinous rice flour and boiled to create a sticky texture and comes available in white or green variations. (It is also prepared with pandan extract, which also infuses it with the sweet scent of vanilla.) It's served warm (my preference) or at room temperature.

Quality palm sugar and grated coconut are key to a delicious *klepon*. These rice cake balls often remind me of the many Indonesian places I've visited and where I have tasted some of the best palm sugar in my life.

Origin: Throughout Indonesia

Preparation time: 40 minutes
Cooking time: 20 minutes

Makes 20–22 rice balls

For the coating:
* 200 g/7 oz (scant 2½ cups) Freshly Grated Coconut (page 38)
* ½ teaspoon salt

For the rice balls:
* 4 pandan leaves, finely chopped
* 5 tablespoons coconut milk
* 250 g/9 oz (2 cups) glutinous rice flour
* 2½ tablespoons rice flour, plus extra for dusting
* ½ teaspoon salt
* 150 g/5½ oz palm sugar, thinly sliced
* 1 tablespoon coconut oil

To make the coating, combine the grated coconut and salt in a heatproof dish and mix well. Spread out the coconut, then place the dish in a steamer basket and steam for 10 minutes. Leave to cool.

To make the rice balls, put the pandan leaves and 150 ml/5 fl oz (⅔ cup) water into a blender and blend well. Strain the mixture through a fine-mesh sieve (strainer) and into a small saucepan. Add the coconut milk and bring it to a simmer over medium heat. Turn off the heat.

In a large bowl, combine the flours and salt and mix well. Pour in the warm coconut-pandan mixture and mix for 3–4 minutes with a wooden spoon until a dough ball forms.

Transfer the mixture to a clean work counter dusted with flour. Using your hands, knead for 2–3 minutes. Set aside for 3 minutes.

Line a baking sheet with baking (parchment) paper. Put a dessert spoon of dough (about 25 g/1 oz) into the palm of your hand and flatten it with your fingers to a thickness of 2 mm/1⁄16 inch.

Put a generous ½ teaspoon of palm sugar in the centre of the dough, then wrap the edge over the sugar and shape it into a ball. Place the rice ball on the baking sheet and repeat with the remaining dough and palm sugar.

Bring a large saucepan of water to a boil and add the coconut oil. (This prevents the rice balls from sticking to each other.) Reduce the heat to medium.

Working in 2 batches, gently lower the rice balls into the pan. Cook for 4–5 minutes until they float to the surface. Using a slotted spoon, transfer the rice balls to the plate of grated coconut and toss to coat. Repeat with the remaining rice balls.

Serve warm or at room temperature. The rice balls will become denser at room temperature.

Banana Fritters
Pisang Goreng

I enjoyed the fritters on a recent visit to Friwen Island in Papua, and they tasted identical to those prepared in my grandmother's kitchen. And the vendor was named Merry, just like my mother.

Indonesia has abundant varieties of bananas suitable for frying, but the most delicious fritters are made with saba banana (*pisang kepok*), a short, flattened and sharply faceted banana from Manado and eastern Indonesia. For convenience, I have used the common Cavendish.

In Manado and eastern Indonesia, the fritters are served plain or sweetened with Palm Sugar Syrup (page 229). Sometimes, we have them with *sambal roa*, an umami-rich condiment made with dried and smoked garfish, chillies and shallots.

Origin: Throughout Indonesia

Preparation time: 15 minutes
Cooking time: 20–25 minutes

Serves 4

* 4 unripe Cavendish bananas
* 90 g/3¼ oz (½ cup) rice flour
* 2½ tablespoons cornflour (cornstarch)
* 1 teaspoon baking powder
* 1 teaspoon sugar
* ½ teaspoon salt
* Sunflower oil, for deep-frying
* 1 quantity Palm Sugar Syrup (page 229), *sambal roa* or Kolak Sauce (page 39), to serve

---

Peel the bananas and cut them in half crosswise. Cut each piece in half lengthwise. You should have 16 pieces in total.

In a medium bowl, combine the rice flour, cornflour (cornstarch), baking powder, sugar and salt and mix well. Gradually whisk in 225 ml (7½ fl oz/scant 1 cup) cold water, until the batter is smooth.

Heat the oil in a deep saucepan over medium heat. The oil is ready when a cube of bread dropped in sizzles on contact and turns golden in 10–15 seconds. (Alternatively, use a thermometer and heat to 180°C/350°F.)

Dip 2 banana pieces into the batter and carefully lower them into the pan. Deep-fry for 2–3 minutes, turning occasionally, until golden. Using a slotted spoon, transfer the fritters to a plate lined with paper towels to drain. With the same spoon, remove any loose batter mixture from the oil as it will burn. Repeat with the remaining banana pieces.

Serve warm with a drizzle of palm sugar syrup, sambal or kolak sauce.

Mung Bean Porridge with Coconut and Pandan
Bubur Kacang Ijo

Oma's mung bean porridge flavoured with ginger and pandan leaves, warming coconut milk and sweet palm sugar has always been my favourite breakfast. When my family moved to Jakarta when I was in my early teens, I was delighted to discover that mung bean porridge was easily obtainable.

Mung beans are readily available, but if you struggle to find pandan leaves, an infusion of ginger will not disappoint.

Origin: Throughout Indonesia

Preparation time: 5–10 minutes, plus overnight soaking time
Cooking time: 25–30 minutes

Serves 8

* 300 g/10½ oz (1½ cups) dried mung beans, rinsed well
* 1 long pandan leaf, tied into a knot
* 10 g/¼ oz fresh root ginger, sliced and crushed
* 400 ml/14 fl oz (1⅔ cups) coconut milk
* 80 g/2¾ oz palm sugar or coconut sugar
* ½ teaspoon salt

Soak the mung beans in a bowl of water overnight, discarding any floating beans.

Drain, then transfer them to a large saucepan. Add 700 ml/24 fl oz (generous 2¾ cups) of fresh water and bring to a boil. Add the pandan and ginger and simmer over medium heat for 40 minutes, until the mung beans are very tender.

Using a ladle, skim any scum from the surface. Stir in the coconut milk, palm sugar and salt. Bring to a boil and simmer for 5 minutes until the sugar has melted.

Serve warm or at room temperature.

Sweet Coconut and Pandan Pancakes
Kue Dadar Gulung Pandan

This classic snack is a taste of my childhood. It is typically filled with sweet and juicy freshly grated coconut, which can be difficult to source outside the tropics. The next best thing? Desiccated coconut soaked in quality coconut milk. It's a clever way to emulate freshly grated coconut without all the hassle of sourcing it or grating it yourself.

Origin: Throughout Indonesia

Preparation time: 20 minutes, plus 1 hour standing time
Cooking time: 45 minutes

Makes 9

For the filling:
- 1 long pandan leaf, cut in half and tied into a knot
- 150 ml/5 fl oz (⅔ cup) palm sugar or coconut sugar
- Pinch of salt
- 200 g/7 oz (scant 2½ cups) Freshly Grated Coconut (page 38)

For the pandan pancakes:
- 4 long pandan leaves, cut into 2-cm/¾-inch lengths
- 250 ml/8 fl oz (1 cup) semi-skimmed milk
- 50 g/1¾ oz (⅓ cup) sifted plain (all-purpose) flour
- 1 teaspoon sugar
- ¼ teaspoon salt
- 2 eggs, lightly beaten
- 2 tablespoons melted butter
- 1 tablespoon coconut oil
- Greek yoghurt, to serve (optional)

To prepare the filling, combine the pandan leaf, palm sugar, salt and 5 tablespoons of water in a saucepan. Bring to a boil, then reduce the heat to medium-low. Simmer for 8–10 minutes until the sugar dissolves and the mixture thickens. Stir in the grated coconut and cook over medium heat for 12–15 minutes, stirring occasionally, until dark brown and caramelized. Discard the pandan leaf. Set aside.

To make the pandan pancakes, combine the pandan leaves and 150 ml/5 fl oz (⅔ cup) milk in a blender and blend well. Strain the mixture through a fine-mesh sieve (strainer) and into a bowl. It should make 100 ml/3½ fl oz (scant ½ cup). Set aside.

Combine the flour, sugar and salt in a separate bowl and mix well. Add the eggs and butter and mix well. Slowly pour in the pandan milk and the remaining 100 ml/3 fl oz (⅓ cup) milk, whisking until smooth. Strain the mixture through a fine-mesh sieve (strainer) and into a jug (pitcher). This will make it easier to pour the batter into the frying pan. Set aside for 1 hour.

Heat a 20-cm/8-inch non-stick frying pan over medium heat. Place a few drops of coconut oil on a paper towel and rub it on the pan.

Pour 3 tablespoons of batter into the pan, swirling the pan gently to create a thin pancake. Cook for 2 minutes, then flip over and cook for another 40 seconds until cooked through. Transfer the pancake to a chopping (cutting) board.

Put 1½–2 tablespoons of the coconut filling along one edge of the pancake. Roll the pancake over the filling, tucking in the sides as you roll it. Transfer to a serving plate and repeat with the remaining pancakes.

Serve as is or with yoghurt, if you wish.

Beef and Egg Martabak
Martabak Telur

This well-known Jakartan snack sees a pancake stuffed with a savoury beef filling, then pan-fried to golden perfection on a large frying pan. The pancake is then rolled towards the centre of the pan and cut into squares. It is served with pickled shallots, cucumber and chillies.

I have fond memories of *martabak* prepared by Sri Owen, the beloved cooking teacher, author and queen of Indonesian food. On a visit to London when I was still living in Jakarta, I received a lunch invitation at her house.

She prepared an authentic *martabak*, and it was absolutely sensational. When I moved to England, Sri gave me a present—a brand-new steel *martabak* pan, about 60 cm/24 inches in diameter.

I have adapted the recipe by using small, ready-made spring roll wrappers, which give a satisfying crunch to the pancakes. You can find them at Asian speciality food shops or use the large wrappers and cut them into quarters.

Origin: Java

Preparation time: 20 minutes
Cooking time: 30 minutes

Makes 10

- 2 tablespoons coconut oil or vegetable oil
- 4 cloves garlic, finely chopped
- 1 onion, finely chopped
- 200 g/7 oz lean minced (ground) beef
- Salt and white pepper, to taste
- 2 eggs, lightly beaten
- 2 spring onions (scallions), thinly sliced

- 20 small spring roll wrappers
- 2 egg whites, lightly beaten, for brushing
- 100 ml/3½ fl oz (scant ½ cup) sunflower oil
- Pickled Shallots and Chillies (page 55), to serve

To make the filling, heat the coconut oil in a frying pan over medium-low heat. Add the garlic and onions and sauté for 7–10 minutes until translucent. Add the minced (ground) beef and sauté for 10 minutes, stirring occasionally. Season with salt and pepper. Transfer to a bowl and set aside to cool. Add the eggs and spring onions (scallions) and mix well.

To make the pancakes, place a spring roll wrapper on a clean work counter. Add a heaped tablespoon of filling to the centre, then flatten slightly. Brush the wrapper edges with egg white and top with another wrapper. Press the edges to seal the parcel. Repeat with the remaining wrappers and filling.

Heat the sunflower oil in a wok over medium heat. Working in batches of 2–3, carefully add the filled pancakes to the pan and pan-fry for 2–3 minutes on each side until golden. Using a slotted spoon, transfer the pancakes to a plate lined with paper towels to drain. Repeat with the remaining pancakes.

Cut each pancake in half into triangles and serve hot with pickled shallots and chillies.

Spicy Empanadas with Smoked Fish
Panada Isi Ikan Asap Pedas

Empanadas were introduced to us by Portuguese explorers, traders and missionaries who came to Manado in the seventeenth century and continue to have a strong cultural presence. The fillings are as varied as the imagination, but we Manadonese are partial to a savoury version filled with spicy smoked tuna and grated young papaya.

For this recipe, I have made a filling of smoked mackerel, young papaya and fresh mint leaves homage to my Oma's recipe. However, an empanada with canned tuna and kohlrabi would make a tasty substitute. Either way, these empanadas make great snacks or tasty picnic fare alongside a fresh mixed salad with a perky dressing.

When I was young, Oma taught me how to make the small dough rounds, then twist and curl the edges with my fingers to seal the empanada 'pocket'. You could simplify the process by pressing the prongs of a fork along the edges.

Origin: Sulawesi

Preparation time: 45 minutes, plus 5 minutes standing time and 1½ hours proving (proofing) time
Cooking time: 35 minutes

Makes 18–20

For the dough:
* 220 ml/7½ fl oz (scant 1 cup) milk or water
* 6 tablespoons butter
* 9 g/¼ oz fast-action (active dry) yeast
* 500 g/1 lb 2 oz (generous 4 cups) plain (all-purpose) flour, sifted, plus extra for dusting
* 1 tablespoon sugar
* ¼ teaspoon salt
* 1 egg, lightly beaten

For the filling:
* 2 tablespoons vegetable oil
* 2 cloves garlic, finely chopped
* 2 banana shallots, finely chopped
* 2 red bird's eye chillies, thinly sliced
* 10 g/¼ oz fresh root ginger, finely grated
* 1 small young green papaya or 1–2 kohlrabi, peeled and grated (250 g/9 oz)
* 1 (250-g/9-oz) skinless smoked mackerel fillet, bones removed, or 1 can drained tuna in water, chopped
* 2 spring onions (scallions), thinly sliced
* Handful of mint leaves, finely chopped
* Salt, to taste
* 1 litre/34 fl oz (4¼ cups) sunflower oil, for deep-frying

To make the dough, combine the milk and butter in a large saucepan and warm over low heat until the butter has melted. Mix well, then turn off the heat. Add the yeast and mix. Set aside for 5 minutes.

Combine the flour, sugar and salt in a large bowl and mix well. Add the dry ingredients to the yeast mixture and mix briefly. Add the egg. Using a wooden spoon, stir until the dough comes together into a ball. Transfer the dough to a lightly floured work counter. Using your hands, knead the dough for 10 minutes until elastic. Place the dough in a greased bowl and cover with a dish towel. Set it aside to prove (proof) for 1 hour until doubled in size. (Ideally, you want to put your bowl in a warm part of your kitchen, between 38–42°C/100–111°F. Alternatively, you could put it in your oven's warming drawer at 40°C/104°F.)

Meanwhile, prepare the filling. Heat the vegetable oil in a frying pan over medium heat. Add the garlic, shallots, chillies and ginger and sauté for 3 minutes until fragrant. Add the papaya and sauté for another 5–7 minutes until soft. Add the smoked mackerel and cook for another 5 minutes. Stir in the spring onions (scallions) and mint and season with salt. Leave to cool.

Knead the dough for 3 minutes or until smooth. Divide the dough into 50-g/1¾-oz balls. Using a rolling pin, roll out each piece into a disc, about 12 cm/4½ inches in diameter and 3 mm/⅛ inch thick.

Place a tablespoon of filling into the centre of a pastry circle. Fold the pastry in half over the filling and press the edges together to form a half-moon shape. Transfer to a baking sheet. Repeat until all the dough and the filling are used. Cover the empanadas with a dish towel and set aside for 30 minutes to rise.

Heat the sunflower oil in a deep saucepan or wok over medium heat. The oil is ready when a cube of bread dropped in sizzles on contact and turns golden in 10–15 seconds. (Alternatively, use a thermometer and heat to 180°C/350°F.)

Working in batches, carefully lower the empanadas into the hot oil and deep-fry for 2 minutes on each side, turning occasionally, until golden brown. Using a slotted spoon, transfer the empanadas to a plate lined with paper towels. Repeat with the remaining empanadas. Serve warm.

Dumplings with Spicy Peanut Sauce
Siomay Bandung

Located amid volcanic hills, national parks and forests is Bandung, the capital city of West Java. It is a popular destination among foodies and home to this popular dish, featuring steamed fish and chicken dumplings, potatoes, cabbage and tofu with a spicy peanut sauce.

Siomay may have been influenced by the Chinese pork dumpling *siu mai,* but these dumplings are entirely different in both ingredients and appearance. This dish brings me back to when I was a teenager and getting together with friends after school or a sporting activity. We would enjoy the snack in Menteng, a district in Jakarta renowned for its street food.

The preparation of *siomay* is often associated with the most wonderful fragrance of makrut limes (*jeruk purut*). Although the citrus fruit yields little juice, it has the most incredible citrus aroma you will ever experience.

Origin: Java

Preparation time: 25 minutes
Cooking time: 20–25 minutes

Serves 8

For the dumplings:
- 185 g/6½ oz mackerel or any white fish fillets, skinless and coarsely chopped
- 100 g/3½ oz chicken breast, coarsely chopped
- 100 g/3½ oz (generous ¾ cup) tapioca flour or sago flour
- 1 egg, lightly beaten
- 2 small spring onions (scallions), thinly sliced
- 2 cloves garlic, grated
- 1 banana shallot, finely chopped
- 2 tablespoons sesame oil
- 1 teaspoon white pepper
- ½ teaspoon salt
- Pinch of granulated sugar

To serve:
- 300 g/10½ oz firm tofu, cut into triangles
- 8 large cabbage leaves, stems trimmed, rolled up
- 250 g/9 oz new potatoes, with or without skin
- 4 eggs
- 2–3 tablespoons Sweet Soy Sauce (page 38)
- 2–3 tablespoons Sriracha (page 54)
- 1 quantity Peanut Sambal (page 52)
- 2–3 tablespoons ketchup
- 4 makrut limes, halved, or 2 limes, cut into wedges

To make the dumplings, combine the fish and chicken in a food processor and purée into a paste. Transfer the mixture into a medium bowl. Stir in the flour and the egg and mix well. Add the remaining ingredients and mix well. Set aside.

Put a tablespoon of mixture into your palm and shape it into a ball. Put it on a plate lined with baking (parchment) paper. Repeat with the remaining mixture.

Place the dumplings and tofu in a large steamer basket and steam for 10–15 minutes. Add the rolled cabbage and steam everything for another 10 minutes.

Meanwhile, put the potatoes in a saucepan and bring to a boil. Boil for 15 minutes.

Put the eggs into a small saucepan of water. Bring to a boil and boil for 10 minutes. Drain, then transfer to a bowl of cold water to stop the cooking process. When cool enough to handle, peel the eggs and cut them in half.

Put the dumplings, tofu, cabbage, potatoes, and eggs on a serving plate. Put the condiments into little bowls and serve with the limes.

Potato and Beef Croquettes
Kroket

The name of this dish infers a Dutch influence. Croquettes are widely available in many varieties from Indonesian street food vendors and bakery shops. They can be filled with cheese and potatoes, cassava or sweet potatoes or beef and vegetable ragout. Processed cheese was used back in the day, but fresh cheeses by artisanal cheese makers in Java and Bali are now more commonly used. Indonesia is not a dairy country, but many people grew up with the familiar taste of milk and cheese. Serve these croquettes in the classic tradition with whole green chillies or a simple salad for a light meal.

Origin: Java

Preparation time: 25 minutes, plus 30 minutes chilling time
Cooking time: 35–45 minutes

Makes 12

For the coating:
* 2 large floury (baking) potatoes, cut into 2.5-cm/ 1-inch chunks (500 g/1 lb 2 oz)
* 100 g/3½ oz (scant 1 cup) grated mature Cheddar
* 3½ tablespoons salted butter
* 1 teaspoon freshly grated nutmeg
* 2 egg yolks
* Pinch of salt
* 1 teaspoon white pepper

For the filling:
* 1 tablespoon olive oil
* 1 tablespoon butter
* 3 cloves garlic, finely chopped
* 200 g/7 oz minced (ground) beef
* 2 carrots, cut into ½-cm/ ¼-inch cubes
* 2 tablespoons chopped parsley or celery leaves
* Salt and white pepper, to taste

For the croquettes:
* 50 g/1¾ oz (⅓ cup) plain (all-purpose) flour
* 100 g/3½ oz (2 cups) panko breadcrumbs
* 2 eggs, beaten
* 500 ml/17 fl oz (generous 2 cups) sunflower oil, for deep-frying
* Sriracha (page 54) or green bird's eye chillies, to serve

To make the coating, simmer the potatoes in lightly salted water for 15–18 minutes until tender. Drain. Using a potato ricer or a food processor, mash the potatoes thoroughly. Transfer to a bowl and cool slightly.

Add the cheese, butter, nutmeg and egg yolks. Season with salt and pepper and mix thoroughly. Cover and set aside.

To make the filling, heat the oil and butter in a frying pan over medium-high heat. Add the garlic and sauté for 1–2 minutes until slightly golden. Add the minced (ground) beef and sauté for 7–8 minutes until brown. Add the carrots and sauté for another 3–4 minutes until the carrots are softened. Stir in the parsley. Season with salt and pepper. Leave to cool.

To make the coating, place the flour and breadcrumbs on separate plates.

Place a heaped tablespoon of the potato mixture into your palm and flatten, about ½ cm/¼ inch thick. Put 2 teaspoons of filling into the centre of the potato patty, then carefully bring the edges up around the filling and shape like a sausage. Roll in flour, dip in egg and coat in the breadcrumbs. Place it on a baking sheet and repeat with the remaining potato mixture and filling. Place the croquettes on a plate, cover and refrigerate for 30 minutes.

Heat the sunflower oil in a large, heavy saucepan over medium-high heat. The oil is ready when a cube of bread dropped in sizzles on contact and turns golden in 10–15 seconds. (Alternatively, use a thermometer and heat to 180°C/350°F.)

Working in batches, carefully lower the croquettes into the hot oil and deep-fry for 3–4 minutes, turning occasionally, until golden brown. Using a slotted spoon, transfer the croquettes to a plate lined with paper towels to drain.

Transfer the croquettes to a plate and serve immediately with green chillies or Sriracha.

Pasty with Vegetables and Rice Noodles
Pastel Sayuran dan Bi Hun

This distant cousin of the Empanada (page 65) has an entirely different pastry texture and filling. Pasties were introduced to Indonesia by the Portuguese and eventually made with local ingredients. (Interestingly, the noodle filling in this vegetarian recipe has Chinese influences.) You will find pasties in big cities around the archipelago.

While they are usually deep-fried, this version is baked with beautiful results. It is best enjoyed with Peanut Sambal (page 52), which I also serve with Siomay (page 66). I simply love the sambal connections across Indonesia.

Origin: Throughout Indonesia

Preparation time: 45–50 minutes, plus 1 hour chilling time
Cooking time: 40–50 minutes

Makes 16–18

For the pastry:
* 450 g/1 lb (scant 4 cups) plain (all-purpose) flour, sifted, plus extra for dusting
* 1 tablespoon sugar
* 1 egg, lightly beaten
* 125 g/4¼ oz salted butter, room temperature
* 125 g/4¼ oz margarine, room temperature

For the filling:
* 50 g/1¾ oz dried glass or rice noodles
* 2 tablespoons sunflower oil
* 4 cloves garlic, finely chopped
* 2–3 banana shallots, finely chopped
* 2 potatoes, cut into ½-cm/¼-inch cubes
* Salt and white pepper, to taste
* 5 carrots, grated (1⅔ cups)
* 75 g/2¾ oz green beans, thinly sliced

* 2 spring onions (scallions), thinly sliced
* Small bunch of parsley, leaves only, chopped
* 1 egg, lightly beaten, for brushing
* 1 quantity Peanut Sambal (page 52), to serve

To make the pastry, put the flour and sugar into a stand mixer fitted with the hook attachment. Mix well. Add the egg, butter and margarine. Gradually pour in 110 ml/3¾ fl oz (scant ½ cup) of hot water, little by little, until a dough forms. Transfer the dough to a chopping (cutting) board and divide it into 8 portions. Wrap each piece in baking (parchment) paper and chill for 1 hour.

To make the filling, prepare the dried noodles according to the package directions. Drain, then cut the noodles into 5-cm/2-inch lengths.

Heat the oil in a frying pan over medium heat. Add the garlic and shallots and sauté for 7–8 minutes until softened. Add the potatoes and sauté for 2–3 minutes, stirring constantly. Add 100 ml/3½ fl oz (scant ½ cup) of water, season with salt and pepper and cook for another 10 minutes until the potatoes are soft and most of the water has evaporated. Add the carrots and green beans and cook for another minute.

Stir in the noodles. If the mixture is too dry, add 1 tablespoon of water. Season to taste with salt and pepper. Add the spring onions (scallions) and parsley and mix well. Leave to cool.

Preheat the oven to 180°C/350°F/Gas Mark 4. Line a baking sheet with baking (parchment) paper. Remove the dough from the refrigerator and set it aside for 5 minutes.

Dust a clean work counter and rolling pin with flour. Roll the dough to a thickness of 3 mm/⅛ inch. Using a ramekin, about 12 cm/4½ inches in diameter, mark out circles. Gather any left-over pastry and mark out more. Makes 16–18 rounds in total.

Dust the pastry round with flour and put 2 tablespoons of filling in the middle of each one. Brush the edges of a pastry with egg, then fold in half over the filling and crimp the edges to form a half-moon shape. Place the pasty on the prepared baking sheet. Repeat with the remaining pasties.

Brush the pasties with egg. Bake for 10 minutes. Reduce the oven temperature to 160°C/325°F/Gas Mark 3 and bake for another 15–17 minutes, or until golden brown.

Serve warm with peanut sambal.

Variations:
- **South Sulawesi-Style Pasty (Jalangkote)**
  Omit the green beans. Replace the potato mixture with 150 g/5½ oz (⅔ cup) grated green papaya and 100 g/3½ oz (generous 1 cup) of finely shredded cabbage. Substitute 50 g/1¾ oz (¼ cup) bean sprouts for the glass noodles.
  Heat 500 ml/17 fl oz (generous 2 cups) sunflower oil in a deep saucepan over medium heat.
  The oil is ready when a cube of bread dropped in sizzles on contact and turns golden in 10–15 seconds. (Alternatively, use a thermometer and heat to 160°C/325°F.) Deep-fry pasties in hot oil for 3–4 minutes until golden brown. Using a slotted spoon, transfer to a plate lined with paper towels to drain. Serve warm with Boiled Sambal (page 53).
- **Spring Rolls (Lumpia Goreng)**
  Transform the pasties into spring rolls (lumpia goreng) with shop-bought wrappers. Put 2 tablespoons of filling along the edge of the spring roll wrapper nearest you. Brush the edges with egg wash or simply dilute 1 tablespoon of rice flour with 3 tablespoons water for vegan. Roll the spring roll tautly, tucking in the edges. Repeat until all the filling is used. Deep-fry in hot oil, about 160°C/325°F, for 3–4 minutes, turning frequently, until golden brown. Transfer to a plate lined with paper towels to drain. Serve warm with Sriracha (page 54).

Salads

Selada

A formal three-course meal was never a part of the traditional Indonesian table, but many classic dishes include mixed tropical fruits and raw, cooked or pickled vegetables seasoned with sauce or dressing. As our salads bear little similarity to traditional Western salads, the chapter name might seem like a misnomer. However, Indonesians do prepare fresh fruit and vegetables as fresh accompaniments in family-style meals that also serve to aid digestion.

Tropical fruits make up a large part of my childhood memories. As a young girl, I would pluck juicy, sweet mangoes, ripe water apples, plump mangosteens and guavas off the branches of our fruit trees. What we didn't grow in our garden could be gathered at the markets – papaya, pineapple, snake fruit, durian, rambutan, banana and so many more. Going to the market was always a visual feast for the eyes.

When the tropical fruits had yet to ripen, we would prepare them in *rujak buah* (page 78), a medley of pineapple, mango and papaya served with spicy, tangy tamarind sauce. Admittedly, I am partial to fruit *rujak* and hunt them out regularly whenever I travel to the archipelago, but other popular variations include *rujak* with raw tubers, unripened bananas with their peels and jicama (*rujak bebek*).

I love serving raw vegetables as an Indonesian-style crudité with shrimp paste sambal (page 80). On a trip to Palembang, South Sumatra, this same dish was served with a fruit sambal accompaniment. It featured white turmeric with a delicate mango flavour (*temupo*) and a type of small black bean (*kabau*) – I still remember my excitement upon discovering these two new ingredients. I cherish these rare and precious moments.

Spicy, Sour and Sweet Vegetables and Fruits
Asinan Jakarta

This tantalizing salad is sweet, spicy and tangy with deep umami notes. I use a julienne vegetable peeler to create short matchsticks from the jicama, which helps to introduce a textural element to the salad.

When serving for large parties, you can prepare this dish several hours before your guests arrive (or even the day before and refrigerate until needed).

Origin: Java

Preparation time: 25 minutes, plus 24 hours pickling time
Cooking time: 15 minutes

Serves 8

For the pickling brine:
* 200 ml/7 fl oz (generous ¾ cup) rice vinegar or apple cider vinegar
* 100 ml/3½ fl oz (scant ½ cup) Simple Syrup (page 39)
* 1 tablespoon salt

For the salad:
* 150 g/5½ oz firm tofu, cut into 1-cm/½-inch cubes
* 2 carrots, grated

* 1 cucumber, seeded and cut into 1-cm/½-inch cubes (optional)
* ¼ white cabbage, finely shredded
* 200 g/7 oz pineapple, cut into 1-cm/½-inch cubes
* 100 g/3½ oz jicama or kohlrabi, cut into matchsticks (optional)
* 50 g/1¾ oz (¼ cup) bean sprouts

* 50 g/1¾ oz (scant ½ cup) roasted peanuts or cashews, coarsely ground, to serve (optional)
* Chopped chives, to garnish

For the spicy peanut sauce:
* 1 teaspoon shrimp paste
* 1 quantity Peanut Sambal (page 52)
* 2 tablespoons Dried Shrimp Powder (page 41)

For the pickling brine, combine all the ingredients in a large bowl. Add 1 litre/34 fl oz (4¼ cups) of water and mix well. Set aside.

For the salad, bring a medium saucepan of water to a boil. Reduce the heat to medium. Add the tofu to a steamer basket or bamboo steamer, place over the pan of simmering water and steam for 10 minutes. Set the tofu aside to cool.

Layer all the ingredients in a large container, then pour in the pickling brine to cover the salad. Cover with a lid and refrigerate for 24 hours.

For the spicy peanut sauce, dry-roast the shrimp paste in a frying pan for 2–3 minutes. Transfer to a pestle and mortar and grind finely. Stir into the peanut sambal, add the dried shrimp powder and mix well.

To serve, place the salad on a serving platter or in individual glasses. Add the peanut sauce, then top with the toasted nuts, if using, and chives.

Variation:
- **Bogor-Style Pickled Vegetables (Asinan Bogor)**
  Add 10 chive bulbs, along with the young stems, to the pickled vegetables. Omit the peanut sauce. In a saucepan, combine 1 large red chilli, 2 red bird's eye chillies, 3 tablespoons sugar and 200 ml/7 fl oz (scant 1 cup) water. Boil for 5–7 minutes until the sugar has dissolved. Transfer the mixture to a blender and blend until smooth. Add 50 ml/1¾ oz fl oz (¼ cup) rice vinegar or apple cider vinegar. Season to taste. Add 1–2 tablespoons of Simple Syrup (page 39) and drizzle the sauce over the salad.

Tropical Fruit Salad with Sweet Tamarind Dressing

Rujak Buah

Rujak buah is a popular dish made by Jakartan street vendors, but the same dish can also be found in Munduk, North Bali, where the fruit is thinly sliced instead. I fondly remember enjoying this dish on a day trip to a beachfront *warung* at Natsepa Beach in Maluku, revelling in the sweeping views of the aquamarine sea and enjoying the calls of street vendors serving young coconut and fried bananas.

This Indonesian snack makes the perfect salad. The honey-like sauce is sweet, sour and spicy, offsetting the crunchy tang of tropical fruit and creating a refreshing, well-balanced dish.

Origin: Throughout Indonesia

Preparation time: 20 minutes
Cooking time: 10 minutes

Serves 8–10

For the sauce:
* 1 teaspoon shrimp paste (optional)
* 3 red bird's eye chillies, thinly sliced or finely ground with pestle and mortar
* 100 g/3½ oz chopped palm sugar or coconut sugar
* 2–3 tablespoons Tamarind Paste (page 44)
* Salt, to taste

For the fruit salad:
* 1 small pineapple, peeled, cored and cut into bite-size chunks
* 1 small firm mango, peeled and cut into bite-size chunks
* 1 small ripe firm papaya, peeled and cut into bite-size chunks
* 1 cucumber, seeded and cut into bite-size chunks

To make the sauce, dry-roast the shrimp paste in a frying pan over medium-high heat for 2–3 minutes. Set aside.

Combine all the ingredients in a small saucepan and add 4–5 tablespoons of water. Bring to a boil, then reduce the heat to medium-low and simmer for 5–7 minutes, until syrupy. Strain, then set aside. The sauce will thicken as it cools to room temperature.

To make the fruit salad, arrange the fruit on a large serving plate, then drizzle the sauce on top.

Variations:
- **Jakartan Fruit and Vegetable Salad (Rujak Bebek)**
  Replace the fruits with 1 small sweet potato, 1 small green banana, 1 jicama, 2 June plums (*kedondong*) and 1 small unripe mango. Peel and coarsely chop all the fruit and add to a blender. Mix until chunky. Serve chilled or at room temperature.
- **Jakarta Wedding Salad (Rujak Pengantin)**
  Omit the papaya, mango and cucumber. Double the pineapple and cut into 1-cm/½-inch cubes. Cut 100 g/3½ oz tofu into small cubes, season with salt and steam for 10 minutes. (Or pan-fry for 5–6 minutes until slightly golden.) Separate the leaves from 2 heads of baby gem lettuce and arrange them on a serving plate. Add pineapple and tofu and drizzle with Spicy Peanut Sauce (page 76).

Lettuce and Pineapple Salad with Sesame Sambal

Selada Campur, Nanas dan Sambal Wijen

Both black and white sesame seeds are commonly used in Indonesian dishes. In Manado, I grew up with sweet black sesame *baos* (a term for Chinese steamed buns) known locally as *bia pong temo*. In Java, white sesame seeds are used to make *onde-onde wijen*, a sesame-coated glutinous rice ball filled with sweetened mung beans. Onde-onde can also be filled with cheese, chocolate and even sweet potatoes.

Wijen paste is probably better known as tahini, the Middle Eastern paste made with white sesame seeds. Indeed, tahini is the base for this popular Central Java sambal recipe, often served as an alternative to the spicy peanut sauce in Vegetable Salad (page 88). The nutty and creamy paste reminds me of the wonderful market in Solo, Central Java, where I first tasted it. I've combined it with chillies, lime leaves and lime juice for fragrance and flavour.

Sesame sambal also makes a fine accompaniment for Compressed Rice (page 198). I have deliberately made the sambal vegan by omitting shrimp paste from the recipe. You could also prepare the salad with different salad leaves (greens), sweetcorn, boiled potatoes, carrots and cucumber – it's an excellent opportunity to exercise your creativity or design a salad to suit your tastes.

Origin: Modern recipe; sambal from Java

Preparation time: 25 minutes

Serves 4–6

For the sesame sambal:
* 4 makrut lime leaves, centre stem removed and thinly sliced (optional)
* 2 red bird's eye chillies, thinly sliced
* 2 cloves garlic, finely chopped
* 5 g/⅛ oz kencur or 10 g/¼ oz grated fresh root ginger
* 4 tablespoons lime juice
* 3 tablespoons tahini
* Salt, to taste

For the salad:
* 1 eating (dessert) apple, cored and cut into matchsticks
* 1 purple endive, leaves separated
* 1 small pineapple, peeled, cored and cut into bite-size chunks
* 100 g/3½ oz (1 cup) radishes, thinly sliced
* 50 g/1¾ oz (2 cups) watercress
* 50 g/1¾ oz (3½ cups) baby salad leaves (greens)

To prepare the sesame sambal, combine all the ingredients and 2 tablespoons of water. Mix well. Set aside.

To make the salad, arrange the vegetables on a large serving plate and serve with a side of dressing for your guests to help themselves. Alternatively, dress the salad and toss well, then serve immediately.

Crudité, Tempeh and Tofu with Shrimp Paste Sambal

Lalapan, Tempe, Tahu dan Sambal Terasi

The rich agriculture of West Java has helped the indigenous Sundanese people thrive, so it comes as no surprise to see the importance of fresh vegetables in their diet.

Lalapan is a classic Sundanese dish of raw vegetables, tempeh and tofu served with a shrimp paste sambal, often served in a small stone mortar. I have replaced some vegetables with more accessible varieties from my local farmer's market, but you could easily swap them out with cabbage, endive and baby sweetcorn. It can be served with rice and chicken or fish for a healthy and balanced meal.

Origin: Java

Preparation time: 20 minutes
Cooking time: 5 minutes

Serves 4–6

For the crudité:
* 2 carrots, halved lengthwise
* 1 small cucumber, cut into 10-cm/4-inch sticks
* 1 baby gem lettuce, halved lengthwise
* 1 red chicory (endive), leaves separated, rinsed and dried
* 100 g/3½ oz (⅔ cup) vine-ripened cherry tomatoes
* 50 g/1¾ oz (½ cup) radishes, halved
* Small bunch of basil (optional)
* 1 quantity Tomato and Shrimp Paste Sambal (page 54), to serve

For the tempeh and tofu:
* 2 cloves garlic, finely chopped
* 1 banana shallot, finely grated
* 1 tablespoon ground coriander
* 1 teaspoon salt
* 200 g/7 oz tempeh, cut into chunky pieces
* 200 g/7 oz firm tofu, cut into triangles
* 400 ml/14 fl oz (1⅔ cups) sunflower oil

For the crudité, arrange the vegetables and bunch of basil, if using, on a platter and refrigerate until needed.

For the tempeh and tofu marinade, combine the garlic, shallot, coriander and salt in a small bowl. Add 200 ml/7 fl oz (generous ¾ cup) of water and mix well. Add the tempeh and tofu and set aside for 5 minutes to marinate.

Heat the oil in a large frying pan over medium heat. Carefully add the marinated tofu and tempeh and deep-fry for 3–4 minutes on each side until golden brown. Using a slotted spoon, transfer the tofu and tempeh to a plate lined with paper towels to drain.

Remove the platter of vegetables from the refrigerator. Place the tempeh and tofu onto the platter and serve with a small bowl of sambal. Enjoy!

Variation:
- **Crudité, Tempeh and Tofu with Aubergine Sambal (Sambal Terong)**
  Serve with Aubergine Sambal (page 50) and gado-gado peanut sauce (page 86).

Prawn and Seaweed Salad with Spiced Coconut Dressing

Lawi Lawi dan Udang

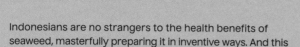

Indonesians are no strangers to the health benefits of seaweed, masterfully preparing it in inventive ways. And this Sulawesi salad is no exception.

It's a winning combination of briny seaweed, succulent prawns and sweet mango lightly dressed in a spicy, creamy coconut dressing. The Balinese have a version of this salad with spices and grated coconut (*rujak bulung*).

The sea grape, sometimes known as 'green caviar', is one of my favourites. You can buy sea grapes in specialist shops or online, but for practicality, I have used dried seaweed in this recipe. You could also replace it with samphire (sea asparagus).

Origin: Sulawesi

Preparation time: 25 minutes, plus 20 minutes soaking time
Cooking time: 5 minutes

Serves 4–6

For the salad:
* 20 g/¾ oz dried wakame or hijiki seaweed
* 2 carrots, coarsely grated
* 1 ripe mango, cut into 1-cm/½-inch cubes
* 2–3 tablespoons coconut oil
* 24 tiger prawns, peeled, deveined and patted dry

* Salt, to taste
* Juice of 2 limes

For the dressing:
* 40 g/1½ oz (½ cup) unsweetened desiccated coconut
* 100 ml/3½ fl oz (scant ½ cup) coconut milk

* 3–5 red bird's eye chillies, finely chopped
* Large bunch of basil, finely chopped
* Salt, to taste

To make the salad, soak the seaweed in a bowl of water for 10 minutes to rehydrate (or follow the package directions).

To make the dressing, combine the coconut and coconut milk in a bowl. Mix well and set aside for 10 minutes. Add the chillies and half of the basil and season with salt. Set aside.

Drain the seaweed. Add the carrots and mango. Set aside.

Heat the oil in a frying pan over medium-high heat. Season the prawns with salt and lime juice. Add the prawns and sauté for 4 minutes until pink. Transfer to a bowl.

Combine the dressing and salad and toss gently. Add the remaining half of the basil and toss again. Top with the prawns and serve immediately.

Variation:
- **Moluccan-Style Fish with Spiced Coconut Dressing (Kohu-Kohu)**
  Replace the salad with 400 g/14 oz smoked mackerel or haddock, 100 g/3½ oz thinly sliced young green beans and 50 g/1¾ oz bean sprouts. Omit the chillies from the dressing and stir in a ½ quantity of Red Spice Paste (page 43).

Raw Tuna in Spicy and Tangy Citrus
Gohu Ikan

The Manado word *gohu* translates to 'pickled' in specific dishes such as *gohu papaya*, where ripe papaya is pickled for at least 24 hours. But in this case, it is used to describe a quick, spicy and tangy marination of tuna.

I first learned of this dish on a visit to a fishing village near Likupang, a hot Indonesian tourist destination in my hometown of Manado. As the story goes, local fishermen would go out to sea with pouches of fresh chillies, shallots, calamansi and salt. When hunger struck, a few freshly caught fish were filleted on the spot and combined with the ingredients in the small bags.

This dish is also a tradition in Maluku, and I've prepared it to much success at several great establishments and gala dinners. Essentially, it's an Indonesian ceviche, full of freshness, heat and the perfect amount of sharpness to bring the flavours to life – and it's incredibly easy to make. Quality is paramount, so you must use high-quality fish. Ask a trusted fish supplier for sashimi-grade tuna.

Origin: Sulawesi and Maluku Islands

Preparation time: 15 minutes, plus 10 minutes chilling time

Serves 4

For the marinade:
* 2–3 red bird's eye chillies, finely chopped
* 2 banana shallots, finely chopped
* Handful of basil, finely chopped

* ½ teaspoon salt
* ¼ teaspoon sugar
* 1 tablespoon groundnut (peanut) oil
* Juice of 4 calamansis or 2 limes

For the tuna:
* 1 (400-g/14-oz) sashimi-grade tuna steak or tuna belly, cut into 1-cm/½-inch cubes
* Micro basil leaves, to garnish (optional)

To make the marinade, combine all the ingredients in a mixing bowl and mix well. Add the tuna to the bowl and refrigerate for 10 minutes.

Remove the mixture from the refrigerator and toss gently. Serve on individual plates topped with micro basil leaves.

Variation:
- **Indonesian Poke Bowls (Poke Bowl Ala Indonesia)**
  Divide 400 g/14 oz (2 cups) cooked rice into 4 bowls. Top each bowl with the tuna mixture. Add sliced avocado, coarsely grated carrots, edamame and corn. Dress with a Chilli and Tomato Sambal (page 48).

Seared Tuna with Chilli and Tomato Sambal
Ikan Tuna dengan Dabu-Dabu

A chilli and green tomato sambal makes a super spicy, yet versatile condiment for fried or barbecued fish at Manadonese restaurants. The sambal can also dress the salad.

Here is a simple and modern twist on a traditional dish, where I've combined tomatoes with avocados to create a delectable sambal with a kick. You could also substitute the tuna with prawns, cooked chicken breast, smoked tofu or even beef.

Origin: Sulawesi

Preparation time: 10 minutes
Cooking time: 5 minutes

Serves 4

* 1 quantity Chilli and Tomato Sambal (page 48)
* 2 ripe avocados, stoned (pitted) and diced
* 1 tablespoon lime juice
* Salt and black pepper, to taste

* 4 (200-g/7-oz) high-quality tuna steaks
* 2 tablespoons coconut oil
* 20 g/¾ oz baby salad leaves (greens)
* Small handful of mint or basil, to garnish

In a small bowl, combine the sambal, avocados and lime juice. Season with salt and mix well. Set aside.

Season the tuna steaks on both sides with salt and pepper.

Heat the oil in a frying pan over high heat. Add the tuna steaks and sear for 30–40 seconds on each side until the surface is opaque. Transfer the tuna to a chopping (cutting) board to rest.

Place the baby leaves on a large serving plate. Slice the tuna into 1-cm/½-inch-thick slices and arrange it on the salad. Top with chilli and tomato sambal and garnish with mint leaves.

Mixed Salad with Spicy and Tangy Peanut Sauce

Gado-Gado

Although very much a traditional Betawi dish, *gado-gado* is a signature Indonesian salad and a meal in itself. I first tasted gado-gado in my early teens from a Jakartan street vendor. Thanks to her incredible performance in assembling the dish, the experience was as much visual entertainment as enjoyment of flavours and textures. She placed a fresh chilli on a large stone mortar and, with a rhythmic rocking motion to her pestle, she ground it with garlic and deep-fried peanuts. She continued to add grated palm sugar, roasted shrimp paste and tamarind water to create a thick, creamy paste. She then tossed together boiled vegetables, tofu, tempeh and compressed rice cakes (*lontong*) with the sauce. The final dish was topped with a boiled egg, crispy shallots and prawn crackers and wrapped in a banana leaf. I paid for my first takeaway meal and enjoyed it on my walk home.

This recipe captures gado-gado's authentic flavours but I've added dry-roasted (rather than deep-fried) peanuts. I also combined a medley of blanched and fresh vegetables to add vibrancy, colour and texture.

Origin: Java

Preparation time: 40 minutes
Cooking time: 25–30 minutes

Serves 4

For the sauce:
* 2–3 red bird's eye chillies, finely chopped
* 2 cloves garlic, finely chopped
* 100 g/3½ oz (scant ½ cup) Peanut-Cashew Butter (page 39)
* 3–4 tablespoons Tamarind Paste (page 44)
* 2 tablespoons coconut sugar
* Salt, to taste

For the salad:
* 12 new potatoes
* 2 eggs

* 50 g/1¾ oz long beans or green beans (optional)
* 50 g/1¾ oz (⅔ cup) shredded white or red cabbage
* 1 carrot, grated
* 60 g/2¼ oz (1¼ cups) baby spinach
* 20 g/¾ oz (scant ½ cup) bean sprouts
* 1 cob sweetcorn, kernels only

For the tempeh and tofu:
* 3 cloves garlic, finely chopped
* 2 teaspoons ground coriander
* 1 teaspoon salt

* 100 g/3½ oz tempeh, cut into 1-cm/½-inch cubes
* 150 g/5½ oz tofu, cut into 1-cm/½-inch cubes
* 200 ml/ 7 fl oz (generous ¾ cup) sunflower oil, for deep-frying

To serve:
* 2 tablespoons Crispy Shallots (page 41)
* 4–8 Rice Crackers (page 42), cassava crackers or prawn crackers (optional)

To prepare the sauce, combine all the ingredients and mix well. Gradually add 150 ml/5 fl oz (⅔ cup) of water and mix until smooth. It should be creamy, tangy, spicy and sweet. Season with salt and set aside.

For the salad, boil the new potatoes in salted water for 15–18 minutes until softened. Drain, then set aside to cool. Halve the potatoes.

Meanwhile, put the eggs into a small saucepan of water. Bring to a boil and boil for 8 minutes. Drain, then transfer to a bowl of cold water to stop the cooking process. When cool enough to handle, peel the eggs and cut them in half.

Bring another saucepan of water to a boil. Fill a large bowl with iced water. Add the long beans to the saucepan, if using, and cook for 3–4 minutes, then immediately transfer to the bowl of iced water and cool for 2–3 minutes (to preserve the vivid green colour). Drain, then cut the beans into 1-cm/½-inch lengths. Add the cabbage to the water and blanch for 30 seconds. Drain.

Combine the cooked vegetables in a large bowl and toss. Add the carrot, baby spinach and bean sprouts and toss again.

For the tempeh and tofu, combine the garlic, coriander, salt and 100 ml/3½ fl oz (scant ½ cup) of water in a large bowl and mix well. Divide the marinade equally between two bowls, then add tempeh to one and tofu to the other.

Heat the oil in a small saucepan over medium-high heat. The oil is ready when a cube of bread dropped in sizzles on contact and turns golden in 10–15 seconds. (Alternatively, use a thermometer and heat to 180°C/350°F.) Carefully lower the tempeh into the oil and deep-fry for 2–3 minutes until golden. Using a slotted spoon, transfer the tempeh to a plate lined with paper towels. Repeat with the tofu for 3–4 minutes.

Spread the sauce onto four plates, then add the mixed vegetables. Add the tempeh, tofu and eggs. Sprinkle with crispy shallots and serve with the extra sauce and rice crackers on the side.

Variations:
- **Bali-Style Gado-Gado (Tipat Cantok)**
  Add 10 g/½ oz finely chopped kencur or 15 g/½ oz fresh root ginger to the sauce.
- **Gado-Gado Crudité (Gado-gado lalapan)**
  Gado-gado can also be served as a crudité. Omit the tofu. Replace all the vegetables, except the potatoes, with 12 baby carrots, 2 endives (separate the leaves), 1 pack of cherry tomatoes, 1 small cucumber (cut into sticks) and fried tempeh (cut into chips and fried). Arrange the vegetables and tempeh on a large serving platter and serve with the dipping sauce in a bowl.

Vegetables with Kencur and Peanut Sauce
Karedok

This raw vegetable dish, a close cousin of *Gado-Gado* (page 86), is served with a spicy and tangy peanut sauce, infused with the distinctive taste and aroma of kencur (also known as aromatic or sand ginger), garlic and herbaceous basil. Cashews have also been added for creaminess.

Some cooks will add shrimp paste or fermented soy pulp *(oncom)*, a byproduct from making tofu, to impart intense umami flavour to the sambal. The latter is a staple in West Java and a novel example of Sundanese resourcefulness when it comes to food waste reduction. The salad can be prepared in advance and kept in the refrigerator. Classic *karedok* sauce is dark brown as the peanuts tend to be deep-fried rather than roasted.

Origin: Java

Preparation time: 25 minutes

Serves 4

For the peanut sauce:
* 2–3 red bird's eye chillies, finely chopped
* 1 clove garlic, finely chopped
* 200 g/7 oz (generous ¾ cup) Peanut-Cashew Butter (page 39) or quality peanut butter
* 10 g/¼ oz kencur or 20 g/¾ oz ginger, finely grated
* 3 tablespoons Tamarind Paste (page 44) or juice of 2 limes
* 2 tablespoons coconut sugar
* 1 teaspoon roasted shrimp paste or 2–3 tablespoons fish sauce (optional)
* Salt, to taste

For the salad:
* 6 cherry tomatoes, cut in half
* 1 carrot, grated
* ½ small cucumber, unpeeled and cut into matchsticks
* 50 g/1¾ oz (¼ cup) bean sprouts
* 50 g/1¾ oz green beans, long beans or runner beans, thinly sliced
* 50 g/1¾ oz sweetheart cabbage, thinly sliced (optional)
* 50 g/1¾ oz (½ cup) radishes, thinly sliced
* Large bunch of basil
* 2 tablespoons Crispy Shallots (page 41), to serve (optional)
* Rice Crackers (page 42), to serve (optional)

To prepare the sauce, combine all the ingredients and 150 ml/ 5 fl oz (⅔ cup) of water in a bowl and mix until smooth. It should taste tangy, spicy and sweet. Season with salt. Set aside.

To make the salad, combine all the ingredients in a large bowl and mix.

Spread half of the sauce on a serving plate, then add the vegetables. Top with the remaining peanut sauce, crispy shallots and rice crackers, if you wish.

Variations:
- **Vegetable Salad (Pecel)**
  Double the green beans, bean sprouts and cabbage. Add 50 g/ 1¾ oz (1½ cups) baby spinach. For the sauce, omit the shrimp paste and add 5 lime leaves, centre stem removed and thinly sliced. Mix all the sauce ingredients, drizzle the sauce around the vegetables and serve with steamed rice.
- **Vegetable Salad with Spiced Tempeh Batter (Lotek)**
  Add 50 g/1¾ oz (1½ cups) baby spinach, boiled eggs and Deep-Fried Spiced Tempeh (page 155). Serve with the peanut sauce.
- **Jakartan Cold Rice Noodles (Ketoprak)**
  Omit all vegetables except the carrot and bean sprouts. Prepare 200 g/7 oz dried vermicelli according to the package directions. Drain and transfer to a bowl of iced water. Season 200 g/7 oz firm tofu with salt and 1 tablespoon ground coriander, then deep-fry or steam them. Put them in a bowl, top with grated carrots and bean sprouts and serve with the peanut sauce.

Solo Steak Salad
Selat Solo

Famed for its hand-decorated and textile batik cloth, Solo (the colloquial name for Surakarta) is the cultural heartland of Java with a deep history influenced by the Dutch, first via the spice trade and then later in the cultivation of tobacco and development of irrigation systems across the dry region.

Selat Solo is a favourite of the ruling Javanese royal family. (I had the privilege of dining at both palaces: Keraton Surakarta and Keraton Mangkunegaran.) The warming spices of nutmeg, cinnamon and cloves – essential ingredients in the famous Dutch shortcrust biscuit (cookies) – are paramount to this dish. Traditionally, beef topside (top round) is braised with spices, sweet soy sauce, potatoes, carrots and green beans. I've deconstructed this recipe by pan-frying rib-eye steaks, which keeps all the classic flavours intact, and incorporating potatoes into a light salad.

Origin: Java

Preparation time: 15 minutes
Cooking time: 25–30 minutes

Serves 4

For the salad:
* 12 new potatoes (150 g/5½ oz)
* Salt and black pepper, to taste
* 2 eggs
* 100 g/3½ oz (⅔ cup) vine-ripened cherry tomatoes, cut into 4 portions
* ½ small cucumber, seeded and cut into bite-size pieces
* 60 g/2¼ oz (2½ cups) watercress
* 50 g/1¾ oz baby gem lettuce, leaves separated, rinsed and patted dry

For the steak:
* 2 (250-g/9-oz) rib-eye steaks
* Salt and black pepper, to taste
* Coconut oil, for brushing

For the sauce:
* 3 tablespoons Sweet Soy Sauce (page 38)
* Juice of 2 limes
* 1–2 teaspoons Speculaas Spice Blend (page 41)
* Salt and black pepper, to taste

To make the salad, bring a saucepan of water to a boil. Add the new potatoes and 1 teaspoon of salt, then boil for 20 minutes until softened. Drain, then set aside to cool.

Add the eggs to a saucepan and cover with cold water. Bring to a boil and boil for 8–10 minutes. Drain, then transfer the eggs to a bowl of cold water to stop the cooking process. When cool enough to handle, peel the eggs.

To prepare the steak, heat a frying pan over high heat. Brush the oil on each side of the steak. Season both sides with salt and pepper. Sear for 2–3 minutes on each side for medium-rare or 3–4 minutes for medium. Set aside to rest.

Reduce the heat to medium-low, then add 3½ tablespoons of water to deglaze the pan. Add the sweet soy sauce, lime juice and spice blend. Season to taste with salt and pepper.

To serve, slice the steaks into strips. Combine all the salad ingredients and toss gently. Divide the salad among serving plates. Slice and fan the steak on top, then drizzle with sauce and serve.

Soups, Sotos and Noodle Soups

Sop, Soto dan Mie

I have my family to thank for my expansive repertoire of soups. Oma Tecla, my late paternal grandmother, would prepare the richest, most flavoursome and fortifying *brenebon* soup (page 98) with tender morsels of pork, hearty red beans and aromatic spices and serve it with Chilli and Tomato Sambal (page 48). Oma Merey, my maternal grandmother, mastered the art of preparing *ikan kuah asam*, a clear fish soup infused with lemongrass, tomato, chillies and basil (page 94). Her signature spicy roast pumpkin soup (page 93) was also a highlight at family gatherings. And every Christmas, Mum made her famous chicken soup with glass noodles, carrots, potatoes, and wood ear mushrooms topped with Chinese parsley.

As a child, I recall well-prepared soups as an essential part of evening meals and always a pleasurable course, warming the being from the inside out – especially during the rainy season when I crave it the most. Manadonese soups often have Dutch or Chinese influence, and I'll sometimes add an assortment of vegetables, pulses (legumes), macaroni and meatballs to clear vegetable or meat broths. But I am also fond of the strong layers of spiced flavours found in the Arabic-influenced Javanese Oxtail Soup (page 97) and goat leg soup (*sop kaki kambing*) loaded with carrots and potatoes.

For those unfamiliar with Indonesian cuisine, soto (also known as coto or sroto) could easily be mistaken for just another bowl of noodle soup or stew – but this happens to be one of the nation's most revered dishes, available across the many regions (especially Java and Sumatra), each with its unique story and personality. My first taste of soto was in Jakarta, and it delivered everything one might expect from this traditional dish: a light broth infused with herbs, spices and a hint of fragrant coconut milk, boosted with noodles (optional) and topped with chopped tomatoes, bean sprouts, Chinese celery, boiled eggs and crispy shallots.

These recipes for soups, sotos and noodle soups are uncomplicated and easy to put together. They're comforting, soul-soothing and designed to be enjoyed with friends and family.

Oma's Spicy Roast Pumpkin Soup
Sup Sambiki Oma

This dish reminds me of my Oma's simple but delicious home cooking. The fragrant combination of ginger, garlic, pumpkin and coconut milk sings of authentic Manadonese flavours.

The Minahasa or Manadonese word for pumpkin is *sambiki*. My grandmother used to prepare it by simmering the pumpkin in water and coconut milk. I prefer to roast the pumpkin first to intensify its flavour. And the Manadonese like to use shallots, but I prefer onions for a touch of sweetness.

Origin: Sulawesi

Preparation time: 15 minutes
Cooking time: 50–55 minutes

Serves 6–8

---

* 1 (1-kg/2 lb 4-oz) pumpkin or butternut squash, peeled, seeded and sliced into 1-cm/½-inch cubes
* 1–1½ teaspoons salt
* 3 tablespoons coconut oil or vegetable oil
* 3 cloves garlic, finely chopped
* 1 onion, finely chopped
* 20 g/¾ oz fresh root ginger, finely grated
* 400 ml/14 fl oz (1⅔ cups) coconut milk, reserving 4–6 tablespoons for drizzling
* Black pepper, to taste

Preheat the oven to 180°C/350°F/Gas Mark 4. Line a baking sheet with baking (parchment) paper.

Place the pumpkin on the prepared baking sheet. Season with ½ teaspoon of salt and 2 tablespoons of oil. Using your hands, mix to coat. Roast for 30–35 minutes until tender. Remove from the oven and set aside.

Heat the remaining 1 tablespoon of oil in a large saucepan over medium heat. Add the garlic and onion and sauté for 5 minutes until softened but not coloured. Add the ginger and sauté for another minute.

Stir in the pumpkin and cook for 2 minutes. Pour in the coconut milk and 200 ml/7 fl oz (generous ¾ cup) of hot water. Bring to a boil, then reduce the heat to medium-low and simmer for 5 minutes. Season to taste with the remaining ½–1 teaspoon of salt and pepper.

Using an immersion blender, blend until smooth. (Alternatively, transfer the mixture to a blender and blend in batches. Pour the soup back into the saucepan.)

Bring the soup to a boil. Season to taste with more salt if needed. Simmer for 8 minutes until piping hot.

Ladle 2–3 spoons of soup into soup bowls. Drizzle each with coconut milk.

Left-over soup can be stored in the freezer for 2 weeks.

Variation:
- **Sweet Potato Soup (Sup Ubi Jalar)**
  Replace the pumpkin with sweet potatoes.

Sour Fish Soup
Ikan Kuah Asam

This restorative Manadonese soup can now be had across Eastern Indonesia. Tinged yellow with turmeric, the clear broth is layered with flavour and deceptively easy to make, requiring no oil or paste. It was my Oma's favourite soup.

She would prepare it with mackerel, prized for its sweet, delicate flesh, and add a few tablespoons of fluffy steamed rice.

Origin: Sulawesi

Preparation time: 15 minutes
Cooking time: 25–30 minutes

Serves 4

* 4 makrut lime leaves, torn
* 2 large tomatoes, finely chopped
* 2 spring onions (scallions), finely sliced
* 1–2 red bird's eye chillies, thinly sliced
* 1 stalk lemongrass, crushed and tied into a knot
* 1 banana shallot, thinly sliced
* Handful of basil, plus extra to garnish
* Salt, to taste
* Juice of 1–2 limes
* 4 (125-g/4¼-oz) skinless firm white fish fillets, cut into bite-size pieces

Bring 800 ml/27 fl oz (3½ cups) of water to a boil in a large saucepan. Add all the ingredients, except the lime juice and fish, and bring to a boil. Reduce the heat to medium and simmer for 20–25 minutes. Season with salt and add lime juice to taste.

Add the fish and cook for 3–4 minutes. Divide the fish into 4 soup bowls and ladle 2–3 spoons of broth on top. Garnish with basil and serve hot.

Variations:
- **Sour Fish Soup with Turmeric (Ikan Parende)**
  Add 10 g/¼ oz fresh thinly sliced turmeric and 15 g/½ oz thinly sliced ginger with the rest of the soup ingredients.
- **Prawn and Sweetcorn Soup (Binte Biluhuta)**
  Replace the salmon with an equal weight of medium shelled prawns, add the kernels from 2 cobs of sweetcorn and cook for 2–3 minutes.

Oxtail Soup
Sup Buntut

Light and comforting, this popular Jakarta soup has a distinctive aroma, courtesy of a spiced infusion of nutmeg, cloves and cinnamon. It requires time, but your patience will be rewarded with juicy, fork-tender morsels of oxtail. The toppings introduce even more texture, flavour and goodness to the dish, while a cooked sambal adds the perfect amount of chilli heat. For a lighter, and more traditional, version, use water instead of beef stock.

Origin: Java

Preparation time: 20 minutes
Cooking time: 2 hours 50 minutes

Serves 4

For the soup:
* 1.5 kg/3 lb 5 oz chopped oxtail, fat trimmed and discarded
* 2.5 litres (2½ quarts) beef stock or water
* 5 makrut lime leaves, torn
* 2 banana shallots, thinly sliced
* 3 cloves garlic, finely chopped
* 10 g/¼ oz fresh root ginger, thinly sliced
* 10 g/¼ oz galangal, thinly sliced
* 1 stick cinnamon
* 1 whole nutmeg, coarsely ground
* 1 teaspoon cloves
* 1 teaspoon black peppercorns
* 4 carrots, chopped into 1-cm/½-inch lengths
* 2 large potatoes, cut into 2-cm/¾-inch cubes
* 2 teaspoons salt
* Juice of 2 limes

For the toppings:
* 2 tomatoes, seeded and chopped
* 3 tablespoons Crispy Shallots (page 41)
* 2 tablespoons finely chopped Chinese parsley or parsley
* 3 tablespoons finely chopped spring onions (scallions)
* 1 large red chilli, thinly sliced (optional)

To serve (optional):
* Steamed rice
* Boiled Sambal (page 53)
* Lime wedges

Place the oxtail into a large saucepan and cover with room-temperature water. Bring to a boil and boil for 5 minutes. Drain, then rinse the oxtail. Repeat.

In the same saucepan, combine the oxtail and beef stock. Add the lime leaves, shallots, garlic, ginger, galangal, cinnamon, nutmeg, cloves and peppercorns. Bring to a boil, then reduce the heat to medium-low and simmer for 2 hours. If needed, cover with more water to keep the oxtail covered.

Add the carrots, potatoes and salt. Simmer for another 45 minutes or until tender and soft. Add the lime juice. Season to taste with more salt. Discard the lime leaves.

To serve, arrange the oxtail and vegetables in 4 large bowls. Ladle in the soup, then top with tomatoes, crispy shallots, Chinese parsley, spring onions (scallions) and chilli, if using. Serve as is or with a bowl of steamed rice, boiled sambal and lime wedges.

Beans and Pork Soup
Brenebon

This dish is an example of Dutch influence on Manadonese cuisine. Traditionally, pig feet give the soup a gelatinous texture, but I've used pork ribs for lightness. A hearty variety of beans and vegetables pack it with extra protein and nutrients.

If you're short on time, consider replacing the dried beans with canned kidney beans and adding them to the saucepan for the last 30 minutes of cooking. The Chilli and Tomato Sambal (page 48) introduces a balanced layer of flavour.

Origin: Sulawesi

Preparation time: 20 minutes
Cooking time: 1–1½ hours

Serves 6–8

* 450 g/1 lb pork loin ribs, cut into pieces
* 250 g/9 oz (1½ cups) dried kidney beans or 10-bean mix, soaked overnight
* 3 spring onions (scallions), chopped

* 1½ teaspoons cloves, finely ground
* 1½ teaspoons freshly ground nutmeg
* 1 teaspoon salt
* 1 teaspoon white pepper

* 3 tablespoons Chinese parsley or celery leaves

To serve:
* 3 tablespoons Crispy Shallots (page 41) and Chilli and Tomato Sambal (page 48)

Combine the ribs and beans in a large saucepan. Add 2 litres/2 quarts of water and bring to a boil. Add half of the spring onions (scallions), the cloves, nutmeg, salt and pepper. Reduce the heat to medium-low, cover and simmer for 1–1½ hours, until the pork falls off the bone.

Transfer the meat to a chopping (cutting) board and let cool slightly. Using a fork, remove the meat from the bone and chop.

Put the pork back into the soup. Add the Chinese parsley and remaining spring onions. Season to taste.

Serve in bowls with crispy shallots and sambal.

Pumpkin, Oyster Mushroom and Coconut Soup
Letak Letuk

Lampung, a province on the southern tip of Sumatra, is renowned for its nature reserve and national parks and home to magnificent wildlife including endangered elephants and Sumatran tigers. I first learned about this local dish at a cooking competition where I was one of the judges – it was a reminder that so many new discoveries of people and traditions can be had in simple yet engaging conversations with local members of the community.

This vegan dish isn't known around the archipelago, but I adore its simple preparation. No oil, no paste – just sliced or chopped ingredients tossed into a pot.

Origin: Sumatra

Preparation time: 20 minutes
Cooking time: 25–30 minutes

Serves 4

* 3 cloves garlic, thinly sliced
* 3 makrut lime leaves, torn
* 2 red bird's eye chillies, thinly sliced
* 1 large banana shallot, thinly sliced in rings

* 400 ml/14 fl oz (1⅔ cups) coconut milk
* 500 g/1 lb 2 oz pumpkin, butternut squash or sweet potatoes, cut into 1.5-cm/⅝-inch cubes
* Salt and black pepper, to taste

* 200 g/7 oz oyster mushrooms, sliced into thirds
* 100 g/3½ oz (3 cups) baby spinach
* Small bunch of basil, leaves and stems chopped

In a medium saucepan, combine the garlic, lime leaves, chillies and shallot. Add half of the coconut milk and 200 ml/7 fl oz (generous ¾ cup) of water and bring to a boil. Add the pumpkin and bring it back to a boil. Cover, then reduce the heat to medium-low and simmer for 20 minutes or until the pumpkin is tender.

Add the remaining half of coconut milk. Season with salt and pepper. Add the mushrooms and cook for 3–4 minutes. Stir in the spinach and basil and cook for another 2 minutes. Season to taste.

Discard the lime leaves. Ladle the soup into bowls and serve.

Variation:
- **Javanese Spinach and Coconut Soup (Sop Bobor)**
Omit the chillies, pumpkin and mushrooms. To the stock, add 4 lime leaves, 15 g/½ oz ginger (or 8 g/¼ oz finely grated kencur), 10 g/¼ oz crushed galangal and 1 stalk crushed lemongrass. After simmering for 20 minutes, add double the amount of spinach and cook for 3–4 minutes. Remove the galangal and lemongrass before serving.

Medan Sour Laksa with Mackerel and Tamarind
Laksa Medan

My dear friend Maria introduced me to this delicious laksa. The glorious torch ginger flowers, also known as a wild ginger bud or *kecombrang,* impart a unique aroma to the dish. Another exotic ingredient called *asam gelugur* (the dried fruit of *garcinia atrovirdis*) brings a hint of sourness. Together, they balance out this mackerel dish.

It's not easy to find asam gelugur here in England, so I've replaced it with tamarind. You can find torch ginger flowers from Asian speciality food shops, but *myoga* (Japanese ginger) is a suitable substitute. Here, I use flat rice noodles but feel free to use any rice noodles. Finally, seek out fresh mackerel from a reputable fish supplier who can clean and fillet the fish. Just be sure to ask for the fish bones and head wrapped separately.

Origin: Sumatra

Preparation time: 25 minutes
Cooking time: 40 minutes

Serves 4–6

For the fish broth:
* 1 (600-g/1 lb 5 oz) mackerel, cleaned and filleted with head and bones reserved
* 2 stalks lemongrass, white part finely chopped and green part crushed
* Salt, to taste
* 2 tablespoons sunflower oil

* 1 quantity Yellow Spice Paste (page 43), prepared without the galangal
* 1 teaspoon shrimp paste or 2 tablespoons fish sauce
* 2 torch ginger flowers, thinly sliced
* 4 tablespoons Tamarind Paste (page 44)
* 3 makrut lime leaves, torn
* 1 tablespoon sugar

For the laksa:
* 200 g/7 oz dried rice noodles
* ½ cucumber, seeded and finely chopped
* 1 large red chilli, thinly sliced
* 1 banana shallot, thinly sliced
* Bunch of mint, to serve

To make the fish broth, bring 1.5 litres/50 fl oz (6¼ cups) of water to a boil in a large saucepan. Add the reserved mackerel head, bones and crushed green parts of the lemongrass. Bring back to a boil. Reduce the heat to medium-low, cover and simmer for 20 minutes. Add the mackerel fillets and simmer for 10 minutes or until cooked thoroughly. Season with salt.

Using a slotted spoon, carefully transfer the fillets to a plate. Set aside. Strain the stock into a bowl and set it aside.

Heat the oil in a large saucepan over medium heat. Add the spice paste and cook for 4–5 minutes until fragrant. Add the shrimp paste and cook for another 2 minutes. Mix well. Add the torch ginger flowers and sauté for 1–2 minutes. Pour in the fish stock and bring to a boil. Reduce the heat to medium-low and simmer for 10 minutes.

Meanwhile, remove the skin from the fish and pull apart the fish with a fork. Carefully remove all bones from the fish. Add the fish, tamarind paste, lime leaves and sugar to the pan. Mix well. Season to taste. You should have a rich broth exploding with sweet, sour and spicy flavours. Discard the lime leaves.

Prepare the dried noodles according to the package directions. Drain, then divide the noodles among the bowls. Ladle hot broth into each bowl, then top with cucumber, chilli, shallot and mint. Serve immediately.

Bogor Tempeh Laksa
Laksa Tempe Bogor

The people of West Java were never ones to waste food, and this Bogor laksa is traditionally prepared with grilled *oncom*, a beautiful orange fermented soy product from this region. Visiting my uncle in Bogor was always a treat, a time to enjoy this laksa with *combro*, a fried snack made with grated cassava, oncom, chillies and basil.

This laksa is often prepared with chicken, but I've opted to use tempeh to keep this dish strictly vegetarian. The broth, beautifully golden from turmeric, lemongrass and lime leaves, is equally fortifying and delicious.

Origin: Java

Preparation time: 20 minutes, plus 10 minutes marinating time
Cooking time: 35–40 minutes

Serves 4

For the spice blend:
* 1 tablespoon coriander seeds
* 1 teaspoon cumin seeds
* 1 teaspoon white peppercorns

For the laksa:
* Salt, to taste
* 250 g/9 oz tempeh, cut into 1-cm/½-inch-thick slices
* 2 tablespoons coconut oil or vegetable oil

* ½ quantity Yellow Spice Paste (page 43)
* 3 green cardamom pods, slightly crushed
* 4 makrut lime leaves, torn
* 1 stalk lemongrass, crushed and tied into a knot
* 600 ml/20 fl oz (2½ cups) coconut milk
* 1–2 tablespoons coconut sugar (optional)

* 200 g/7 oz dried rice noodles
* Handful of basil
* Juice of 1 lime
* Boiled Sambal (page 53), to serve

For the toppings:
* 2–4 eggs
* 50 g/1¾ oz (¼ cup) bean sprouts
* 2 tablespoons Crispy Shallots (page 41, optional)

To make the spice blend, dry-roast the spices in a small frying pan over medium heat for 4–5 minutes. Leave to cool slightly. Transfer to a pestle and mortar and grind to a fine powder. Set aside.

For the laksa, put ½ teaspoon of the spice blend into a medium bowl. Add 100 ml/3½ fl oz (scant ½ cup) of water and ½ teaspoon salt and mix well. Add the tempeh, stir to coat and marinate for 10 minutes.

Heat a griddle pan over high heat. Working in batches, add the tempeh and grill for 2–3 minutes on each side. Transfer to a plate. Repeat with the remaining tempeh, then cut into 1-cm/½-inch cubes.

Heat the oil in a large saucepan over medium heat. Add the yellow spice paste and sauté for 4 minutes. Add the remaining spice blend, cardamom and half of the tempeh. Mix well and cook for 1 minute. Add the lime leaves and lemongrass. Pour in the coconut milk and 300 ml/10 fl oz (1¼ cups) of water. Season with coconut sugar, if using, and salt. Bring to a boil, then reduce the heat to medium-low and simmer for 20 minutes.

Meanwhile, put the eggs into a small saucepan of water. Bring to a boil and boil for 10 minutes. Drain, then transfer to a bowl of cold water to stop the cooking process. When cool enough to handle, peel the eggs and halve them.

Prepare the dried noodles according to the package directions. Drain, then transfer to a bowl of cold water. Drain again, then set aside.

Discard the lime leaves. Add half of the basil and the lime juice to the broth and cook for 1 minute. Season to taste.

Divide the noodles into 4 bowls. Ladle 2–3 spoons of hot broth into each bowl. Top with eggs, grilled tempeh, bean sprouts, crispy shallots and the remaining basil. Serve with boiled sambal.

Variation:
- **Jakarta Laksa (Laksa Betawi)**
  This laksa has a deep and rich umami flavour. Add 1 teaspoon shrimp paste and 2 additional large red chillies to the paste. To your spice blend, add 1 teaspoon dried shrimp. Replace the tempeh with 100 g/3½ oz firm tofu (cut into 1-cm/½-inch cubes), 100 g/3½ oz shelled prawns and 4 boneless, skinless chicken thighs, thinly sliced. Add the chicken and tofu to the broth and cook for 10 minutes. Add the prawn and cook for another 2–3 minutes. Omit the bean sprouts topping and add melinjo crackers (optional).

Chicken Soto with Turmeric and Lemongrass
Soto Ayam Lamongan

This is my ultimate comfort food, especially on a grey day in England. The explosion of flavours and textures brings a smile to my world.

Nearly every community around the archipelago, and the world for that matter, has its version of chicken soup and chicken noodle soup. Layered with flavour, this light dish captures both.

Here, we have a clear broth with turmeric, lemongrass and glass noodles or rice vermicelli, making this dish gluten-free and dairy-free! Additional toppings, a touch of lime juice and spoons of sambal make it even more flavoursome. In some regions, coconut milk is added.

Origin: Java

Preparation time: 20 minutes
Cooking time: 55 minutes

Serves 8

For the soto:
* 1 tablespoon sunflower oil
* 1 quantity Yellow Spice Paste (page 43)
* 1 (1.2-kg/2 lb 12-oz) chicken, cut into 8 pieces and skin removed
* 4 makrut lime leaves, torn
* 2 stalks lemongrass, crushed
* Salt, to taste
* 200 g/7 oz dried rice vermicelli or glass noodles

For the toppings:
* 4 eggs (optional)
* 2 large tomatoes, seeded and cut into ½-cm/¼-inch cubes
* 150 g/5½ oz (1½ cups) shredded cabbage
* 3 tablespoons bean sprouts
* 3 tablespoons chopped Chinese celery or celery leaves
* 4 tablespoons Koya (page 42)
* 8 slices lime, halved

To serve:
* 8 lime slices
* 1 quantity Boiled Sambal (page 53)
* Melinjo crackers or prawn crackers

To make the soto, heat the oil in a large saucepan over medium heat. Add the spice paste and sauté for 3–4 minutes. Add the chicken and cook for 5 minutes, stirring occasionally. Add the lime leaves, lemongrass and 1.5 litres/50 fl oz (6¼ cups) of water. Season with salt. Bring to a boil, then cover and reduce the heat to medium-low. Simmer for 45 minutes, skimming any scum from the surface with a ladle.

Meanwhile, prepare the dried noodles according to the package directions. Drain, then transfer to a bowl of cold water. Drain again, then set aside.

Put the eggs, if using, into a small saucepan of water. Bring to a boil and boil for 10 minutes. Drain, then transfer to a bowl of cold water to stop the cooking process. When cool enough to handle, peel the eggs and cut them in half.

Transfer the chicken to a chopping (cutting) board and let cool. When cool enough to handle, pull the meat away from the bone and cut into slices. Set aside.

Put the noodles into bowls. Add the tomatoes, cabbage, bean sprouts and chicken. Ladle 2–3 spoons of hot broth into the bowls. Sprinkle with Chinese celery and koya. Add half an egg and a lime slice to each bowl. Serve with sambal and melinjo crackers on the side.

Variations:
- **Chicken Soto Banjar (Soto Banjar)**
  Replace the yellow spice paste with White Spice Paste (page 43). When frying the paste, add 3 green cardamom pods, 2 star anise, 1 (5-cm/2-inch) stick of cinnamon and 1 teaspoon each of ground nutmeg and clove. Omit the koya.
- **Jakartan Soto with Noodles (Soto Mie Jakarta)**
  Replace the yellow spice paste with White Spice Paste (page 43). Replace the chicken with beef topside (top round) or cheeks and cook for 1½ hours, or until the beef is tender. Replace the rice noodles with egg noodles. Omit the koya and egg. Serve with Boiled Sambal (page 53) and Spring Rolls (page 70) as well.

Beef and Coconut Soto
Soto Betawi

Soto often starts with a clear broth, but the Betawi version is thicker with a subtle curry-like flavour. The delicious soup base consists of a beef broth enriched with coconut milk and infused with herbs and spices. Adventurous eaters enjoy it with offal, pan-fried kidney, tripe or liver.

This lighter adaptation of the traditional soto has beef, coconut milk, spices and herbs stewed low and slow to tender perfection. Serve it on its own or with a bowl of rice or Compressed Rice (page 198).

Origin: Java

Preparation time: 15 minutes
Cooking time: 1 hour 45 minutes

Serves 4

For the beef:
* 600 g/1 lb 5 oz quality stewing beef or topside (top round), cut into 1-cm/½-inch cubes
* Salt and black pepper, to taste
* 2 tablespoons coconut oil or sunflower oil, plus extra if needed
* ½ quantity White Spice Paste (page 43)
* 4 makrut lime leaves, torn

* 1 tablespoon ground coriander
* 1 teaspoon freshly grated nutmeg
* 600 ml/20 fl oz (2½ cups) coconut milk
* Steamed rice, to serve

For the toppings:
* 2 large ripe tomatoes, cut into ½-cm/¼-inch cubes

* 2 limes, cut into wedges
* 1 spring onion (scallion), finely chopped
* Small bunch of Chinese parsley or celery leaves
* 1 quantity Crispy Shallots (page 41)
* 1 quantity Boiled Sambal (page 53, optional)
* Melinjo crackers (optional)

Season the beef with salt and pepper. Heat the oil in a large saucepan over medium heat. Working in batches, add the beef and sear for 2–3 minutes on all sides until browned. Transfer to a plate.

In the same saucepan, add the spice paste and cook for 4–5 minutes over medium heat until fragrant. If the mixture is dry, add a bit more oil.

Return the beef to the pan, mix well and sauté for another minute. Stir in the lime leaves, coriander and nutmeg. Pour in 500 ml/17 fl oz (generous 2 cups) of water and half of the coconut milk. Season with salt. Bring to a boil, then reduce the heat to medium-low and simmer for 1½ hours until the meat is tender. Stir in the remaining coconut milk and cook for another 5 minutes. Season with salt and pepper.

Put the toppings in individual bowls. Serve family-style with sides of toppings and steamed rice on the table.

Variation:
- **Jakartan Spiced Beef Soto (Soto Tangkar)**
  Add 600 g/1 lb 5 oz ribs and cut them into single ribs. Replace the white paste with a full quantity of Red Spice Paste (page 43). Omit the nutmeg and Chinese parsley. Add 1 teaspoon toasted ground cumin, 2 tablespoons Tamarind Paste (page 44) and another 400 ml/14 fl oz (1⅔ cups) water to the stock. Dice 2 tomatoes and add just before serving.

Makassar Beef Coto
Coto Makassar

This dish always brings back fond childhood memories of eating out with my family at a popular restaurant in Manado. Makassar beef coto is a well-known Makassar restaurant dish prepared with herbs and spices and thickened with finely ground peanuts.

Beef cheeks have an unctuous, melt-in-the-mouth tenderness in this slow-cooked favourite. You could also replace it with topside (top round) if you wish.

Origin: Sulawesi

Preparation time: 25 minutes
Cooking time: 2 hours 15 minutes

Serves 4–6

For the paste:
* 5 cloves garlic, coarsely chopped
* 2 banana shallots, coarsely chopped
* 2 red bird's eye chillies
* 15 g/½ oz fresh root ginger, thinly sliced
* 10 g/¼ oz galangal, thinly sliced

For the spice blend:
* 1 (2-cm/¾-inch) stick cinnamon
* 1 tablespoon coriander seeds
* 1 teaspoon cumin seeds
* ½ teaspoon cloves

For the beef:
* 2 tablespoons coconut oil or vegetable oil
* 1 kg/2 lb 4 oz beef cheeks or topside (top round), cut into 2-cm/¾-inch cubes
* Salt and black pepper, to taste
* 5 makrut lime leaves
* 1 stalk lemongrass, crushed and tied into a knot
* 2 tablespoons miso paste
* 100 g/3½ oz (scant 1 cup) finely ground raw peanuts
* Juice of 1 lime

For the toppings:
* 3 tablespoons Crispy Shallots (page 41)
* 2 spring onions (scallions), thinly sliced

To serve:
* Steamed rice
* Miso Sambal (page 51)

To make the paste, combine all the ingredients in a small blender and blend into a smooth paste. Set aside.

To prepare the spice blend, dry-roast the spices in a frying pan over medium heat for 4–5 minutes. Leave to cool. Transfer the mixture, except for the cinnamon, into a spice grinder and grind to a fine powder. Set aside.

To prepare the beef, heat the oil and paste in a medium saucepan over medium heat. Stir for 5–6 minutes.

Season the beef with salt and pepper. Add the beef to the pan and sauté for 5 minutes until the meat is coated in the paste. Add the spice blend, cinnamon stick, lime leaves, lemongrass and miso. Mix well. Add 1.5 litres/50 fl oz (6¼ cups) of water and bring to a boil. Reduce the heat to medium-low and simmer for 1 hour. Using a ladle, skim any scum from the surface. Add the peanuts and cook for another hour, until the beef is tender.

Add the lime juice, then season to taste with salt and pepper. Ladle the soup into bowls and sprinkle with crispy shallots and spring onions (scallions). Serve with steamed rice and miso sambal.

Vegetable and Miso Noodle Soup

Mie Tek-Tek Sayuran dengan Tauco

I grew up in Jakarta with *tek-tek* noodles. 'Tek-tek' is the rapping sound of a wooden stick hitting the side of the cart, made by street food vendors looking for evening business and keen to attract the attention of hungry patrons. Sadly, online meal delivery services are replacing this great tradition.

Simple, quick, and easy to make, *mie tek-tek* can be prepared in endless variations. I enjoy it with chicken breast, chicken liver or eggs, and I like this version for its ample umami undertones courtesy of the miso. I deliberately omitted sweet soy, relying on the sweetness from the sweetcorn, which also adds vibrant colour to the soup. Finish it with a bit of vinegary tang and chilli heat for a wonderfully memorable meal.

Origin: Modern recipe

Preparation time: 15 minutes
Cooking time: 15 minutes

Serves 4

* 2 tablespoons coconut oil
* 4 cloves garlic, finely chopped
* 2 tablespoons miso paste
* 350 g/12 oz (2 cups) sweetcorn
* 2 red bird's eye chillies, finely chopped
* 250 g/9 oz fresh egg noodles
* 2 tablespoons light soy sauce
* 100 g/3½ oz (3 cups) baby spinach
* 1 tablespoon rice vinegar or apple cider vinegar
* Salt and white pepper, to taste
* 3 spring onions (scallions), sliced
* 2 tomatoes, cut into 1-cm/½-inch cubes
* 1 quantity Crispy Shallots (page 41, optional)

Heat the oil in a large saucepan over medium heat. Add the garlic and sauté for 2–3 minutes until golden brown. Turn the heat off. Add 1 litre/34 fl oz (4¼ cups) boiling water to the pan.

In a small bowl, combine the miso and 3½ tablespoons hot water and mix well.

Put half of the sweetcorn and half the miso mixture into a blender and blend until smooth. Pour the mixture into the pan, then add the remaining half of the miso mixture. Bring to a boil, then reduce the heat to medium and simmer for 5 minutes. Add the remaining sweetcorn and the chillies.

Bring a separate saucepan of water to a boil. Add the fresh noodles and simmer for 3 minutes. Drain, then transfer to a bowl of cold water. Drain again. Drizzle the soy sauce over the noodles and mix. Divide the noodles among 4 bowls.

Add the baby spinach to the pan and cook for 30 seconds, or until just wilted. Add the vinegar and pepper. Adjust the seasoning to taste. It should be sweet, sour and spicy with a hint of miso. .

Ladle the soup over the noodles and top with sweetcorn, spring onions (scallions) and tomatoes. Finish with a sprinkle of crispy shallots, if using.

Spicy Noodle Soup with Smoked Fish and Pak Choy

Mi Kuah dengan Ikan Cakalang Fufu dan Sawi

Fufu in Manadonese and Minahasan means 'smoked'. My grandmother would buy smoked skipjack tuna (*cakalang fufu*) from the fish smokeries at the local markets. Smoked tuna is a labour-intensive and lengthy process, using coconut husks to create a distinctive aroma.

Here, I opt for smoked haddock, which is far easier to find, and serve it traditionally with a vinegar sambal for a touch of spice and tang, offsetting the delicate broth with fried garlic and spring onions (scallions). This recipe works well with smoked tofu and smoked chicken breast.

Origin: Sulawesi

Preparation time: 10 minutes
Cooking time: 20 minutes

Serves 4

For the smoked fish broth:
* 2 tablespoons vegetable oil
* 5 cloves garlic, finely chopped
* 2 spring onions (scallions), coarsely chopped
* 1 stalk celery, coarsely chopped
* 300 g/10½ oz smoked tuna or haddock, skin-on and cut into 2 pieces
* Salt and black pepper, to taste
* 2 tablespoons lime juice

For the noodles:
* 400 g/14 oz fresh egg noodles
* 4 pak choy

For the toppings:
* 2 small spring onions (scallions), thinly sliced
* 2 tablespoons celery leaves, finely chopped
* 2–4 tablespoons Crispy Shallots (page 41)
* Vinegar Sambal (page 53), to serve

To make the smoked fish broth, heat the oil in a saucepan over medium heat. Add the garlic and cook for 1 minute until golden brown. Reduce the heat to low. Add the spring onions (scallions), celery and 800 ml/27 fl oz (3½ cups) coconut milk and bring to a boil. Add the fish, then reduce the heat to medium-low. Simmer for 15 minutes. Season with salt and pepper. Do not stir frequently as you want to keep the fish intact.

Using a slotted spoon, transfer the fish to a chopping (cutting) board. Using two forks, remove the skin and pull apart the flesh into smaller bite-size pieces.

In a small bowl, combine the lime juice and 3 tablespoons of water. Season with salt. Drizzle the mixture over the fish. Set aside.

Adjust the seasoning of the broth, adding more salt if needed. Strain the broth through a fine-mesh sieve (strainer) into a large bowl. Set aside.

To make the noodles, bring a large saucepan of water to a boil. Add the fresh noodles and cook for 1 minute. Add the pak choy stalks and cook for 45 seconds. Add the leaves and cook until just wilted. Drain, then transfer to a large bowl.

Pour the broth over the noodles. Place the fish on top and sprinkle with spring onions, celery leaves and crispy shallots. Serve immediately with the sambal on the side.

Rice Noodle Soup with Meatballs
Mie Bakso

This satisfying bowl of noodles and meatballs in a clear and hearty broth is perhaps the most celebrated street food in Jakarta. When former US president Barack Obama delivered a speech at the University of Indonesia many years ago, he proclaimed *bakso, enak ya!* meaning 'bakso is delicious, right!'

There are so many elements of this dish to enjoy. The broth has a spicy and tangy character courtesy of vinegar. There is a myriad of sauces to accompany this classic dish, all depending on your taste. There's the *saos tomat*, which refers to tomato ketchup, or the *kecap*, which is short for *kecap manis*.

The meatballs are traditionally made by hand, using two cleavers on a chopping (cutting) board to create a fine meatball paste. Still, it's time-consuming (and, arguably, dangerous for the uninitiated). A blender or food processor works perfectly well in the home kitchen. It'll serve you well to prepare a big batch of the meatballs and freeze them when you need a quick topping for fried rice or noodles or stir-fried vegetables.

Origin: Jakarta

Preparation time: 40 minutes
Cooking time: 2 hours 20 minutes

Serves 8

For the beef stock:
* 2 kg/4 lb 8 oz beef bones, fat trimmed
* 8 cloves garlic, coarsely chopped
* 3 stalks celery
* 2 whole nutmegs, coarsely ground with a mortar and pestle (1 teaspoon)
* 1 tablespoon sea salt
* 1 tablespoon white pepper

For the meatballs:
* 2 tablespoons sunflower oil
* 8 cloves garlic, finely chopped
* 500 g/1 lb 2 oz beef topside (top round), fat removed and coarsely chopped
* 1 teaspoon white pepper
* 1 egg
* 200 g/7 oz (1½ cups) tapioca flour

For the noodles and condiments:
* 300 g/10½ oz fresh or dried rice noodles
* 4 large pak choy, halved and cut into 1-cm/½-inch lengths
* 2 teaspoons rice or apple cider vinegar
* 4 tablespoons tomato sauce
* 4 tablespoons Sweet Soy Sauce (page 38)
* 4 teaspoons light soy sauce
* 4 teaspoons Sriracha (page 54)
* 4 tablespoons Crispy Shallots (page 41)
* 2 tablespoons chopped celery leaves
* Boiled Sambal (page 53), to serve

To make the stock, combine the beef bones and 2 litres/2 quarts of water in a stockpot and bring to a boil. Drain, then rinse the bones. This assures a clear broth.

In the same stockpot, combine the bones, garlic, celery, nutmeg, salt and pepper. Add 2 litres/2 quarts of water and bring to a boil. Reduce the heat to medium-low, then cover and simmer for 2–3 hours. Strain into a medium saucepan and set aside.

To make the meatballs, heat the oil in a small frying pan over medium heat. Add the garlic and sauté for 1–2 minutes until golden brown. Set aside.

In a blender or food processor, combine the fried garlic, meat and pepper and process until fine. Add the egg, flour and 50 g/1¾ oz cold water and mix until smooth.

Fill a saucepan halfway with water and bring to a simmer. Scoop a small handful of the meatball mixture in one hand and make a gentle fist. Gently squeeze the paste up through the hole between your thumb and index finger until you have a small ball about the size of a large grape. Scoop the meatball with your other hand and gently lower it into the pan. Repeat with the remaining mixture. Simmer the meatballs for 6–7 minutes until they float to the surface. Using a slotted spoon, remove one of the meatballs and cut it in half to check that it's cooked through.

Put the meatballs into the broth and bring to a boil. Reduce the heat to medium-low and simmer for 10 minutes.

To make the noodles, prepare the noodles according to the package directions. Drain, then transfer to a bowl of cold water. Drain again, then set aside.

Add the pak choy to the stock and cook for 45 seconds. Using a slotted spoon, transfer the pak choy to a plate.

Place the noodles into individual bowls and add the pak choy. Top with 3–4 meatballs, then ladle 2 spoons of stock into each bowl. Season each bowl with vinegar, tomato sauce, soy sauces and Sriracha. Sprinkle with crispy shallots and celery leaves. Serve immediately with the sambal.

Satays

Sate

Satay is Indonesia's most recognizable dish, especially chicken satay served with a tangy-sweet-spicy peanut sauce.

As skewered meats were not part of the Manadonese diet, satay was never part of my upbringing. My parents brought me and my siblings to a satay vendor when we relocated to the capital city. It was the first time I tasted skewered chicken with the complex flavour profile of a well-made peanut sauce – completely unlike the jarred peanut butter that I had known! From then on, I knew few things would compare to the taste of skewered meat or seafood grilled over hot coconut charcoals.

Java is home to satay, and you can find chicken, beef, pork, goat, seafood and tempeh on most menus. Seasonings and preparations are equally varied across the island: the cut of the meat will vary or, sometimes, roasted candlenuts, cumin and coriander are added into the peanut sauce. And since my hometown was without its version of satay, I couldn't resist the opportunity to create a Manadonese-flavoured Pork Satay (page 116) for a local Jakartan publication. I often serve this and other satays such as *beef satay marrangi* on their own or the Balinese Seafood Satay with a fragrant chilli and lemongrass sambal (page 47).

Readers can truly experience a range of Indonesian flavours and travel the country – Bali, Madura, Ponorogo or Padang – through all the regional variations of this national dish. Why not give them all a try?

A few practical barbecue (grill) tips:
- A barbecue is the preferred way to cook authentic satay, but a griddled (grill) pan on a stove will do.
- Soak your bamboo skewers in water first before loading them with ingredients.
- Grilling satay requires a small rack to hold the skewers. Consider investing in a small but efficient hibachi grill.
- Ran out of skewers? No need to panic, simply pan-fry or roast the meat and serve with or without satay sauce. You may not have the aroma from the barbecue, but the meat will still deliver on flavour.

Seafood Satay
Sate Lilit

This amazing and distinctive seafood satay is one of Bali's many contributions to our national culture. The flavours of the sea, the aroma of lemongrass and the vibrancy of fresh chillies and lime make *sate lilit* a firm favourite among my Balinese friends.

The finely chopped seafood is seasoned and wrapped around lemongrass skewers, then grilled to perfection and served with a bright sambal. You'll need lots of lemongrass – since we only require the white parts, you can reserve the green sections for curries. Best of all, they are completely unique when traditionally skewered with stalks of lemongrass.

Origin: Bali

Preparation time: 30 minutes
Cooking time: 10 minutes

Makes 10 skewers

- 12 stalks lemongrass
- ½ quantity Yellow Spice Paste (page 43)
- 300 g/10½ oz skinless white snapper, haddock or seabass fillets, coarsely chopped
- 300 g/10½ oz shelled prawns, coarsely chopped
- 4 makrut lime leaves, centre stem removed and thinly sliced
- 1 tablespoon ground coriander
- 2 tablespoons unsweetened desiccated coconut
- 1 tablespoon coconut sugar or brown sugar
- ½ teaspoon salt
- 1 teaspoon black pepper
- 2 tablespoons coconut oil, for brushing

To serve:
- Chilli and Lemongrass Sambal (page 47)
- Vegetables with Spiced Coconut (page 156)
- Steamed rice (optional)

Finely slice 2 lemongrass stalks, white part only, and combine with the paste. Set aside.

Combine the fish and prawns in a food processor and process until finely chopped. Transfer to a large bowl, then add the spice paste, lime leaves and ground coriander. Add the desiccated coconut and sugar. Season with salt and pepper and mix well.

Scoop a generous tablespoon of the mixture into your palm, put some lemongrass paste on top and mould the seafood mixture around a lemongrass stalk, leaving plenty of room to create the handle. Repeat with the remaining lemongrass stalks and mixture.

Preheat a charcoal barbecue or griddled (grill) pan over high heat. Brush each satay with coconut oil. Add the skewers to the barbecue and grill for 6–8 minutes, turning often, until cooked through. Serve with sambal, vegetables and steamed rice, if you wish.

Variations:
- **Bali Duck Satay (Sate Lembat)**
  Replace the fish and prawns with minced duck (remove the skin and most of the fat first). Use flat bamboo skewers instead of lemongrass stalks.
- **Lombok Beef Satay (Lombok Sate Pusut)**
  Substitute the seafood with minced (ground) beef and use flat bamboo skewers. Serve without the sambal.
- **Bali Fish Cake (Bali Perkedel Ikan)**
  Gently shape the seafood mixture into 4–6 patties, about 2.5 cm/1 inch thick. Heat 2–3 tablespoons coconut or sunflower oil in a large frying pan over medium heat. Pan-fry for 4–5 minutes until golden. Serve with vegetables with spiced coconut and sambal.

Chicken Satay
Sate Ayam

This moreish dish originates from Madura Island, just off the coast of East Java, where a dry climate encourages livestock farming. The Madurese are known to be entrepreneurial and have successfully raised the status of chicken satay to become a national dish, like our Beef Rendang (page 134). It was also a firm favourite with my sons while they were growing up – a weekend treat.

Try to keep the chicken pieces on the smaller side to ensure a greater infusion of flavour. You can serve chicken satay as a snack or a complete meal with steamed rice or compressed rice.

Origin: Java

Preparation time: 25 minutes, plus 30 minutes marinating time
Cooking time: 5–10 minutes

Makes 12–14 skewers

For the satay:
* 600 g/1 lb 5 oz chicken thighs, boneless and skinless, cut into 2-cm/¾-inch chunks
* 2 cloves garlic, grated
* 2 tablespoons Sweet Soy Sauce (page 38)
* 1 tablespoon coconut oil or vegetable oil
* ½ teaspoon salt
* Juice of 1 lime

For the peanut sauce:
* 2–3 red bird's eye chillies, finely chopped
* 2 cloves garlic, finely chopped
* ¼ teaspoon salt
* 4 heaped tablespoons Peanut-Cashew Butter (page 39)
* 2–3 tablespoons Sweet Soy Sauce (page 38)
* Juice of 2 limes

To serve:
* Crispy Shallots (page 41)
* 1 lime, sliced
* Steamed or Compressed Rice (page 198)

Soak 14 long bamboo skewers in water for 1 hour.

To make the satay, combine all the ingredients in a medium bowl. Cover and set aside to marinate for 30 minutes in the refrigerator.

To make the peanut sauce, combine all the ingredients in a bowl. Gradually add 100 ml/3½ fl oz (scant ½ cup) of water and mix well. It should be thick enough to coat the back of a spoon. Season to taste with salt. Set aside.

Preheat a charcoal barbecue or a griddled (grill) pan over high heat. Add 2 tablespoons of peanut sauce into the chicken mixture and mix well. Thread 4 chicken pieces onto each skewer. Grill for 2–3 minutes on each side, turning often, until cooked through.

Transfer the skewers to a plate. Drizzle over a little peanut sauce, then garnish with crispy shallots. Serve with slices of lime and a side of the remaining peanut sauce and rice.

Variation:
- **Ponorogo Chicken Satay (Sate Ponorogo)**
  Ponorogo is in East Java, about 300 km (185 miles) away from Madura Island. The Ponorogo satay has more layers of spices than the classic Madura chicken satay.
  Cut the chicken into thin, long strips. Add 1 tablespoon of ground coriander to the marinade. Thread each bamboo skewer with 2 pieces of chicken.
  For the sauce, sauté 1 finely chopped shallot in oil for 3–4 minutes. Add 1 teaspoon each of ground coriander and cumin to the pan, then combine the mixture with the remaining sauce ingredients.

Pork Satay with Chilli, Ginger and Lime
Sate Babi Rica-Rica

Rica-rica is a sambal from Manado, North Sulawesi. The name translates to 'chilli' in the local dialect and, to be expected, this spicy condiment has fiery intensity.

The spiciness is also attributed to the red ginger, distinctively coloured, local to Manado and smaller than your typical ginger. For this recipe, I have reduced the number of bird's eye chillies, but you can add as many as 20 if you're feeling adventurous. You can also try this dish using prawns, chicken or fish fillets.

Origin: Sulawesi

Preparation time: 10 minutes, plus 10 minutes marinating time
Cooking time: 15–20 minutes

Makes 12–14 skewers

For the rica-rica:
* 2 cloves garlic, coarsely chopped
* 2 banana shallots, coarsely chopped
* 2–3 red bird's eye chillies
* 2 large red chillies
* 20 g/¾ oz ginger, thinly sliced
* 2 tablespoons coconut oil or sunflower oil
* Juice of 1 lime
* Salt, to taste

For the satay:
* 600 g/1 lb 5 oz pork tenderloin, cut into 2-cm/ ¾-inch cubes
* ½ teaspoon salt
* Juice of 1 lime
* 1 tablespoon coconut oil

To serve:
* Steamed rice
* Spiced Vegetable Stew (page 151)

Soak 14 long bamboo skewers in water for 1 hour.

To make the rica-rica, combine all the ingredients, except the oil, lime and salt, in a blender and blend to a fine paste. Set aside.

Heat the oil in a frying pan over medium heat. Add the paste and sauté for 6–7 minutes. Season with lime juice and salt and sauté for another 2 minutes. Set aside.

To make the satay, season the pork with salt, half of the rica-rica paste and the lime juice. Mix well and set aside to marinate for 10 minutes.

Preheat a charcoal barbecue or a griddled (grill) pan over high heat. Thread 4 pieces of pork onto each skewer. Grill the pork for 5–6 minutes, brushing it with marinade and turning often, until cooked through. Transfer the skewers to a plate.

Serve as is or with the steamed rice, spiced vegetable stew and the remaining rica-rica.

Beef Satay
Sate Maranggi

As this satay is already full of flavour, it requires no sauce. After the satays have been marinated, grill them on the barbecue. This recipe can also be prepared with lamb tenderloin, chicken, fish fillets, tempeh or tofu.

Origin: Java

Preparation time: 30 minutes, plus 1 hour chilling time
Cooking time: 15–20 minutes

Makes 12 skewers

* ½ quantity Red Spice Paste (page 43), prepared without galangal
* 8 g/¼ oz kencur, peeled and thinly sliced (optional)
* 2 tablespoons sunflower oil
* 600 g/1 lb 5 oz beef tenderloin, cut into 2-cm/¾-inch cubes
* 2 tablespoons Sweet Soy Sauce (page 38)
* Juice of 1–2 limes
* 1 tablespoon sliced palm sugar or coconut sugar
* 1 teaspoon ground coriander
* 1 teaspoon salt
* 1 teaspoon black pepper
* 2 tablespoons coconut oil
* Steamed Cassava (page 145) or steamed rice, to serve (optional)

Soak 12 long bamboo skewers in water for 1 hour.

Combine the red spice paste and kencur in a small blender and blend into a smooth paste.

To make the satay, heat the sunflower oil in a frying pan over medium-low heat. Add the paste and sauté for 5 minutes until slightly dry. Set aside to cool.

In a large bowl, combine the beef, paste, soy sauce, lime juice, palm sugar, coriander, salt and pepper. Mix and refrigerate for 1 hour.

Preheat a charcoal barbecue or griddled (grill) pan over high heat. Thread 4 pieces of beef onto each skewer. Combine the coconut oil with the left-over marinade. Brush oil over each satay. Sear for 1 minute on each side. Brush the meat with the marinade and cook for another 2–3 minutes on each side, until cooked through.

Serve with steamed cassava or rice, if you wish.

Goat Satay
Sate Kambing

Java is said to be the home of satay. This satay starts with a tangy sweetness and finishes with a lingering heat, thanks to the fresh chillies in the soy sambal.

If you're looking to vary the flavour, replace the goat with lamb tenderloin.

Origin: Java

Preparation time: 35 minutes, plus 1 hour marinating/soaking time
Cooking time: 10–15 minutes

Makes 20 skewers

For the soy and chilli sambal:
* 3 red or green bird's eye chillies, thinly sliced
* 2 large tomatoes, seeded and cut into ½-cm/¼-inch cubes
* 1 banana shallot, finely chopped
* 3 tablespoons Sweet Soy Sauce (page 38)
* Juice of 1 lime
* Salt, to taste

For the marinade:
* 5 makrut lime leaves, centre stem removed and thinly sliced
* 1 banana shallot, finely chopped
* 3 tablespoons Sweet Soy Sauce (page 38)
* 2 tablespoons lime juice
* Salt and black pepper, to taste

For the satay:
* 1 kg/2 lb 4 oz goat or lamb tenderloin, cut into 2-cm/ ¾-inch cubes

* 1 teaspoon salt
* ½ teaspoon black pepper
* 2 tablespoons coconut oil, for brushing

To serve:
* 2 tablespoons Crispy Shallots (page 41)
* Sorghum (page 210) or couscous

Soak 20 long bamboo skewers in water for 1 hour.

To prepare the sambal, combine all the ingredients and mix well. To prepare the marinade, combine all the ingredients in a large bowl and mix well. Set both aside.

To prepare the satay, season the goat with salt and pepper and add to the marinade. Leave to marinate in the refrigerator for 1 hour.

Preheat a charcoal barbecue or a griddled (grill) pan over high heat. Thread 4 pieces of goat meat onto each skewer. Brush each skewer with the marinade and grill for 5–6 minutes, turning often, until cooked through. Transfer the satay to a plate and sprinkle with crispy shallots. Serve with the sambal and sorghum.

Tempeh Satay with West Sumatra Sauce
Sate Tempe Saos Padang

The well-known beef satay from Padang, West Sumatra, inspired this vegetarian recipe. Traditionally, beef (or offal) would be stewed in an aromatic broth, then cut into cubes, skewered and grilled over charcoals.

This plant-based recipe delivers a vibrant curry flavour, courtesy of earthy cumin and coriander, a fiery turmeric bumbu and a hint of coconut.

Origin: Modern recipe

Preparation time: 30 minutes
Cooking time: 1 hour 5 minutes

Makes 12 skewers

For the spice blend:
- 1 tablespoon coriander seeds, roasted
- 1 teaspoon cumin seeds, roasted
- 1 teaspoon black pepper

For the satay:
- 2 tablespoons coconut oil
- ½ quantity Yellow Spice Paste (page 43)
- 600 g/1 lb 5 oz tempeh, cut into 2-cm/¾-inch pieces
- 3 makrut lime leaves, torn
- 2 stalks lemongrass, crushed and tied into a knot
- 1 litre/34 fl oz (4 cups) coconut water or water

- Salt, to taste
- 1 tablespoon rice flour
- 2–3 tablespoons Crispy Shallots (page 41)
- Ginger Coconut Rice (page 198) and Vegetables with Spiced Coconut (page 156), to serve

---

Soak 12 long bamboo skewers in water for 1 hour.

To prepare the spice blend, combine all the ingredients in a frying pan and dry-roast for 5–6 minutes over medium-low heat until fragrant, stirring occasionally to prevent them from burning. Transfer to a spice grinder or pestle and mortar and grind to a fine powder.

To prepare the satay, heat the oil in a medium saucepan over medium heat. Add the spice paste and cook for 4–5 minutes. Add the tempeh, lime leaves and lemongrass. Pour in the coconut water, making sure the tempeh is fully covered. Add 1 teaspoon salt and bring to a boil. Reduce the heat to medium-low, cover and simmer for 20 minutes. Gently turn the tempeh and cook for another 20 minutes. Set aside.

Using a slotted spoon, transfer the tempeh to a plate. Add 200 ml/ 7 fl oz (scant 1 cup) of water to the pan and mix well. Strain the mixture through a sieve (strainer) into another saucepan.

Preheat a charcoal barbecue or a griddled (grill) pan over high heat. Thread 4 pieces of tempeh onto each skewer and grill for 2–3 minutes on each side.

In a small bowl, combine the rice flour with 3½ tablespoons of water and mix well. Quickly whisk the rice flour mixture into the saucepan. Bring to a boil, then reduce the heat to medium-low and simmer for 5–7 minutes. Season to taste with salt. Keep warm over low heat.

Transfer the tempeh skewers to a plate and pour the sauce on top. Top with crispy shallots. Serve with coconut rice and vegetables.

Curries

Kari, Gulai

When my family left Manado to move to Jakarta, I missed my Oma and her food terribly: the smell of her kitchen, the bountiful herb garden and, most of all, the curried chicken and potato dish with turmeric, ginger, chillies, lemongrass and coconut milk (page 129). I often think of her and our home in Manado when preparing this dish for my own family.

Indonesian curries are distinguished by their use of fresh root spices, regional dried spiced blends and herbs and tend to be soupier than Indian or Thai curries. My first introduction to an authentic goat curry dish was at a Java restaurant in Manado. My sisters and I still talk about that dish to this day: fork-tender morsels of meat in a balanced curry-spiced broth infused with fragrant coconut milk. We are grateful to have sampled so many dishes and developed our palates at such a young age.

Most curries begin with a fragrant spice paste, which is then enhanced with a spice blend (such as coriander seeds, cloves, nutmeg, cinnamon, cumin and black pepper) and fresh lime leaves, lemongrass, turmeric leaves, curry leaves or pandan give it a beautiful fragrance. Creamy coconut milk will infuse it with richness while a sharp, acidic element – in the form of a citrus juice or an indigenous fruit such as dried starfruit, *belimbing wuluh* known as *asam sunti* or *asam gelugur*, dried garcinia fruit – balances it all out. I find it challenging to source specific citrus and dried fruits outside of Indonesia but I find that tamarind and lime juice make excellent substitutes.

A good Indonesian curry is wonderfully harmonious with distinctive yet balanced flavours to ensure no single note dominates. It's best served with a bowl of steamed rice. Lace Bread (page 210) is the preferred choice in some parts of Sumatra, perfect for mopping up all that delicious sauce.

Vegetable Curry
Sayur Lodeh

This simple and delicate Javanese curry is said to have once been part of the feast within local cultural ceremonies. These days, it is the ultimate source of comfort – hearty soul food without the chilli heat seen in so many of our other dishes.

Vegetables such as unripe jackfruit, young fern, bamboo shoots and moringa leaves are widely used in the traditional recipe, but most vegetables will work. This delicious version features aubergine (eggplant), pumpkin, spinach and green beans.

Origin: Java

Preparation time: 20 minutes
Cooking time: 15 minutes

Serves 4–6

- 2 tablespoons coconut oil
- 1 quantity White Spice Paste (page 43)
- 400 g/14 oz pumpkin or butternut squash, cut into 1.5-cm/⅝-inch cubes
- 3 makrut lime leaves, torn
- 2 salam leaves or bay leaves (optional)
- 1 long stalk lemongrass, crushed and tied into a knot
- 400 ml/14 fl oz (1⅔ cups) coconut milk
- 1 (300 g/10½ oz) aubergine (eggplant), cut into 1.5-cm/⅝-inch cubes
- ½ teaspoon salt
- 100 g/3½ oz French or runner beans, cut into 5-cm/2-inch segments
- 50 g/1¾ oz (1⅔ cups) spinach
- Steamed brown rice, to serve (optional)

Heat the oil in a large saucepan over medium heat. Add the spice paste and cook for 4–5 minutes until fragrant. Add the pumpkin, lime leaves, salam leaves, if using, and lemongrass. Pour in half of the coconut milk and 400 ml/14 fl oz (1⅔ cups) of water. Bring to a boil, then reduce the heat to medium, cover the pan and simmer for 5 minutes.

Add the aubergine (eggplant) and salt, then cover and simmer for 15–17 minutes until the vegetables are softened. Add the green beans and the remaining coconut milk and simmer for 3–4 minutes. Add the spinach and cook for 1 minute. Season to taste with salt.

Serve with steamed rice, if you like.

Variations:
- **Javanese Smoked Fish Curry (Mangut Lele)**
  Replace the vegetables with 600 g/1 lb 5 oz smoked mackerel, cod or haddock, cut into 2-cm/¾-inch cubes. Add 2 tablespoons Tamarind Paste (page 44) and the juice of 1 lime to the pan of lime leaves and simmer for 10 minutes. Add the fish, 2 sliced mild green chillies and 2–3 whole green bird's eye chillies. Cook for 4–6 minutes or until the fish is cooked thoroughly. Season to taste.
- **Manadonese Smoked Fish Curry (Ikan Asap Santan)**
  Omit the pumpkin and spinach. Once the aubergine is soft, add 500 g/1 lb 2 oz smoked mackerel, cod or haddock and 2–3 whole red bird's eye chillies. Cover and cook for 4–6 minutes or until the fish is cooked thoroughly. Add a handful of basil and serve.

Tempeh and Jackfruit Curry
Nangka dan Tempe Gulai

The popularity of tempeh spread from Java across to the archipelago. Jackfruit curry is a West Sumatra speciality, but the addition of tempeh brings something new to this delightful vegan dish. This incredibly simple yet flavourful curry has a vibrant reddish-orange colour, thanks to the combination of chillies.

Fresh raw jackfruit is widely available these days, but you can also used canned jackfruit. Here, firm, raw canned jackfruit is cooked with tempeh, but if you choose to use the soft canned variety, simply add it in for the last 20–25 minutes of cooking.

Origin: Sumatra

Preparation time: 10 minutes
Cooking time: 1 hour 10 minutes

Serves 6–8

- 1 quantity Red Spice Paste (page 43)
- 1 teaspoon ground coriander
- 1 teaspoon black pepper
- 4 makrut lime leaves, torn
- 2 stalks lemongrass, crushed and tied into a knot

- 800 ml/27 fl oz (3½ cups) coconut milk
- 250 g/9 oz tempeh, cut into 2-cm/¾-inch pieces
- 1 (565-g/1 lb 4-oz) can firm jackfruit
- 1 turmeric leaf (optional)

- 1 teaspoon salt
- 2 large red chillies, thinly sliced, to garnish
- Steamed rice or rice noodles, to serve

In a medium saucepan, combine the paste, coriander, pepper, lime leaves, lemongrass and half the coconut milk. Add 400 ml/14 fl oz (1⅔ cups) of water and bring to a boil. Reduce the heat to medium and cook for 20 minutes.

Add the tempeh, jackfruit and turmeric leaf, if using. Season with salt and pepper and bring to a boil. Reduce the heat to medium-low and simmer for 50 minutes, until the jackfruit has softened. Add the remaining coconut milk. Season to taste.

Garnish with chillies and serve with rice or noodles.

Mussel Curry
Kari Remis

Living in the UK, I often crave Scottish mussels, which are perfect for this soupy curry. While mussel curry isn't necessarily a common Indonesian dish, it is infused with the delightful flavours of lemongrass, turmeric, makrut lime leaves and a hint of chilli.

Origin: Modern recipe

Preparation time: 15 minutes
Cooking time: 15–20 minutes

Serves 4

- 1 tablespoon coriander seeds
- 1 tablespoon coconut oil
- 1 quantity Yellow Spice Paste (page 43)
- 400 ml/14 fl oz (1⅔ cups) coconut milk
- 4 makrut lime leaves, torn

- 2 salam leaves or bay leaves
- 1 stalk lemongrass, crushed and tied into a knot
- Juice of ½–1 lime
- Salt, to taste
- 1 kg/2 lb 4 oz mussels, cleaned

Place the coriander seeds in a small frying pan and dry-roast for 2–3 minutes over medium-low heat until fragrant, stirring occasionally to prevent them from burning. Leave to cool. Using a pestle and mortar, grind the mixture to a fine powder.

Heat the oil in a wok or medium saucepan over medium heat. Add the paste and ground coriander and sauté for 4–5 minutes.

Add the coconut milk, lime leaves, salam leaves, lemongrass and lime juice. Pour in 200 ml/7 fl oz (scant 1 cup) of water and mix well.

Season with salt. Bring to a boil, then reduce the heat to medium. Cover and simmer for 5–7 minutes to infuse the herbs and spices.

Rinse the mussels under cold running water and discard any that have already opened. Add the mussels to the pan and cook for 3–4 minutes, until opened. Discard the lemongrass, lime leaves and any unopened mussels. Season to taste. Divide the mussels and broth into 4 large bowls. Serve.

Chicken with Turmeric and Coconut Milk

Ayam Tuturuga

Ayam tuturuga is a vivid childhood food memory from Manado, a representation of the notoriously spicy cuisine of my birthplace, Tuturuga. This particular dish was always a highlight during Christmas, alongside pork in bamboo and grilled turmeric-spiced fish wrapped in palm leaves.

The Manadonese term *tuturuga*, derived from the Portuguese *tartaruga*, means 'turtle'. Oma said this dish was named after the fact that its cooking vessel, a covered wok, looked like a turtle.

Origin: Sulawesi

Preparation time: 20 minutes
Cooking time: 30–35 minutes

Serves 8

- 1.2 kg/2 lb 12 oz bone-in chicken thighs, skin removed
- Salt and black pepper, to taste
- Juice of 1 lime or 2 calamansi
- 2 tablespoons coconut oil
- 1 quantity Yellow Spice Paste (page 43)
- 2–3 large potatoes, cut into 2-cm/¾-inch chunks
- 3 makrut lime leaves, torn
- 2 stalks lemongrass, crushed and tied into a knot
- 1 pandan leaf, tied into a knot (optional)
- 1 turmeric leaf (optional)
- 800 ml/27 fl oz (3½ cups) coconut milk
- Small bunch of basil

To serve:
- Ginger Coconut Rice (page 198)
- Spiced Vegetable Stew (page 151)

Season the chicken with salt, pepper and the juice of 1 lime.

Heat the oil in a large saucepan or wok over medium heat. Add the spice paste and cook for 1–2 minutes. Add the chicken and cook for 2–3 minutes. Add the potatoes, lime leaves, lemongrass and pandan and turmeric leaves, if using. Pour in the coconut milk and 300 ml/10 fl oz (1¼ cups) of water. Mix well and season with salt.

Bring to a boil, then reduce the heat to medium-low. Cover and simmer for 25–30 minutes, until the chicken is cooked through. Add half the basil and stir until just wilted. Season to taste. Discard the lemongrass and lime leaves.

Garnish with the remaining basil. Serve with ginger coconut rice and vegetables.

Variations

- **Java Chicken Curry (Kari Jawa)**
  After cooking the paste, add 1 teaspoon each of ground coriander and cumin. Omit the pandan, turmeric and basil leaves. Slice 2 carrots into ½-cm (¼-inch) rounds, add them to the pan once the chicken has been cooked through and cook for 5 minutes. Cut 50 g/1¾ oz green beans into 2-cm/¾-inch lengths, add them to the pan, and cook for another 5 minutes. Transfer into a serving bowl and sprinkle with 2–3 tablespoons Crispy Shallots (page 41). Serve with white or brown rice.

- **North Sumatra Chicken and Potato Curry (Gulai Ayam dan Kentang Medan)**
  Reduce the turmeric in the spice paste to 5 g/⅛ oz. Add 4 Kashmiri chillies, soaked in hot water for 5 minutes. Grind together with the spice paste. Add 1 teaspoon ground coriander, 4 slightly crushed cardamom pods and 3 star anise. Omit the pandan, turmeric and basil leaves. Add a small bunch of curry leaves. Serve with Lace Bread (page 210).

Chicken Curry with Pineapple
Gulai Ayam Nanas

South Sumatra has a rich and fascinating history, and the city of Palembang was formerly the base of the Srivijaya – a Malay Buddhist empire – in the seventh century. It was one of the most important trading hubs between China and Persia but also a centre for Buddhist learnings where monks from India, China and Java gathered.

This soupy curry is milder and more delicate than those from the northern part of the island. This recipe's inspiration was drawn from a dish of fish dumplings in a turmeric-coconut broth (*celimpungan*) but with a pineapple twist.

Origin: Sumatra

Preparation time: 10 minutes
Cooking time: 15–20 minutes

Serves 4

- 8 boneless, skinless chicken thighs, cut into bite-size pieces
- ½ teaspoon salt
- Black pepper, to taste
- Juice of 1 lime
- 60 ml/2 fl oz (¼ cup) coconut oil or sunflower oil

- 1 quantity Yellow Spice Paste (page 43)
- 1 small pineapple, peeled, cored and cut into 2-cm/ ¾-inch cubes
- 4 makrut lime leaves, torn
- 1 stalk lemongrass, crushed and tied into a knot

- 400 ml/14 fl oz (1⅔ cups) coconut milk
- 1 large red chilli, thinly sliced, to garnish

To serve:
- Steamed rice
- Water Spinach with Chilli and Miso (page 146)

Season the chicken with salt, pepper and lime juice. Set aside.

Heat 2 tablespoons of oil in a saucepan over medium heat. Add the yellow spice paste and cook for 4–5 minutes. Add the chicken, pineapple, lime leaves and lemongrass and mix well. Cook for 1–2 minutes, then pour half of the coconut milk and 400 ml/14 fl oz (1⅔ cups) of water. Bring to a boil, then reduce the heat to medium-low. Cover and simmer for 10–12 minutes until the chicken is cooked and the pineapple is softened. Add the remaining coconut milk. Season to taste. Discard the lemongrass and lime leaves.

Garnish with the chilli and serve with rice and vegetables.

Variation:
- **West Sumatra Chicken Curry (Ayam Kalio)**
  Omit the pineapple. Add 3 asam kandis or the juice of 1 lime with the chicken. Cook, uncovered, until the sauce has thickened and reduced by half.

Chicken Curry with Potatoes and Vegetables
Kare Ayam, Kentang dan Sayuran

While Sumatrans like rich, complex curries with layers of spices, the Javanese prefer delicate and light curries such as this. This soupy curry has no trace of cardamom or cloves, yet it still has ample curry flavour. It is the ultimate one-pot meal and best served with a bowl of steamed rice.

Origin: Java

Preparation time: 20 minutes
Cooking time: 25 minutes

Serves 8

* 1 teaspoon coriander seeds
* 1 teaspoon cumin seeds
* 600 g/1 lb 5 oz chicken breast, sliced into bite-size pieces
* Salt and black pepper, to taste
* Juice of 1 lime
* 2 tablespoons coconut oil
* 1 quantity Yellow Spice Paste (page 43)
* 4 carrots, cut into bite-size pieces
* 3 potatoes, cut into 1-cm/ ½-inch cubes
* 800 ml/27 fl oz (3½ cups) coconut milk
* 5 makrut lime leaves
* 2 salam leaves or bay leaves
* 2 stalks lemongrass, crushed
* 3 tablespoons Crispy Shallots (page 41, optional)
* Steamed rice, to serve

Place the coriander and cumin in a small frying pan and dry-roast for 5–6 minutes over medium-low heat until fragrant, stirring occasionally to prevent them from burning. Leave to cool.

Using a pestle and mortar, grind the mixture to a fine powder.

Season the chicken with salt, pepper and lime juice.

Heat the oil in a wok or medium saucepan over medium-high heat. Add the ground cumin and coriander and cook for few seconds. Add the paste and sauté for 4–5 minutes.

Stir in the carrots and potatoes and cook for a few seconds. Add the coconut milk, lime leaves, salam leaves and lemongrass and mix well. Pour in 200 ml/7 fl oz (generous ¾ cup) water and season with salt. Bring to a boil, then reduce the heat to medium-low. Cover and simmer for 10–12 minutes until the vegetables are tender. Add the chicken and cook for 6–8 minutes. Season to taste. Discard the lemongrass and lime leaves.

Sprinkle with crispy shallots, if using. Serve with rice.

Fragrant Chicken Curry
Opor Ayam

This classic Javanese chicken curry is truly popular during *Idul Fitri*, the Indonesian holiday that concludes the fasting month of Ramadan. Whenever I prepare this dish, I fondly remember the happy celebration of this holiday with my Muslim friends in Jakarta.

Tradition calls for the use of a free-range chicken known as *ayam kampung* (meaning 'village chickens'). The meat is tougher and lean, quite different from broiler chicken. I use skinless chicken thigh pieces, but it could easily be made into a vegetarian dish by adding tofu or tempeh instead.

This curry is often accompanied by a simple Shallot Sambal (page 50) and *ketupat,* a parcel (package) of palm leaves stuffed filled with rice, which is then boiled and expanded with cooked rice. After it's been cooled to room temperature, it is cut and presented to guests to enjoy.

Origin: Java

Preparation time: 20 minutes
Cooking time: 40 minutes

Serves 6

For the paste:
* 2 tablespoons coconut oil or sunflower oil
* 1 quantity White Spice Paste (page 43)

For the spice blend:
* 3 whole cloves
* 1 (2-cm/¾-inch) stick cinnamon
* 1 tablespoon coriander seeds
* 1 teaspoon cumin seeds
* 1 teaspoon black peppercorns
* ½ teaspoon freshly grated nutmeg

For the curry:
* 12 bone-in chicken thighs, skin removed
* 1 teaspoon salt
* 1 teaspoon black pepper
* Juice of 1 lime
* 1 tablespoon coconut oil or vegetable oil
* 4 makrut lime leaves, torn
* 2 salam leaves or bay leaves
* 1 stalk lemongrass, crushed and tied into a knot
* 1 teaspoon coconut sugar or brown sugar
* 800 ml/27 fl oz (3½ cups) coconut milk

To serve:
* Steamed rice or Compressed Rice (page 198)
* Green vegetables

To make the paste, combine the oil and the spice paste in a small blender and blend into a smooth paste.

To make the spice blend, combine all the ingredients, except the nutmeg, in a frying pan and dry-roast for 5–6 minutes over medium-low heat until fragrant, stirring occasionally to prevent them from burning. Remove the pan from the heat and let cool.

Transfer the spices into a spice grinder and grind into a fine powder.

To prepare the curry, season the chicken with salt, pepper and lime juice. Heat the oil in a frying pan over medium heat. Add the paste and cook for 3–4 minutes. Add the chicken and spice blend and mix well. Stir in the lime leaves, salam leaves and lemongrass and cook for 2 minutes.

Add the coconut sugar, half of the coconut milk and 200 ml/7 fl oz (scant 1 cup) of water. Season with salt and pepper. Bring to a boil, then reduce the heat to medium-low. Simmer for 20 minutes until the sauce has reduced and thickened. Add the remaining coconut milk and cook for another 5 minutes, until the chicken is tender. Season to taste with salt.

Serve with steamed rice and vegetables.

Duck Curry
Sie Itik

Regarded as a national ingredient, duck features prominently in Indonesian cuisine. The domestic Alabio duck breed is highly prized for its meat as much as its eggs.

My first experience with duck curry was during a trip to Aceh in North Sumatra. Not only did it taste deliciously complex, spices such as cumin and fennel seeds revealed a Middle Eastern influence.

Asam gelugur, the sun-dried slices of fruit from the *garcinia atroviridis* tree, add the much-needed acidity to brighten the dish. These fruits are not easy to find outside the archipelago, so we use tamarind instead and marinate the duck in lime juice.

Origin: Sumatra

Preparation time: 30 minutes
Cooking time: 1 hour 50 minutes

Serves 6

For the spice blend:
* 3 whole cloves
* 2 green cardamom pods
* 2 star anise
* 1 (3-cm/1¼-inch) cinnamon stick
* 1 tablespoon coriander seeds
* 1 teaspoon black peppercorns
* 1 teaspoon cumin seeds
* 1 teaspoon fennel seeds
* ½ teaspoon freshly grated nutmeg

For the spice paste:
* 5 dried Kashmiri chillies
* 2–4 red bird's eye chillies
* 3 banana shallots, coarsely chopped
* 3 cloves garlic, coarsely chopped
* 1 large red chilli
* 10 g/¼ oz fresh root ginger, coarsely chopped
* 10 g/¼ oz galangal, coarsely chopped

For the duck:
* 8 skinless duck legs
* Salt and black pepper, to taste
* Juice of 1 lime

* 2 tablespoons coconut oil
* 3 makrut lime leaves, torn
* 1 stalk lemongrass, crushed and tied into a knot
* Small bunch of curry leaves
* 1 pandan leaf, tied into a knot (optional)
* 800 ml/27 fl oz (3½ cups) coconut milk
* 2 tablespoons Tamarind Paste (page 44)

To serve:
* Steamed rice
* Pickled Pineapple (page 55)

To prepare the spice blend, combine all the ingredients in a large frying pan. Dry-roast for 5–6 minutes over medium-low heat until fragrant, stirring occasionally to prevent them from burning. Remove the pan from the heat and let cool.

Remove the cinnamon stick, cardamom and star anise and set aside. Transfer the remaining spice mixture into a spice grinder and grind into a fine powder.

To make the spice paste, combine the Kashmiri chillies and 100 ml/3½ fl oz (scant ½ cup) hot water in a bowl. Set aside for 5 minutes to soften the chillies, then drain and coarsely chop. Combine all the ingredients in a small blender and blend into a smooth paste. Set aside.

To prepare the duck, trim off as much fat as possible. (Reserve the fat for another use. Rendered duck fat is great for roasted potatoes or to sauté with aromatics in a fried rice.) Season the duck legs with salt, pepper and lime juice. Set aside.

Heat the oil in a frying pan over medium heat. Add the spice paste and mix for 4–5 minutes. Stir in the spice blend, then add the duck, lime leaves, lemongrass, curry leaves and pandan leaf, if using. Add the reserved cinnamon, star anise and cardamom. Add half of the coconut milk and 200 ml/7 fl oz (scant 1 cup) of water. Mix and bring to a boil. Season with salt and pepper. Reduce the heat to medium-low, cover and simmer for 1½ hours.

Stir in the tamarind paste and the remaining coconut milk. Cook for another 10 minutes. Season to taste with salt and pepper.

Serve with steamed rice and pickled pineapple.

Variation:
- **Aceh-Style Fish Curry (Ikan Gulai Aceh)**
  For the spice blend, use the coriander and fennel seeds and omit the rest. Replace the duck legs with 8 (150-g/5½ oz) white fish fillets of your choice, each cut into large chunks. For the sauce, omit the lemongrass and makrut lime leaves. Add 2 large, chopped tomatoes and the juice of 2 limes and cook for 15 minutes. Season with salt and pepper. Add the fish and cook for 4–5 minutes until the fish flakes easily. Serve with steamed rice.

Beef Rendang
Rendang Daging Sapi

Beef rendang requires no introduction. This iconic Indonesian dish originated in Minangkabau, West Sumatra and the provincial capital of Padang, a hub and settlement for traders from China and the Middle East and a rich trading past dating back to the 17th century. If only the crumbling buildings in the old part of the city could talk, what tales they could share from this colourful period in Indonesian history!

The term *rendang* signifies a specific technique where a dish is boiled for an extended time to reduce the coconut milk, then slow-cooked for over an hour to tenderize the meat. This stage creates a stewed curry known as *kalio*.

To make a classic rendang, the braising liquid must be further reduced. It is then fried over high heat to create rich caramelization and intensified flavour. This luscious and succulent dish is unlike anything you've ever tasted.

Rendang is usually made with beef (in the past, people of Minangkabau used buffalo meat), but it can be substituted with goat, lamb, chicken, tempeh or jackfruit. Across West Sumatra, there are many variations on the rendang theme, with baby potatoes and even ferns as the main ingredients. I learned of a meatball rendang from a 70-year-old lady in Payakumbuh, Uni Emi, who keeps local culinary traditions alive. I also sampled eel rendang further north in Lintau, which is prepared with up to 20 types of local leaves.

In the rare event that you have any rendang left-over, you'll discover a greater intensity of flavour the following day. It would be perfect with fresh rice or even in a sandwich.

The key to a delectable rendang is the use of coconut milk with at least 19 per cent fat content, which is vital to create the right consistency.

Origin: Sumatra

Preparation time: 15 minutes
Cooking time: 2 hours 15 minutes

Serves 6–8

- 1.2 litres/40 fl oz (5 cups) coconut milk
- 1 quantity Red Spice Paste (page 43)
- 2 tablespoons Tamarind Paste (page 44)
- 7 makrut lime leaves, torn

- 2 star anise
- 2 stalks lemongrass, crushed and tied into a knot
- 1 (3-cm/1¼-inch) cinnamon stick
- 1 turmeric leaf (optional)
- 1 teaspoon salt
- 1 teaspoon black pepper

- 1.2 kg/2 lb 12 oz topside (top round) beef, cut into 2.5-cm/1-inch cubes
- Steamed rice, to serve

To prepare the base, combine all the ingredients, except the beef, in a large saucepan or wok and mix well. Add the beef and mix well. Boil for 1 hour, stirring occasionally to prevent the mixture from sticking, until the liquid has reduced by half. Reduce the heat to medium-low and simmer for another hour until the meat is tender.

Increase the heat to high. Cook for 12–15 minutes, stirring constantly to prevent the mixture from sticking to the pan, until the liquid has evaporated and the rendang is dark brown and caramelized. Season to taste. Serve with steamed rice.

Variations:
- **Meatball Rendang (Rendang Bulat)**
  Replace the beef with an equal amount of minced (ground) beef. Finely grind 100 g/3½ oz (1¼ cups) roasted desiccated coconut, then combine with 4 finely grated garlic cloves. Combine the beef, coconut and garlic in a food processor and process until smooth. Shape the mixture into 20-g/¾-oz meatballs. Cook the spices and coconut milk over medium-high heat until the liquid has reduced by three-quarters. Add the meatballs and cook for 20 minutes until the liquid has completely evaporated and the rendang is dark brown.
- **Tempeh Rendang (Rendang Tempe)**
  Replaced the beef with an equal amount of tempeh, cut into 2.5-cm/1-inch cubes. Cook for 1½ hours until the mixture is dry. It will be paler than a beef rendang.
- **Jackfruit Rendang (Rendang Nangka)**
  Replace the beef with 3 (each 565-g/20-oz) cans of firm jackfruit in water, drained. Add the jackfruit to the spiced coconut base. Cook for 1½ hours until the mixture is dry. It will be much lighter in colour than a beef rendang.
- **Goat Rendang (Rendang Kambing)**
  Replace the beef with goat meat.

Beef Curry
Tongseng

This central Java dish is popular among street food vendors across Jakarta. Originally prepared with goat meat in a curry stew, this adaptation combines a rib-eye steak with a fragrant curry infusion of spices, coconut milk and sweet soy sauce.

It's the perfect example of how Indonesians adopt food influences from neighbouring India, the Middle East and China. This dish comes together quickly with the steak, which could be easily substituted with goat tenderloin, fish or tofu.

Origin: Java

Preparation time: 20 minutes
Cooking time: 20 minutes

Serves 4

- 2 tablespoons coconut oil
- ½ quantity Yellow Spice Paste (page 43)
- 1 stalk lemongrass, crushed and tied into a knot
- 2 salam leaves or bay leaves
- 2 spring onions (scallions), finely chopped
- 1 tablespoon ground coriander
- ½ teaspoon white pepper

- 400 ml/14 fl oz (1⅔ cups) coconut milk
- 2 tablespoons Sweet Soy Sauce (page 38)
- 2 tablespoons sunflower oil
- 2 (200-g/7-oz) rib-eye steaks
- Salt, to taste
- 2 tomatoes, cut into wedges
- 200 g/7 oz sweetheart cabbage, thinly sliced

- 50 g/1¾ oz (1½ cups) baby spinach
- Ginger Coconut Rice (page 198) or brown rice
- 2 tablespoons Crispy Shallots (page 41)
- Melinjo crackers (optional)

Heat the coconut oil in a frying pan over medium heat. Add the paste and cook for 3–4 minutes. Add the lemongrass, salam leaves, half of the spring onions (scallions), the ground coriander, and pepper and mix well. Stir in the coconut milk, sweet soy sauce and 200 ml/7 fl oz (scant 1 cup) of water. Bring to a boil, then reduce the heat to medium-low. Cover and simmer for 7–8 minutes until slightly thickened.

Heat the sunflower oil in a frying pan over high heat. Season the steaks with salt and pan-fry for 3–4 minutes on each side. Transfer the steaks to a plate, then rest for 3 minutes.

Add 7 tablespoons of water to the pan and deglaze. Add the deglazing liquid to the coconut mixture. Stir in the tomatoes and cook for 2 minutes. Add the cabbage and cook for 1 minute. Add the spinach and cook until just wilted. Season with salt and pepper.

Slice the steak into ½-cm/¼-inch strips. Divide the rice among 4 wide bowls. Arrange the steak on one half of each bowl, then add the vegetables and sauce to the other half. Top with crispy shallots and melinjo crackers, if using. Serve immediately.

Variation:
- **Tempeh and Tofu Curry (Tongseng Tempe dan Tahu)**
  Replace the beef with 250 g/9 oz each of tempeh and firm tofu, cut into 2-cm/¾-inch cubes. Add the tempeh and tofu to the curry base mixture and bring to a boil. Reduce the heat to medium-low and simmer, uncovered, for 30 minutes. Season to taste.

Lamb Curry
Gulai Korma Domba

Korma is the Indonesian term for dates, a fruit that is, interestingly enough, entirely absent from this recipe. My grandmother and mum never prepared goat or lamb dishes, but I've always enjoyed the flavour.

This reminds me of a Javanese goat curry (*gulai kambing*) I first had when I was ten years old. Asam gelugur is traditionally used to make this curry light and aromatic, but I've opted for tamarind instead.

Origin: Sumatra

Preparation time: 15 minutes
Cooking time: 1 hour 50 minutes–2 hours 20 minutes

Serves 6–8

For the spice blend:
* 6 whole cloves
* 1 teaspoon coriander seeds
* 1 teaspoon cumin seeds
* 1 teaspoon fennel seeds
* 1 tablespoon black peppercorns

For the curry:
* 2 tablespoons coconut oil
* 1 quantity Red Spice Paste (page 43)
* 1.2 kg/2 lb 12 oz lamb stew meat, cut into 2-cm/¾-inch cubes
* 2 star anise
* 2 green cardamom pods, crushed
* 1 teaspoon freshly grated nutmeg
* 5 makrut lime leaves, torn

* 2 stalks lemongrass, crushed and tied into a knot
* 800 ml/27 fl oz (3½ cups) coconut milk
* ½ teaspoon salt
* 2 salam leaves or bay leaves
* ½ pandan leaf, tied into a knot (optional)
* 3 tablespoons Tamarind Paste (page 44)
* 2 red large chillies, thinly sliced, to garnish

To make the spice blend, combine all the ingredients in a frying pan. Dry-roast over medium heat for 6–8 minutes until fragrant, stirring occasionally to prevent them from burning. Remove from the heat and let cool.

Transfer the spices into a spice grinder and grind into a fine powder.

To make the curry, heat the oil in a large frying pan over medium heat. Add the paste and cook for 4–6 minutes, stirring continually. Add the spice blend and cook for 1 minute. Add the lamb and cook for 5 minutes, stirring well. Add the star anise, cardamom, nutmeg, lime leaves and lemongrass. Pour in half of the coconut milk and 300 ml/10 fl oz (1¼ cups) of water. Season with salt. Add the salam leaves and pandan, if using. Bring to a boil, then reduce the heat to low. Cover and simmer for 1½–2 hours, until the meat is tender.

Add the remaining coconut milk and the tamarind paste and mix well. Increase the heat to high and cook for 5 minutes. Season to taste. Discard the lime leaves and lemongrass. Garnish with chillies.

Variation:
- **Prawn Curry (Gulai Udang)**
  Replace the lamb with king prawns. Replace the tamarind with the juice of 2 limes. Cook the curry base until reduced by two-thirds. Add the prawns and cook for 3–4 minutes.

North Bali Pork Curry
Kuah Balung

Balinese curry dishes may be less popular than those from Sumatra or Java, but they are delicious nonetheless.

This North Balinese curry was inspired by Ayu Kreshna, the founder of Rumah Intaran Cookery School and a local food campaigner. Her kitchen reminds me of Oma's open-plan kitchen in Manado, back in the mid-seventies, where she would prepare food over an open fire.

If you're looking for an even more authentic taste, replace the ginger in the Yellow Spice Paste with 8 g/¼ oz kencur.

Origin: Bali

Preparation time: 20 minutes
Cooking time: 1 hour 25 minutes

Serves 8

- 1 tablespoon coriander seeds
- 1 teaspoon white peppercorns
- 2 tablespoons coconut oil
- 1 quantity Yellow Spice Paste (page 43)
- 1.2 kg/2 lb 12 oz baby pork ribs, cut into two-rib portions
- 2 stalks lemongrass, crushed and tied into a knot
- 4 makrut lime leaves, torn
- 4 salam leaves or bay leaves

- ½ whole nutmeg
- 1 litre/34 fl oz (4¼ cups) coconut milk
- 1 teaspoon salt
- 300 g/10½ oz bottle gourd or butternut squash, cut into 2-cm/¾-inch cubes
- 3 long peppers or 1 tablespoon black peppercorns

To serve:
- Steamed rice or Turmeric Coconut Rice (page 201)
- Roasted Aubergine (page 148)
- Shallot Sambal (page 50)

Combine the coriander seeds and peppercorns in a frying pan and dry-roast for 4–5 minutes over medium-low heat until fragrant, stirring occasionally to prevent them from burning. Remove the pan from the heat and cool completely.

Transfer to a spice grinder and grind into a fine powder.

Heat 1 tablespoon of oil in a large wok or frying pan over medium heat. Add the paste and cook for 4 minutes until the mixture is dried out. Add the pork ribs, lemongrass, lime leaves, salam leaves, nutmeg and spice blend. Pour in half of the coconut milk and 750 ml/25 fl oz (3 cups) of water. Add the salt. Bring to a boil, then reduce the heat to medium-low. Cover and simmer for 1 hour, or until the ribs are tender.

Add the bottle gourd, long peppers and the remaining coconut milk. Bring to another boil, then reduce the heat to medium-low and simmer for another 15 minutes, or until the bottle gourd has softened. Season to taste.

Serve with rice, vegetables and sambal.

Tempeh, Tofu and Vegetables

Tempe, Tahu dan Sayur

A friend once asked me to describe the vegetables I grew up with in Manado. I recalled indigenous ferns, breadfruits, papaya flowers and the popular water spinach otherwise known as morning glory. When I moved to Jakarta, I discovered the delights of other vegetables and legumes such as the distinct and *nutty jengkol* (*left*), also known as the bitter bean. But the outside world introduced us to other vegetables – including carrots, tomatoes, aubergines (eggplants) and potatoes – that have also become staples in our cuisine.

Steamed root vegetables, plantain and corn combined with a serving of spicy sambal (page 145) and various vegetable stir-fries bring back memories of my Oma in her kitchen. Whenever adding aromatics of lemongrass, basil and lime leaves to vegetable dishes, she would insist *supaya bau enak*, meaning 'for the delicious fragrance'.

Introduced to Indonesia by Chinese migrants, soybeans are an excellent source of protein and key to making tofu, tempeh, miso and soy sauce. I first tasted tempeh goreng – fried tempeh seasoned with ground garlic, shallots, coriander and salt – in Java. It was a revelation that so much flavour and texture could be had in such a common and inexpensive dish. And I've been a fan since that day.

As we continue to move towards plant-based diets, I've found that tofu and tempeh are good sources of protein and provide sustenance and variety in our diets, which inspired me to feature more vegan recipes in the cookbook. This includes Spiced Tofu and Tempeh Braised in Coconut Water (page 154), Bogor Tempeh Laksa (page 100) and Tempeh Satay (page 119). As we know, good food has the power to nurture and lift spirits.

Sweetcorn Fritters with Chilli and Tomato Sambal

Perkedel Jagung dan Dabu-Dabu

Served as a snack or as part of a meal, these sweet and crunchy fritters are absolutely irresistible. Best of all, they're unbelievably simple to make.

Traditionally, the fritters are made with fresh sweetcorn on the cob but you can substitute canned (or frozen) sweetcorn so long as you drain out all the water. (This ensures a crunchy fritter.) Makrut lime leaves infuse the fritters with a wonderful fragrance.

Dabu-dabu is a fresh and versatile chilli-tomato sambal similar to tomato salsa. The sambal can be prepared in advance but to preserve the freshness of the tomatoes, add the lime juice, salt and oil just before serving.

Origin: Sulawesi

Preparation time: 15 minutes
Cooking time: 10–20 minutes

Serves 4

- 250 g/9 oz (1½ cups) sweetcorn
- 3 makrut lime leaves, centre stem removed and thinly sliced
- 2 cloves garlic, grated
- 2 spring onions (scallions), finely chopped

- 1–2 red bird's eye chillies, finely chopped
- 1 banana shallot, finely chopped
- 6 tablespoons rice flour
- 4 tablespoons cornflour (cornstarch)
- ½ teaspoon salt
- ½ teaspoon white pepper

- 500 ml/17 fl oz (generous 2 cups) sunflower oil, for deep-frying
- 1 quantity Chilli and Tomato Sambal (page 48), to serve

If using canned sweetcorn, drain well and squeeze out as much water as possible from the kernels. Transfer the sweetcorn to a food processor and blend for 10 seconds until a coarse purée.

In a large bowl, combine the sweetcorn, lime leaves, garlic, spring onions (scallions), chillies and shallot and mix well. Stir in the rice flour and cornflour (cornstarch). Season with salt and pepper. The batter should be thick but easy to mix. If needed, add 2–3 tablespoons of cold water to thin it out slightly.

Heat the oil in a wok or deep saucepan over medium heat. The oil is ready when a cube of bread dropped in sizzles on contact and turns golden in 10–15 seconds. (Alternatively, use a thermometer and heat to 180°C/350°F.)

Scoop a tablespoon of the mixture and flatten it slightly into a patty. Repeat with the remaining mixture. Carefully lower 5–6 into the pan and deep-fry for 2–3 minutes on each side until golden brown. Using a slotted spoon, transfer the cooked fritters to a plate lined with paper towels. Repeat with the remaining fritters.

Place the fritters on a serving dish and serve with the sambal.

Variation:
- **Samarinda Sweetcorn Fritters (Empal Jagung)**
  Omit the lime leaves and chillies. Add a small bunch of Chinese parsley or celery leaves, chopped, and 1 tablespoon ground coriander. Omit the sambal.

Grilled Sweetcorn with Green Sambal and Lime

Jagung Manis Oles Sambal Ijo

Boiled, steamed or barbecued, sweetcorn is always on the Indonesian table. We love it steamed in its husk and served with steamed fresh peanuts in the shell and edamame, as prepared by Indonesian street food vendors. Barbecued sweetcorn is a personal favourite.

Origin: Throughout Indonesia

Preparation time: 15 minutes
Cooking time: 15–20 minutes

Serves 4

* 2 tablespoons coconut oil
* 1 quantity Green Sambal (page 51)
* Juice of 1 lime
* 4 cobs sweetcorn, husks and silky strands removed
* Chopped basil, to garnish (optional)

Preheat your barbecue or griddled (grill) pan over medium-high heat.

In a small bowl, combine the oil, sambal and lime juice. Brush a little of the mixture over the sweetcorn. Add the cobs to the barbecue and grill for 10–12 minutes, brushing on a little more of the sambal and turning occasionally.

Transfer to a plate, then drizzle over the remaining sambal and garnish with basil.

Steamed Sweet Potatoes, Plantains, Sweetcorn and Cassava with Sambal

Ragam Makanan Kukus dan Sambal

Many Indonesian communities enjoy tubers as their main carbohydrate source. The vegetables can be roasted, but I steam them simply as a matter of personal preference. This recipe makes the perfect accompaniment to grilled seafood, braised fish and stir-fried vegetables with a side of sambal, of course, for good measure.

Origin: Throughout Indonesia

Preparation time: 10 minutes
Cooking time: 50–55 minutes

Serves 8

* 1 kg/2 lb 4 oz cassava, peeled, washed and cut into 10-cm/ 4-inch lengths
* 1 kg/2 lb 4 oz sweet potatoes, unpeeled and chopped into 4–5 pieces
* 2 cobs sweetcorn, cut into thirds
* 1 plantain, unpeeled and cut into 3–4 lengths
* Your choice of sambal (pages 47–54)

Arrange the cassava and sweet potatoes in a large steamer basket and steam for 30 minutes or until softened. Add the sweetcorn and plantain and steam for another 20–25 minutes.

Serve with your choice of sambal.

Water Spinach with Chilli and Miso
Tumis Kangkung dengan Cabe dan Tauco

Water spinach is a celebrated vegetable in Indonesian cuisine, distinguished by its delicious juicy texture and hollow stems. In fact, the sought-after variety in North Sulawesi is prized for its larger leaves and stems.

It can be enjoyed a number of ways: stir-fried or boiled with sambal or added to *Gado-Gado* (page 86) and Vegetable Salad (page 88). You can find fresh water spinach online, but it is also stocked at Asian speciality food shops. If water spinach is unavailable, replace it with spinach.

Origin: Sumatra

Preparation time: 10 minutes
Cooking time: 5–10 minutes

Serves 4

* 200 g/7 oz water spinach or regular spinach
* 2 tablespoons dark miso paste
* 2 tablespoons coconut oil
* 2 cloves garlic, finely chopped
* 2 red bird's eye chillies, thinly sliced
* 10 cherry tomatoes, halved
* Salt, to taste

Discard any hard stalks or wilted leaves from the water spinach. Wash the spinach thoroughly, shake dry and cut the leaves and stems into 3-cm/1¼-inch lengths. Put the leaves and stalks into separate bowls. Mix the miso with 4 tablespoons of water. Set aside.

Heat the oil in a wok or a frying pan over medium heat. Add the garlic and chillies and sauté for 2–3 minutes, until the garlic is golden. Increase the heat to high. Add the water spinach stems and tomatoes and stir-fry for 2–3 minutes, until the stalks have softened. Add the leaves and cook for 3–4 minutes, until heated through and the leaves have just wilted. Stir in the miso mixture and cook for another minute. Season to taste.

Variations:
- Stir-Fried Water Spinach with Papaya Flowers (Tumis Kangkung dengan Bunga Pepaya)
  Omit the miso. Parboil 100 g/3½ oz papaya flowers. With the water spinach, add the papaya flowers, 1 crushed stalk lemongrass and 3 torn lime leaves. You could also add 100 g/3½ oz smoked haddock, cod or bacon, cut into small cubes.
- Water Spinach with Shrimp Paste and Tomato Sambal (Pelecing Kangkung)
  Omit the miso and cherry tomatoes. Sauté the garlic with a chopped banana shallot for 2–3 minutes. Add ½ teaspoon shrimp paste and cook for 2 minutes. Add 2 finely chopped tomatoes and lime leaves, with the centre stems removed and thinly sliced, and stir-fry for 5 minutes. Season with salt and a pinch of sugar. In a separate saucepan, blanch the water spinach for 2 minutes and refresh with iced water. Transfer to a place and top with the tomato sambal.
- Stir-Fried Bean Sprouts (Tumis Tauge)
  Omit the miso. Add 2 tablespoons fried anchovies or 4 finely chopped anchovy fillets to the garlic and chillies. Replace the water spinach with 200 g/7 oz (2 cups) bean sprouts.
- Stir-Fried Leafy Vegetables (Rumpu Rampe)
  This classic dish from Sumba and Flores Island combines water spinach with fresh moringa leaves, papaya leaves, cassava leaves and papaya flowers. Omit the miso and tomatoes. Grind 2 whole dry-roasted candlenuts and add, along with 1 large sliced banana shallot, to the garlic and chillies. Replace the vegetables with 250 g/9 oz spinach.

Roasted Aubergine with Spicy Pili Sauce
Terong Saos Kacang Kanari Pedas

Pili nuts are similar to almonds but with a richer, creamier taste. They are plentiful in Maluku, a province comprised of nearly a thousand islands. The province was once known as the Moluccas or The Spice Islands, a historic trading hub for the visiting merchants from China, India and, later, Medieval Europe (page 25).

One of the best places to find pili nuts is in the Banda Islands. Known locally as *kacang kanari*, pili nut trees have a vital function by offering shade for nutmeg, which could only be found in Banda in the sixteenth century. (Seedlings were eventually carried to other countries around the world.)

Origin: Maluku

Preparation time: 30 minutes
Cooking time: 30–35 minutes

Serves 2–4

For the aubergines (eggplants):
* 2 large aubergines (eggplants)
* 2 tablespoons melted coconut oil
* Salt and black pepper, to taste
* Small bunch of basil, leaves only, to garnish

* Steamed rice or Turmeric Coconut Rice (page 201), to serve

For the sauce:
* 100 g/3½ oz (scant 1 cup) natural pili nuts or almonds with skin
* 2 tablespoons coconut oil

* 2 cloves garlic, finely chopped
* 1 banana shallot, finely chopped
* 2–3 red bird's eye chillies, sliced
* 1–2 tablespoons lime juice
* Salt, to taste
* ½ teaspoon white pepper

To make the aubergines (eggplants), preheat the oven to 220°C/425°F/Gas Mark 7.

Using a sharp knife, cut the aubergine into 5-cm/2-inch pieces. Place in a roasting pan, drizzle with the oil and season with salt and pepper. Roast for 30–35 minutes until soft.

To make the sauce, place the pili nuts on a baking sheet and roast on the lowest rack of the oven for 10–12 minutes.

Heat the oil in a saucepan over medium heat. Add the garlic and shallot and sauté for 2–3 minutes until fragrant. Add the chillies and sauté for another 2–3 minutes. Set aside.

In a blender, combine the pili nuts, garlic mixture and 200 ml/7 fl oz (generous ¾ cup) of water and blend until thick and smooth. If necessary, add a little water. Transfer to a bowl, then add the lime juice. Season with salt and pepper.

Transfer the aubergines to a large serving plate and drizzle with the sauce. Garnish with basil leaves and serve with rice.

Variation:
- **Padang-Style Aubergines (Terong Balado)**
  Replace the sauce with Balado Sambal (page 51) and mix with the aubergines.

Stir-Fried Tempeh and Vegetables
Oseng Tempe dan Sayuran

Oseng in the Javanese dialect means 'stir-fry'. As one of my favourite plant-based dishes, this medley of vegetables owes its delightful fragrance to the sliced galangal. Simply sauté the garlic and shallots, then add in the tempeh and cook everything together. It makes for a flavoursome and fuss-free topping for a rice bowl, perfect for a mid-week lunch or dinner option.

Origin: Java

Preparation time: 15 minutes
Cooking time: 10–15 minutes

Serves 2

* 2 tablespoons coconut oil
* 3 cloves garlic, finely chopped
* 2 large chillies, thinly sliced
* 1 large banana shallot, finely chopped
* 10 g/¼ oz galangal, cut into 1-cm/½-inch slices
* 250 g/9 oz tempeh, cut into 1-cm/½-inch cubes

* 2–3 tablespoons Sweet Soy Sauce (page 38)
* 2 salam leaves or bay leaves
* Salt, to taste
* 50 g/1¾ oz (1 cup) button (white) mushrooms, thinly sliced

* 100 g/3½ oz green beans or runner beans, cut into 2-cm/¾-inch lengths
* 2 large tomatoes, sliced into wedges
* ½ teaspoon white pepper
* Steamed rice, to serve

Heat the oil in a wok or large frying pan over medium heat. Add the garlic, chillies, shallot and galangal and sauté for 4–5 minutes. Mix in the tempeh, sweet soy sauce, salam leaves and 100 ml/3½ fl oz (scant ½ cup) of water. Season with salt. Bring to a boil, then reduce the heat to medium-low and simmer for 2–3 minutes.

Add the mushrooms and stir-fry for 2–3 minutes until the liquid has reduced by half. Add the green beans and tomatoes and cook for 2–3 minutes until the beans are cooked through. Season with salt and pepper. Discard the galangal and salam leaves, then serve.

Spiced Vegetable Stew
Rica Rodo

Rica in Manadonese means chillies and generally signals a fiery dining experience. Rest assured, I have reduced any hazardous spiciness to a more comfortable level. Back in Manado, this dish would be prepared with long beans (they can grow up to a metre/yard in length) and slender aubergines (eggplants). Here, I combine green beans and dark purple aubergine. Aromatic lemongrass and makrut lime leaves make this dried stew extra special, and tomatoes introduce pops of colour.

Origin: Sulawesi

Preparation time: 15 minutes
Cooking time: 25 minutes

Serves 4

* 2 tablespoons coconut oil
* 2 red bird's eye chillies, thinly sliced
* 2 cloves garlic, thinly sliced
* 1 banana shallot, finely chopped
* 1 aubergine (eggplant), cut into 1-cm/½-inch cubes

* 1 long stalk lemongrass, crushed and tied into a knot
* 4 makrut lime leaves, torn
* Salt, to taste
* 100 g/3½ oz green beans, sliced into 1-cm/½-inch lengths
* 200 g/7 oz (2 cups) sweetcorn kernels

* 2 large tomatoes, chopped into 1-cm/½-inch cubes
* Small bunch of basil, finely chopped

To Serve:
* Steamed rice
* Chicken curry of your choice (page 125–130)

Heat the oil in a large frying pan or wok over medium heat. Add the chillies, garlic and shallot and sauté for 3–4 minutes until fragrant. Add the aubergine (eggplant), lemongrass, lime leaves and 3½ tablespoons of water. Season with salt. Sauté for another 8 minutes over medium heat until the aubergine has softened.

Add the green beans and cook for 3 minutes. Add another 4 tablespoons of water and cook for 2 minutes. Stir in the sweetcorn and tomatoes and cook for 4 minutes. Add the basil and cook for another 1–2 minutes. Season to taste.

Serve with steamed rice and chicken curry.

Tempeh

Spelled *tempe* in Indonesia, tempeh (pronounced tem-PAY) is a fermented soybean widely consumed in Indonesia. Allegedly, soybeans were introduced to Indonesia from China in 1,000 CE. Some of the earliest mentions of tempeh are found in the *Serat Centhini,* an ancient twelve-volume manuscript of Javanese stories and philosophies.

Highly nutritious and a rich source of protein, it is often described as having a nutty-mushroom flavour and excellent texture. It also absorbs flavour well, making it incredibly versatile. Moreover, these days, tempeh is produced not only with soybeans but also with many different types of beans.

Most Indonesian tempeh dishes hail from Java. It can be prepared as fried chips *(tempe keripik)*, deep-fried as a delicious snack to be enjoyed any time of the day (page 155); slow-cooked in a hearty vegetable stew with aubergines (eggplants), long beans and coconut milk (page 123); or combined in a spicy dish featuring shallots, ginger, tomatoes and sambal *(sambal goreng tempe).*

And with a growing movement towards plant-based diets, tempeh is becoming more widely available.

Spiced Tofu and Tempeh Braised in Coconut Water

Tahu dan Tempe Bacem

Cooking with light but flavourful coconut water has been a great tradition across Indonesia for centuries. In this recipe, the tempeh and tofu are braised with coconut water, ground coriander, sweet soy and tamarind until all the liquid is absorbed.

Then, the tempeh and tofu are pan-fried in a little oil to add caramelization and sweetness.

Origin: Modern recipe

Preparation time: 25–30 minutes
Cooking time: 1 hour

Serves 4

For the spiced tofu and tempeh:
* 3 cloves garlic, finely chopped
* 2 banana shallots, finely chopped
* 1 tablespoon ground coriander
* 1 tablespoon coconut sugar
* 1 litre/34 fl oz (4¼ cups) coconut water
* 4 tablespoons Tamarind Paste (page 44)
* 10 g/¼ oz galangal, halved and crushed
* 3 makrut lime leaves, torn
* 3 salam leaves or bay leaves
* 2 short stalks lemongrass, crushed and tied into a knot
* 3 tablespoons Sweet Soy Sauce (page 38)
* Salt, to taste
* 250 g/9 oz firm tofu, cut into 3-cm/1¼-inch cubes
* 250 g/9 oz tempeh, cut into 1.5-cm/¾-inch slices
* 2 tablespoons coconut oil

For the salad:
* 4 tablespoons light soy sauce
* 1 tablespoon Sweet Soy Sauce (page 38)
* Juice of 2 limes
* 1 large red chilli, thinly sliced
* 1 red bird's eye chilli, thinly sliced
* 1 carrot, coarsely shredded
* ½ small cucumber, peeled into ribbons
* 50 g/1¾ oz (½ cup) radishes, thinly sliced
* 50 g/1¾ oz (1½ cups) baby spinach

To make the spiced tofu and tempeh, combine the garlic, shallots and ground coriander in a small blender. Finely grind. Transfer the mixture to a medium saucepan, then add the coconut sugar, coconut water, tamarind paste, galangal, lime and salam leaves, lemongrass and sweet soy sauce. Bring to a boil, then reduce the heat to medium-low and simmer for 5 minutes. Season with salt. Mix well. Discard the lime leaves and lemongrass.

Score both sides of the tempeh slices to help it absorb the seasoning. Add the tofu and tempeh to the pan. Cover and cook over medium heat for 30 minutes. Uncover and cook for another 20–25 minutes, until the liquid has evaporated.

Meanwhile, prepare the salad. Combine the soy sauces, lime juice and chillies in a bowl and mix well. Arrange the mixed vegetables on a large serving platter. Set aside.

Heat the oil in a large frying pan. Working in batches to avoid overcrowding, add the tempeh and tofu and pan-fry for 1–2 minutes on each side until nicely browned.

Transfer to the serving plate and serve warm with the salad on the side. Drizzle the dressing over the salad. Serve.

Variation:
- **Padang-Style Fried Chicken (Ayam Pop)**
Replace the tempeh and tofu with 8 skinless chicken thighs. Omit the sweet soy sauce, tamarind paste and chillies. Add 10 g/¼ oz thinly sliced ginger and the juice of 2 limes. Combine all the ingredients together, add 1 teaspoon salt and bring to a boil. Reduce the heat to medium-low and simmer until the chicken is cooked thoroughly. Heat 2 tablespoons of coconut oil in a frying pan over medium-low heat. Add the chicken and cook for 1–2 minutes each side. Then add to the pan after the lime leaves and lemongrass have been discarded and follow the remaining recipe. Serve with Chilli and Tomato Sambal (page 48).

Sambal Tempeh in Lettuce Cups
Sambal Goreng Tempe Disajikan diatas Daun Selada

This sambal tempeh has a sweet, spicy and nutty flavour, often served in Java and Bali with rice and different vegetables and protein known as *nasi campur* ('mixed rice') or added to *nasi tumpeng,* a cone-shaped turmeric coconut rice with different vegetables and protein. It also makes a delightful topping on crunchy, refreshing baby Cos or romaine lettuce.

Origin: Java

Preparation time: 20 minutes
Cooking time: 20 minutes

Serves 4–6

* Sunflower oil, for deep-frying
* 250 g/9 oz tempeh, cut into thick matchsticks
* Salt, to taste
* 4 cloves garlic, finely chopped
* 1 banana shallot, thinly sliced
* 2–3 red bird's eye chillies, thinly sliced
* 10 g/¼ oz galangal, cut into ½-cm/¼-inch-thick slices (optional)
* 3 tablespoons Tamarind Paste (page 44)
* 3 tablespoons Sweet Soy Sauce (page 38)
* 4 makrut lime leaves, torn
* 2 baby gem lettuces, leaves separated and dried
* Cress, to garnish

Heat 400 ml/14 fl oz (1⅔ cups) oil in a saucepan or a wok over medium heat. The oil is ready when a cube of bread dropped in sizzles on contact and turns golden in 10–15 seconds. (Alternatively, use a thermometer and heat to 180°C/350°F.)

Season the tempeh with salt. Carefully lower half of the tempeh into the oil and deep-fry for 6–8 minutes until golden brown. Using a slotted spoon, transfer the tempeh to a plate lined with paper towels to absorb the oil. Repeat with the remaining tempeh. Set aside. Cool the pan and oil slightly. Pour most of the oil into a bowl, reserving 2 tablespoons in the pan.

Heat the pan over medium heat. Add the garlic and shallot and sauté for 3–4 minutes until softened. Add the chillies and galangal and sauté for 3 minutes. Stir in the tamarind paste, sweet soy sauce and lime leaves. Season with a pinch of salt. Stir in the tempeh and cook for 2–3 minutes. Set aside.

Arrange large lettuce leaves on a serving platter. Cut the small lettuce hearts into 4-cm/1½-inch strips and add to the platter. Discard the galangal and lime leaves from the tempeh mixture. Fill each leaf with the tempeh mixture. Garnish with cress and serve.

Deep-Fried Spiced Tempeh
Tempe Mendoan

Thin sheets of tempeh are dipped into a spiced batter and deep-fried to crispy perfection – completely opposite to the soft texture of the classic Javanese dish.

Origin: Java

Preparation time: 15 minutes
Cooking time: 15 minutes

Serves 8

* 250 g/9 oz tempeh, cut into 8–10 thin slices
* 100 g/3½ oz (⅔ cup) plain (all-purpose) flour
* 50 g/1¾ oz (4½ tablespoons) rice flour
* 2 cloves garlic, finely chopped
* 2 tablespoons chopped chives
* 2 tablespoons chopped spring onion (scallions)
* 1 teaspoon ground coriander
* 1 teaspoon salt
* 1 teaspoon baking powder
* 300 ml/10 fl oz (1¼ cups) sunflower oil, for deep-frying

Place the tempeh on a baking sheet lined with paper towels. Set aside for 10 minutes.

In a large bowl, combine all the ingredients, except the tempeh and oil, and mix well. Pour in 250 ml/8 fl oz (1 cup) of water and whisk until smooth.

Heat the oil in a wok or saucepan over medium heat. The oil is ready when a cube of bread dropped in sizzles on contact and turns golden in 10–15 seconds. (Alternatively, use a thermometer and heat to 180°C/350°F.)

Dip a slice of tempeh into the batter, then carefully lower it into the wok. Repeat with a second slice of tempeh. Deep-fry for 2–3 minutes on each side, until slightly golden. Transfer to a plate lined with paper towels to drain. Repeat with the remaining tempeh.

Serve.

Vegetables with Spiced Coconut
Urap

Urap is a classic vegetable dish available in several regions of Indonesia. Featuring several blanched vegetables in a wonderful paste and a spiced coconut dressing, it's a light and delicious meal for a sunny day!

The purists will insist on kencur for this dish, but since it's difficult to find, replace it with ginger – I consider it a small sacrifice well worth making just to enjoy this dish. I also combine fresh and blanched vegetables for texture and colours.

You can prepare the spiced coconut mixture a couple of hours in advance. Just set it aside to cool and keep it chilled in the refrigerator until needed.

Origin: Java and Bali

Preparation time: 20 minutes
Cooking time: 20 minutes

Serves 4

* ½ teaspoon shrimp paste or 2 tablespoons fish sauce
* 2 tablespoons coconut oil
* ½ quantity Red Spice Paste (page 43), made with kencur instead of ginger
* 3 salam leaves or bay leaves
* 200 g/7 oz Freshly Grated Coconut (page 38)
* 4 makrut lime leaves, centre stem removed and thinly sliced

* ½ teaspoon sugar
* Salt, to taste
* 50 g/1¾ oz long beans or green beans
* 100 g/3½ oz sweetheart cabbage, thinly sliced
* 50 g/1¾ oz spinach
* 2 carrots, coarsely grated
* 50 g/1¾ oz (1 cup) bean sprouts
* Large bunch of basil, leaves only

To serve:
* Steamed rice or Turmeric Coconut Rice (page 201)
* Seafood Satay (page 112)

Dry-roast the shrimp paste in a small frying pan over medium-high heat for 2–3 minutes. Transfer to a pestle and mortar and grind to a fine powder.

Heat the oil in a frying pan or wok over medium heat. Add the paste (or fish sauce) and salam leaves and cook for 3–4 minutes. Add the coconut and lime leaves to the pan. Season with sugar and salt and cook for another 4–5 minutes. Set aside to cool.

Fill a saucepan with 1.5 litres/50 fl oz (6¼ cups) of water and bring to a boil. Prepare a large bowl of iced water. Add the beans and blanch for 7 minutes. Transfer the beans to the bowl of iced water to stop the cooking.

Bring the pan of water back to a boil. Add the cabbage and blanch for 2 minutes. Add the spinach and blanch for a minute. Transfer the cabbage and spinach to the bowl of iced water. Drain the vegetables, then cut the beans into 1-cm/½-inch segments. Set aside.

In a large bowl, combine the carrots, bean sprouts and blanched vegetables. Add the coconut mixture and toss well. Stir in the basil.

Serve with your choice of rice and seafood satay.

Variation:
- **Molucca-Style Smoked Fish and Vegetables with Spiced Coconut (Kohu-Kohu)**
  Prepare the red spice paste with ginger (not kencur). Add 200 g/7 oz smoked mackerel, with or without skin, torn into bite-size pieces. Rub the juice of 2 calamansi or 1 lime into the fish. Season with salt. Add the fish into the coconut mixture and simmer for 5–7 minutes. Set aside to cool, then toss well with the vegetables.

Crunchy Tempeh
Kering Tempe

This versatile dish can be enjoyed as a snack, added to rice dishes, sprinkled over salads or stir-fried with noodles. Its super nutty flavour is enhanced with sweet, spicy notes and hints of umami, making it a delightful accompaniment for vegetables, fish or chicken dishes.

The tempeh and the peanuts should be roasted until crispy. You could also fry them to achieve the same results.

Origin: Java

Preparation time: 15 minutes
Cooking time: 30 minutes

Serves 4

For the tempeh:
* 250 g/9 oz tempeh, cut into matchsticks
* Salt, to taste
* 150 g/5½ oz (1¼ cups) blanched peanuts (optional)
* 30 g/1 oz dried baby anchovies, shallow-fried until crunchy (optional)

For the bumbu:
* 3 tablespoons coconut oil
* 4 cloves garlic, finely chopped
* 1 large banana shallot, thinly sliced
* 2–3 red bird's eye chillies, thinly sliced
* 2 large red chillies, thinly sliced
* 5 makrut lime leaves, centre stem removed and thinly sliced
* 1 stalk lemongrass, crushed and tied into a knot
* 5 tablespoons coconut sugar
* 1 tablespoon sugar
* Salt, to taste

To make the tempeh, preheat the oven to 200°C/400°F/Gas Mark 6.

Season the tempeh with salt. Place the tempeh and peanuts, if using, on separate baking sheets, spreading them out in a single layer. Roast for 18–20 minutes, stirring halfway, until golden and crunchy.

Meanwhile, make the bumbu. Heat the oil in a frying pan over medium heat. Add the garlic and shallot and sauté for 3–4 minutes. Add the chillies, lime leaves and lemongrass and sauté for another 3 minutes. Add both sugars and stir until dissolved. Season with salt.

Stir in the tempeh, peanuts and baby anchovies, if using, and mix well to coat. Leave to cool. Leftovers can be stored in an airtight jar at room temperature for up to a week.

Fish and Seafood

Ikan dan Hasil Laut

Indonesia is surrounded by oceans and the more than 17,000 islands have large rivers and lakes full of freshwater fish – it is heaven for fish lovers.

Plentiful, affordable, and easy to source, fish and seafood have been a part of my diet since I can remember. Our dinner table often featured fish or seafood in some shape or form: snapper, mackerel, tuna, sardines, king prawns, squid, catfish and the lesser known gurami. Fish and seafood would also be preserved, and salted fish (*ikan asin*), smoked fish and fermented shrimp paste (*ikan asap dan tera*) were frequently used to flavour dishes. Christmas feasts always included whole barbecued fish smothered in a spiced paste and wrapped in a young palm leaf. This can be a challenge to create, so I tend to prepare a stew version of this dish, with spiced turmeric, herbs and tomatoes (page 174).

More often than not, my travels across the archipelago took me to far-flung locations and remote islands where the inhabitants made up a modest community and time stood seemingly still. On these extraordinary trips, I would feast on the delicious bounties of the sea – such as Barbecued Seafood with Sambals (page 177) – with picturesque blue skies and powdery white sandy beaches that backdropped our meal. These privileged occasions were never lost on me.

This chapter brims with a delightful collection of easy recipes that can be prepared with simple techniques and just a handful of ingredients. In the UK, I seek out locally sourced fish and seafood and I encourage you to do the same. Just be sure to invest in the best-quality seafood and have your fishmonger clean and gut the fish for you.

Salmon with Spiced Tamarind and Vegetables

Filet Salmon Panggang dengan Bumbu Rujak dan Sayuran

The spiced tamarind here is a lovely complement to fish, and also suits roasted vegetables and tofu. If you need inspiration for a mid-week supper, look no further.

Origin: Modern recipe

Preparation time: 15 minutes
Cooking time: 20 minutes

Serves 4

For the tamarind sauce:
* 1 tablespoon coconut oil
* ½ quantity Yellow Spice Paste (page 43)
* 2 tablespoons tamarind paste
* ½–1 teaspoon shrimp paste or 2–3 tablespoons fish sauce
* 4 makrut lime leaves
* 1 stalk lemongrass, crushed and tied into a knot
* 100 ml/3½ fl oz (scant ½ cup) coconut milk
* 2 tablespoons Sweet Soy Sauce (page 38)
* Salt, to taste

For the salmon and vegetables:
* 200 g/7 oz (1⅓ cups) vine-ripened cherry tomatoes
* 1 tablespoon vegetable oil
* Salt and black pepper, to taste
* 4 (200-g/7-oz) lightly smoked salmon fillets
* 100 g/3½ oz (1½ cups) spinach

Preheat the oven to 180°C/350°F/Gas Mark 4.

To make the tamarind sauce, heat the oil in a frying pan over medium heat. Add the paste and sauté for 3–4 minutes. Add the tamarind paste, shrimp paste (or fish sauce), lime leaves and lemongrass. Sauté for 1–2 minutes and mix well.

Add the coconut milk and sweet soy sauce and simmer for 4–5 minutes until the mixture has thickened. Season to taste with salt. Set aside.

To prepare the salmon and vegetables, put the tomatoes in a bowl. Drizzle with the oil and season with salt and pepper. Toss well to coat. Transfer the mixture to one side of a large roasting pan. Put the salmon fillets on the other side. Pour the tamarind sauce over the salmon. Bake for 10–12 minutes.

Scatter the spinach in the empty areas of the roasting pan and return to the oven. Bake for another 2 minutes, then mix. Bake for another 2–4 minutes, until the salmon is cooked through.

Arrange the spinach on a serving platter or individual plates. Add the salmon on top and finish with the cherry tomatoes. Drizzle some of the sauce on top.

Variation:
- Salmon with Miso Sambal and Vegetables (Filet Salmon Panggang dengan Sambal Tauco dan Sayuran)
  Replace the tamarind sauce with Miso Sambal (page 51).

Pan-Fried Mackerel with Fried Rice

Ikan Tenggiri dengan Nasi Goreng

Makrut ime leaves are an essential part of Indonesian cuisine. We also use the fruit of the lime tree which we call *jeruk purut*. Wrinkly and with very little juice, it is prized for its fragrance.

This simple dish is great for using up left-over rice: it has a satisfying combination of saltiness and tang from the mackerel, sweetness from the peas, heat from the chillies and the fresh aromas of lime and basil.

Origin: Modern recipe

Preparation time: 10 minutes
Cooking time: 10 minutes

Serves 2

For the fried rice:
* 1 tablespoon coconut oil
* 2 cloves garlic, finely chopped
* 1 banana shallot, finely chopped
* 2–3 green bird's eye chillies, thinly sliced

* 8 makrut lime leaves, centre stem removed and thinly sliced
* 150 g/5½ oz (scant 1 cup) day-old cooked rice
* 200 g/7 oz (1⅓ cups) frozen peas
* Salt, to taste
* Small handful of basil

For the fish:
* 1 tablespoon coconut oil
* 2 (150-g/5½-oz) mackerel fillets
* Salt and black pepper, to taste
* Juice of 1 lime
* Tomato, Chilli and Basil Sambal (page 53), to serve

To make the fried rice, heat the oil in a frying pan over medium heat. Add the garlic and shallots and sauté for 2–3 minutes. Add the chillies, anchovies and lime leaves and cook for another minute. Stir in the rice and peas. Season with salt. Keep warm on low heat.

To make the fish, heat the oil in a large frying pan over medium heat. Season both sides of the mackerel fillets with salt, pepper and lime juice. Gently place the mackerel, skin-side down, into the pan. Pan-fry for 3–4 minutes until the skin is golden brown. Flip over and pan-fry for another 2 minutes. Transfer to a plate.

Reheat the pan of fried rice over medium heat to ensure the rice is hot. If the rice is dry, add a tablespoon of water to the mixture. Stir in the basil.

To serve, divide the rice between 2 plates and top with the mackerel and sambal.

Turmeric-Spiced Fish in Banana Leaf

Ikan Pepes

Pepes is a term used to describe savoury food wrapped in banana leaves. Popular fillings include turmeric-spiced tofu (*pepes tahu*), seasoned mushrooms (*pepes jamur*), minced (ground) duck or pork (in Bali) and, in this case, filleted fish.

As the French use baking (parchment) paper to steam their fish (*en papillote*), Indonesia has a similar practice in using banana leaves to fulfil the task. Steamed or grilled over charcoals, the result is the most flavourful and delicately cooked fish.

Interestingly, the Manadonese *woku* refers to a whole fish wrapped with spices and herbs in young palm leaves and then cooked over charcoal. The same dish can be cooked in a wok, which is known as *blanga* in local dialect, and is known as *woku blanga*.

I use an oven for the sake of practicality, but an outdoor barbecue is ideal in the summer. If you cannot get hold of banana leaves, baking (parchment) paper will suffice for roasting in the oven, but you'll miss out on the distinctive aromas between the banana leaves and spices.

Origin: Java

Preparation time: 15 minutes
Cooking time 15 minutes

Serves 4

For the spice paste:
* ½ quantity Yellow Spice Paste (page 43)
* 2 tablespoons lime juice
* Salt, to taste

For the fish:
* 4 banana leaves, cut into 50-cm/20-inch squares
* 4 (200-g/7-oz) thick cod fillets
* Salt, to taste
* 2 tomatoes, thinly sliced
* 1 long stalk lemongrass, quartered
* 4 makrut lime leaves, torn
* Bunch of basil, leaves only

To serve:
* Steamed rice or Turmeric Coconut Rice (page 201)
* Stir-Fried Leafy Vegetables (page 146)

To make the spice paste, combine the yellow spice paste and lime juice and mix well. Season to taste.

To prepare the fish, preheat the oven to 180°C/350°F/Gas Mark 4.

Place a banana leaf on a clean, dry chopping (cutting) board and add a cod fillet to the centre. Season the fish with salt and spread ½ teaspoon of paste on each side of the fillet. Top with the tomatoes, lemongrass and lime and basil leaves. Fold the leaf to wrap the fish securely into a parcel (package) and secure the ends with cocktail sticks. Place it on a baking sheet. Repeat with the remaining parcels. Bake for 10–12 minutes. Discard the lime leaves.

Serve with rice and stir-fried vegetables.

Variation:
- **Whole Fish Wrapped in Banana Leaf (Pepes Ikan Utuh)**
  Replace the fillets with 4 whole sea bream or sea bass. Prepare a full quantity of yellow spice paste. Using a sharp knife, make 4–5 shallow, diagonal slashes on each side of fish. Season with salt. Spread the paste all over the inside and outside of the fish, then prepare recipes as instructed. Bake for 22–25 minutes.

Braised Sweet, Sour and Spicy Fish

Ikan Asam Manis Pedas

This simple yet refreshing dish originates from the Bangka and Belitung islands, just east of South Sumatra. Tradition calls for starfruit, as seen in the photo, but this recipe has lime juice and tamarind paste for the sake of convenience.

You can pan-fry either a whole fish or fillets, the choice is yours. If you're feeling brave, add a couple of whole bird's eye chillies, which will add heat and soften during the cooking.

Origin: Sumatra

Preparation time: 25 minutes
Cooking time: 15 minutes

Serves 4

* 2 tablespoons coconut oil or sunflower oil
* 1 teaspoon shrimp paste or 2 tablespoons fish sauce
* 1 quantity Yellow Spice Paste (page 43)

* 2 tablespoons Tamarind Paste (page 44)
* ½ teaspoon salt
* 4 red bird's eye chillies
* ½ cucumber, seeded and cut into 1-cm/½-inch slices (optional)
* Juice of 1 lime

* ¼–½ teaspoon sugar
* 4 (200-g/7-oz) white fish fillets
* 100 g/3½ oz (3 cups) baby spinach
* Steamed brown rice or Sweetcorn Rice (page 201)

Heat the oil in a frying pan over medium heat. Add the shrimp paste and cook for 2–3 minutes. (If you are using fish sauce, it can be added later with the water.) Add the spice paste and cook for 4–5 minutes until fragrant. Stir in the tamarind paste and 300 ml/ 10 fl oz (generous 1¼ cups) of water and mix well. Season with salt.

Add the whole chillies and cucumber, if using, and cook for 2 minutes. Add the lime juice and sugar and mix well. Add the fish and cook for 3–4 minutes on each side, until cooked through.

Transfer the fish to a serving plate and spoon over the sauce on top, leaving 3 tablespoons in the pan.

Add the baby spinach to the pan and cook until just wilted. Season with salt, then transfer to a serving plate. Serve with rice.

Variation:
- **Braised Fish with Spring Onion (Scallions) and Lime (Pesmol Ikan)**
  This is a classic Sundanese (West Java) and Betawi dish. Omit the shrimp paste and tamarind paste and add 3 thinly sliced spring onions (scallions), 1 teaspoon ground coriander, 1 stalk lemongrass (crushed) and 4 makrut lime leaves to the pan.

Grilled Turbot with Green and Red Sambals
Ikan Panggang Sambalijo dan Merah

Preparing a whole fish is not an everyday occurrence for us, but it's easy to do and makes a spectacular presentation. When I was younger, my grandmother and mother would prepare skipjack tuna with yellow spice paste and herbs, wrapped in palm leaves and barbecued for our Christmas feasts. Serving it with red and green sambals was a representation of the season.

The desire to return to good times was never stronger than when our world went into lockdown. One day, I was at the supermarket, and my longing for something special was found in a beautiful fresh turbot on display at the fish counter. This recipe is the result.

Turbot is at its best in spring and summer and more difficult to find in the colder months. You could easily prepare this with sea bass, bream or halibut.

Origin: Modern recipe, sambal from Sulawesi and Sumatra

Preparation time: 15 minutes, plus 1 hour standing time
Cooking time: 40 minutes

Serves 4

* 1 (1.5–2-kg/3 lb 5 oz–4 lb 8-oz) whole turbot
* 12 baby carrots, peeled
* 1 teaspoon coconut oil
* Juice of 1½ limes
* Salt and black pepper, to taste
* 28 vine-ripened cherry tomatoes

* 1 quantity Green Sambal (page 51)
* ½ quantity Tomato, Chilli and Basil Sambal (page 53)
* Steamed sweet potatoes, to serve

Set the fish aside for 1 hour at room temperature. Pat-dry with paper towels.

Preheat the oven to 200°C/400°F/Gas Mark 6. Grease a baking sheet.

In a bowl, combine the carrots, coconut oil and the juice of ½ lime. Season with salt and pepper. Mix well, then set aside.

Place the fish on the prepared baking sheet. Using a sharp knife, cut 4–5 shallow, diagonal slashes on each side of fish. Season with salt and the juice of 1 lime. Spread the green sambal on one half and tomato sambal on the other half. Add the carrots and bake for 20 minutes. Add the tomatoes and bake for another 10 minutes, until the fish is cooked through. Leave to rest for 10 minutes.

Using a knife, ease chunks of fish from the bones onto a large platter. Add the carrots and tomatoes and garnish with the basil. Serve with the cooking juices and a side of steamed sweet potatoes.

Grilled Jumbo King Prawns with King's Sambal

Udang Gala Panggang dengan Sambal Raja

Raja, meaning 'king', is used to describe this roasted vegetable sambal from the city of Samarinda. It combines eggs with roasted aubergines (eggplant) and long beans.

While the traditional dish calls for two calamansi, I've replaced it with lime for its sharp acidity. It makes an incredible accompaniment to fresh grilled seafood.

Origin: Kalimantan

Preparation time: 30 minutes
Cooking time: 30 minutes

Serves 4

For the sambal:
* 1 large aubergine (eggplant), cut into 1-cm/½-inch cubes
* Salt, to taste
* 3 tablespoons coconut oil
* 2 eggs
* 4 large red chillies, coarsely chopped
* 3 banana shallots, sliced
* 2–3 red bird's eye chillies, coarsely chopped

* 75 g/2¾ oz long beans or green beans, cut into 2-cm/¾-inch lengths
* 1 teaspoon shrimp paste or 2–3 tablespoons fish sauce
* Juice of 1 lime
* 1 teaspoon coconut sugar or granulated sugar

For the prawns:
* 12–16 jumbo king prawns in their shells, rinsed well and patted dry
* Salt, to taste
* Juice of 1 lime
* 2 tablespoons coconut oil
* Steamed sweet potatoes, cassava (page 145) or rice, to serve

To make the sambal, preheat the oven to 200°C/400°F/Gas Mark 6.

Season the aubergine (eggplant) with salt and 1 tablespoon coconut oil. Mix well and place on a roasting pan. Roast for 18–20 minutes.

Put the eggs into a small saucepan of water. Bring to a boil and boil for 10 minutes. Drain, then transfer to a bowl of cold water to stop the cooking process. Set aside.

Combine the chillies and shallots in a small blender and blend into a paste. (Alternatively, use a pestle and mortar.) Set aside.

Transfer the roasted aubergine to a bowl and set aside. Heat the remaining 2 tablespoons of oil in a frying pan over medium heat. Add the beans and stir-fry for 2–3 minutes, until crisp-tender. Using a slotted spoon, transfer the beans to a plate.

Add the shrimp paste to the same frying pan and dry-roast over medium-high heat for 1–2 minutes. Stir in the chilli paste (and the fish sauce, if using) and cook for 5–6 minutes. Add the beans, aubergine and lime juice. Mix well, then season with salt and coconut sugar. Add 3½ tablespoons of water and bring to a boil. Reduce the heat to medium-low and simmer for 3–4 minutes. Season to taste. Set aside.

Preheat the grill (broiler).

To prepare the prawns, cut the prawns, including the head, in half lengthwise. Add the salt, lime juice and coconut oil and mix to coat. Transfer to a baking sheet and grill for 6 minutes, until the prawns are opaque and the shell turns deep orange. Transfer the prawns to a large serving plate.

Peel and slice the eggs into quarters. Add the eggs and sambal to the plate. Serve with steamed sweet potatoes, cassava or rice.

Spicy Seafood Stew with Tomato and Lemongrass
Seafood Woku Blanga

Woku is a blend of spices and herbs unique to the cuisine of my hometown Manado in North Sulawesi. It is a spicy turmeric paste enhanced with lemongrass, makrut lime leaves, spring onions (scallions), tomato and basil. Traditionally, the paste was spread on a whole fish, then wrapped in young palm leaves *(daun woka)* and cooked over coconut-husk charcoal.

The Manadonese prepare this dish with chunky pieces of fish in a wok *(blanga)*, but I have opted for fish fillet and prawns in this recipe. (The sauce makes the perfect foil for rice or pasta.)

The Manadonese are renowned for their love of spice, but I have softened the heat by reducing the quantity of chillies in the paste and adding plenty of tomatoes. I use good-quality canned San Marzano tomatoes, which are readily available in England, but you could replace this with two chopped tomatoes and double the amount of water for a traditional preparation.

Origin: Sulawesi

Preparation time: 15 minutes
Cooking time: 20 minutes

Serves 4

* 2 tablespoons sunflower oil
* 1 quantity Yellow Spice Paste (page 43)
* 2 stalks lemongrass, crushed and tied into a knot
* 4 spring onions (scallions), sliced
* 4 makrut lime leaves, torn

* 1 (400-g/14-oz) can chopped tomatoes
* Bunch of basil
* 1 pandan leaf, tied into a knot (optional)
* 1 turmeric leaf (optional)
* ½ teaspoon salt, to taste

* 2 (500-g/1 lb 2-oz) skinless cod fillets, cut into bite-size pieces
* 250 g/9 oz tiger prawns (jumbo prawns), peeled and deveined
* 2 tablespoons lime juice
* Steamed rice or cooked pasta, to serve

Heat the oil in a large, heavy frying pan over medium heat. Add the spice paste and cook for 5–6 minutes until fragrant. Add the lemongrass, spring onions (scallions), lime leaves, tomatoes and half of the basil, the pandan and turmeric leaves, if using. Mix well.

Pour in 100 ml/3½ fl oz (scant ½ cup) of water and bring to a boil. Reduce the heat to medium-low, cover and simmer for 10 minutes, stirring occasionally. Season with salt.

Season the fish and prawns with salt and lime juice, then add to the pan. Cover and simmer for 2–3 minutes, until the fish is just cooked through. Add the remaining basil. Season to taste with more salt and lime juice if needed. Discard the lemongrass and lime leaves.

Serve with rice or pasta.

Fried Sea Bream with Tomato and Sweet Soy Sambal

Ikan Goreng dengan Sambal Tomat Kecap

A good-quality, organic and unrefined coconut oil is best for this dish. With a lovely aroma, it's perfect for the intense high heat needed to crisp up the skin. In West Java, fried freshwater fish is art on a plate. Traditionally, you need to submerge the fish in a vast amount of oil, but I prefer to shallow-fry the fish, which is healthier.

Origin: Throughout Indonesia

Preparation time: 15 minutes
Cooking time: 20 minutes

Serves 2

For the fish:
* 6 tablespoons coconut oil, for shallow-frying
* 2 whole sea breams, patted dry with paper towels
* Juice of 2 limes
* Salt, to taste
* Basil leaves, to garnish

For the tomato and sweet soy sambal:
* 2 cloves garlic, finely chopped
* 2 banana shallots, thinly sliced
* 2 red bird's eye chillies, finely chopped
* 1 (400-g/14-oz) can Italian tomatoes

* 2 tablespoons Sweet Soy Sauce (page 38)
* Salt, to taste

To serve:
* Steamed rice
* Stir-Fried Leafy Vegetables (page 146)

Heat the oil in a large wok or frying pan over medium heat. Season the fish with lime juice and salt. Gently place a fish into the pan and cook for 5 minutes on each side. (For a crispier skin, pan-fry for another 2–3 minutes on each side.) Using a slotted spoon, carefully transfer the bream to a plate lined with paper towels to drain. Repeat with the other fish. Reserve the oil.

To make the sambal, heat 2 tablespoons of the reserved oil in a clean frying pan over medium heat. Add the garlic and shallots and sauté for 2–3 minutes. Add the chillies and sauté for another 2 minutes. Add the tomatoes and bring to a boil. Reduce the heat to medium-low and simmer for 5 minutes. Add the sweet soy sauce and season with salt.

Garnish the fish with basil. Serve with rice, vegetables and sambal.

Variation:
- **Grilled Fish (Ikan Panggang)**
  Grill (broil) the fish or bake in a 180°C/350°F/Gas Mark 4 for 20–25 minutes. Serve with the sambal.

Fish with Chillies and Torch Ginger

Ikan Arsik

This dish is famous for its mouth-numbing Szechuan peppercorns, while fragrant torch ginger flowers and the fresh chive root (*bawang batak*) bring something unique to this local speciality. Chive bulbs are not widely available, but I find that chive leaves give the right taste sensation.

Arsik was often prepared with a whole carp and served at weddings and ceremonies, but you can use a variety of fish, even prawns.

Origin: Sumatra

Preparation time: 30 minutes
Cooking time: 15 minutes

Serves 4

* 2 tablespoons coconut oil
* 1 quantity Yellow Spice Paste (page 43)
* 6 chive bulbs and stems (see Note)
* 5 dried asam gelugur or juice of 2 limes
* 4 makrut lime leaves, torn

* 2 stalks lemongrass, crushed and tied into a knot
* 2 torch ginger flowers, thinly sliced (optional)
* Small bunch of fresh green or 2 tablespoons dried Szechuan peppercorns
* ½ teaspoon salt

* 4 ginger flower fruit (*asam cikala*), halved
* 4 (175-g/6-oz) white fish fillets
* Juice of 1 lime
* 100 g/3½ oz green beans
* Steamed rice and Stir-Fried Leafy Vegetables (page 146), to serve

Heat the oil in a large frying pan over medium heat. Add the paste and cook for 4–5 minutes. Add half of the chives, the asam gelugur, lime leaves, lemongrass, torch ginger flowers, if using, Szechuan peppercorns and salt. Add 500 ml/17 fl oz (generous 2 cups) of water and bring to a boil. Reduce the heat to medium-low and simmer for 10 minutes until the liquid has reduced by a third.

Season the fish with lime juice and salt. Add the fish and green beans and cover. Cook for 6–8 minutes, turning the fish halfway through the cooking time.

Add the remaining chives. Season to taste with more lime juice and salt if desired.

Serve with steamed rice and stir-fried vegetables.

Note: If unavailable, chive bulbs and stems can be replaced with the same amount of spring onions (scallions) and 2 tablespoons chopped chives.

Barbecued Seafood with Sambals
Seafood Bakar dengan Ragam Sambal

A successful Indonesian seafood barbecue requires a simple process: firstly, prepare the sambals; secondly, make a simple marinade and the yellow spice paste; and thirdly, cook quickly to avoid over-cooking fresh fish.

This recipe showcases a delicious bounty of seafood and sambals, from Acehnese sambal to a spicy and sour version from South Sulawesi's capital of Makassar. If variety is the spice of life, then seafood lovers rejoice. The sambals can be prepared a day in advance.

Origin: Throughout Indonesia

Preparation time: 1 hour
Cooking time: 25 minutes

Serves 12

* 12 jumbo tiger prawns, unpeeled
* ½ quantity Yellow Spice Paste (page 43)
* 6 tablespoons coconut oil
* Juice of 4 limes
* Salt, to taste
* 2 (450-g/1-lb) sea bream
* 2 (500-g/1 lb 2-oz) mackerel

* 3 tablespoons Sweet Soy Sauce (page 38)
* 10 (300 g/10½ oz) baby squid
* 6 cobs sweetcorn
* 1 quantity Green Sambal (page 51)
* Basil leaves, to garnish (optional)

To serve:
* 2 limes, cut into wedges
* 1 quantity Chilli and Lemongrass Sambal (page 47)
* 1 quantity Chilli and Tomato Sambal (page 48)
* 1 quantity Tomato and Sweet Soy Sambal (page 176)
* Steamed rice
* 1 quantity Crudité (page 80)

Clean and rinse the prawns under cold running water. Leave unpeeled with the tail intact, then make a cut from the tail through to the head, turn it face down on a chopping (cutting) board and flatten gently. Don't worry if the shell loosens slightly.

In a small bowl, combine the spice paste, 2 tablespoons of coconut oil, juice of 1 lime and salt.

Using a sharp knife, cut 4–5 shallow, diagonal slashes on each side of the bream and mackerel. Set aside.

Preheat a barbecue (grill) over high heat. In a small bowl, combine the remaining 3 tablespoons of oil, sweet soy sauce, the juice of 3 limes and salt and mix well. Rub the marinade over half the fish and prawns. Rub the yellow spice paste marinade over the remaining fish and prawns. (Don't flavour the squid with lime juice as this will make the flesh rubbery.) Rub the remaining 1 tablespoon coconut oil over the baby squid and season with salt.

Add the fish to the barbecue and grill for 5–6 minutes until the flesh separates easily from the bone. Brush left-over marinade on the top side of the fish. Turn over and grill for another 5–6 minutes.

Brush the sweetcorn with a third of the green sambal and add to the barbecue. Grill for 5–7 minutes, turning occasionally.

Add the prawns and grill for 2–3 minutes on each side until the skin of the prawns changes colour to deep red-orange and the flesh turns white.

Add the squid and grill for 2–3 minutes, turning every 30 seconds until slightly charred.

Transfer the seafood to a serving platter. Garnish with basil leaves, if using, and serve immediately with lime wedges, sambals, steamed rice and crudité.

Meat and Poultry

Daging dan Unggas

Indonesia's most iconic meat dishes are Beef Rendang (page 134) and satays (page 111). When I prepare them at home, my family devours them quite happily. Both my sons are now grown-up and have lives of their own in London, but they always request beef rendang and my Indonesian Roast Chicken (page 183) whenever they visit. And I happily oblige.

While Indonesia has the largest Muslim population in the world, pork dishes are plentiful outside of these communities. Crispy Pork Belly with Sambal (page 188) is a classic representation of Kalimantan's delectable cuisine. On special occasions, my family would prepare pork with chillies and herbs in bamboo, but I find it is just as easy to cook it in a wok or pot (page 187).

Indonesians rarely use ovens to prepare meat and poultry, but I was determined to include a tasty oven-baked recipe. The Chicken with Galangal, Lime, Aubergine and Sweet Potatoes (page 184) is the perfect marriage of Indonesian flavours and a Western cooking technique. I serve this traybake with a Chilli and Salt Sambal (page 47). The organic and free-range chicken known as *ayam kampung*, meaning 'village chicken', is commonly used in Indonesia. As it's flavourful yet lean, I like to braise the chicken first with spices and coconut water before adding it to recipes.

This chapter features a varied collection of dishes that can be made in Western homes. It includes some of the most celebrated recipes from the archipelago as well as favourites from our home.

Indonesian Fried Chicken
Ayam Goreng Kampung

Indonesian fried chicken is prepared differently across the archipelago. The preferred local free-range chicken (*ayam kampung*) has tough, lean meat with delightful flavour. The chicken is twice-cooked, braised with a mild white or yellow spice paste and then deep-fried.

Some Javanese use spices and coconut water to tenderize the chicken, which is then deep-fried and served with crumbs of tasty, crunchy batter (*kremes*) and sambal.

Aceh fried chicken is also twice-cooked, braised with Yellow Spice Paste (page 43) and deep-fried with pandan, lime and curry leaves.

Serve this dish with rice and Lalapan (page 80) for mega umami flavour.

Origin: Throughout Indonesia

Preparation time: 10 minutes
Cooking time: 55 minutes

Serves 8

* 16 chicken drumsticks with skin
* 1–2 teaspoons salt
* Juice of 2 limes
* 2 tablespoons coconut oil
* 1 quantity Yellow Spice Paste (page 43)
* Sunflower oil, for deep-frying
* Steamed rice, to serve
* Crudité, Tempeh and Tofu with Shrimp Paste Sambal (page 80), to serve

---

Season the chicken with salt and lime juice. Heat the coconut oil in a large saucepan over medium heat. Add the paste and sauté for 4–5 minutes. Add the chicken and 200 ml/7 fl oz (scant 1 cup) of water and mix well. Bring to a boil. Reduce the heat to medium-low and simmer for 45 minutes, until the meat nearly falls off the bone. Using a slotted spoon, transfer the chicken to a plate.

Heat enough sunflower oil for deep-frying in a large wok or frying pan. The oil is ready when a cube of bread dropped in sizzles on contact and turns golden in 10–15 seconds. (Alternatively, use a thermometer and heat to 180°C/350°F.) Carefully lower the drumsticks into the oil and deep-fry for 2–3 minutes on each side, until slightly golden. Transfer the fried chicken to a plate lined with paper towels to drain.

Serve immediately with steamed rice, crudité and shrimp paste sambal.

Variation:
- Aceh Fried Chicken (Ayam Tangkap)
  Use the juice of 1 lime only. Add 4 tablespoons of Tamarind Paste (page 44) with the chicken and water. To the oil, add 3 finely chopped pandan leaves, 15 slightly torn makrut lime leaves and a small bunch of fresh or dried curry leaves. Serve with the rice and crudité. Omit the sambal.

Roast Chicken
Ayam Taiwang

Roast chicken is the ultimate comfort food, and this version from Lombok Island is no exception. The key ingredient is *kencur*, otherwise known as aromatic or sand ginger. It can be replaced with double the amount of ginger though it will lack the same distinct aroma. You may serve it with rice, steamed cassava or a mixed salad for a light meal.

Origin: Nusa Tenggara

Preparation time: 25 minutes, plus 1 hour marinating and 30 minutes standing time
Cooking time: 1 hour 30 minutes

Serves 4

For the chicken:
* 1 (1.5 kg/3 lb 5-oz) whole chicken
* 1 teaspoon salt
* 1 teaspoon black pepper
* 2 tablespoons coconut oil
* Juice of 2 limes
* 3 large tomatoes, finely chopped
* 1 teaspoon palm sugar or brown sugar

For the paste:
* 1 teaspoon shrimp paste or 2–3 tablespoons fish sauce
* 8 large red chillies
* 4 cloves garlic, thinly sliced
* 3–4 red bird's eye chillies (optional)
* 2 banana shallots, thinly sliced
* 1 (5-cm/2-inch) piece kencur, peeled and thinly sliced
* Salt, to taste

To serve:
* Steamed brown rice
* Water Spinach with Chilli and Miso (page 146)

To prepare the chicken, cut along the backbone with kitchen scissors and remove. Press firmly on the breastbone to flatten it. Pat-dry with a paper towel, then season with salt, pepper, 1 tablespoon of coconut oil and lime juice. Set aside.

To make the paste, dry-roast the shrimp paste in a small frying pan over medium-high heat for 2–3 minutes. Transfer to a small blender, add the remaining ingredients and blend into a smooth paste.

Heat the remaining tablespoon of coconut oil in a frying pan over medium heat. Add the paste and cook for 4–5 minutes until the mixture is slightly dry. Add the tomatoes and sauté for 4–5 minutes, until thickened. Keep stirring over low heat. Add the sugar. Mix well and season to taste. Set aside to cool.

Spread the paste all over it. Put the chicken on a large plate and marinate in the refrigerator for 1 hour.

Preheat the oven to 200°C/400°F/Gas Mark 6. Set aside the chicken at room temperature for 30 minutes.

Put the chicken into a baking dish lined with baking (parchment) paper. Cook for 60–75 minutes, until the chicken is cooked through. Serve with steamed brown rice and stir-fried vegetables.

Chicken with Galangal, Lime, Aubergine and Sweet Potatoes

Ayam Panggang, Terong dan Ubi Manis

Travel allows us to taste local dishes in their most authentic form, and my visit to Wae Rebo village in Manggarai Regency, East Nusa Tenggara, was so special for that very reason. Located 1,200 metres (nearly 4,000 feet) above sea level, it required a four-hour drive from the nearest airport and an additional four-hour hike on top of that. The seven homes were most unusual, shaped like inverted cones.

Here, the food is a far cry from the layers of familiar spices enjoyed throughout the rest of Indonesia. Wae Rebo's cuisine uses very little spice and few ingredients, but the dishes burst with unexpected flavour. This chicken recipe was inspired by a fried chicken dish from this village, which only uses galangal and ginger for flavouring. I have added lime juice for tang.

This dish makes for a delicious, fuss-free traybake and an ideal mid-week supper.

Origin: Modern recipe

Preparation time: 15 minutes
Cooking time: 45 minutes

Serves 6

- 15 g/½ oz fresh root ginger, finely grated
- 10 g/¼ oz galangal, finely grated
- 3 tablespoons coconut oil
- Juice of 2 limes

- 2 aubergines (eggplants), cut into 5-cm/2-inch chunks
- 2 sweet potatoes, cut into 5-cm/2-inch chunks
- 1 teaspoon salt
- Black pepper, to taste

- 12 skin-on, bone-in chicken thighs
- 2 spring onions (scallions), thinly sliced, to garnish (optional)
- Shallot Sambal (page 50), to serve

Preheat the oven to 200°C/400°F/Gas Mark 6.

Combine the ginger, galangal, 1½ tablespoons coconut oil and the lime juice in a small bowl. Set aside.

In a large bowl, combine the aubergine (eggplant) and sweet potatoes. Season with salt and pepper and toss. Set aside.

Put the chicken, skin-side up, in a large baking dish. Pour the ginger mixture on top. Using your hands, rub the mixture into the chicken.

Drizzle the remaining 1½ tablespoons coconut oil over the vegetables and toss to coat. Arrange the vegetables around the chicken and roast for 20 minutes. Turn the vegetables over and cook for another 25–30 minutes until the chicken is cooked through and the juices run clear.

Garnish with the spring onions (scallions) and serve with sambal.

Variation:
- **Chicken with Turmeric Paste and Lime (Ayam Panggang Bumbu Kuning dan Air Jeruk)**
  Replace the ginger and galangal mixture with 1 quantity of Yellow Spice Paste (page 43). Mix the yellow spice paste, lime juice, salt and coconut oil. Rub the paste into the chicken and follow the remaining recipe instructions.

Pan-Seared Duck Breast with Soy Sambal
Dada Bebek dengan Sambal Kecap

This dish demonstrates how a simple sambal can have a mega impact. Sambal soy – easily made with sweet soy, chopped chillies, lime and sometimes chopped tomatoes – adds sweet, sour and spicy notes.

Origin: Modern recipe

Preparation time: 25 minutes
Cooking time: 20 minutes

Serves 4

For the soy sambal:
* 2–3 red bird's eye chillies, finely chopped
* 6 tablespoons Sweet Soy Sauce (page 38)
* Juice of 2 limes

For the duck:
* 4 (120-g/4¼-oz) duck breasts
* Sea salt, to taste
* 4 large pak choy, halved
* Steamed rice, to serve

To make the soy sambal, combine all the ingredients in a medium bowl. Set aside.

To prepare the duck, set aside the duck at room temperature for 20–25 minutes.

Preheat the oven to 180°C/350°F/Gas Mark 4.

Score the duck skin in a criss-cross pattern. Season both sides with salt. Add the duck, skin-side down, to a large ovenproof frying pan over medium heat. (The duck will start in a cold pan.) Cook for 10–12 minutes until golden and the fat has rendered. Flip over and cook for another 2 minutes. Transfer the pan to the oven and cook for 6–8 minutes, medium-rare to medium. Transfer the duck to a chopping (cutting) board and set it aside to rest.

Pour the rendered fat from the pan into a small bowl and reserve for another use. (It's excellent for roasted potatoes.) Heat the pan over medium heat. Place the pak choy, cut-side down, in the pan and cook for 2 minutes. Reduce the heat to low and cook for 1–2 minutes until the vegetables are slightly tender. Turn over and cook for another minute. Remove the pan from the heat.

Slice the duck in half and arrange on serving plates. Add the pak choy and drizzle with 2 tablespoons of soy sambal. Serve with steamed rice.

Spiced Pork Stew with Turmeric, Chillies, Nutmeg and Cloves
Tinorangsak

Nutmeg and clove trees are plentiful around Indonesia, but we rarely use the young leaves for cooking – except in this dish and in Spiced Tea (page 243). I love to prepare green sambal with cashew and green chillies using young nutmeg and clove leaves.

This pork stew recipe belongs to my grandmother. This dish was always part of our Christmas feast. It is said to have been a ceremonial dish from centuries ago.

The stew would be prepared in a segment of bamboo lined with banana leaves. The pork, herbs and spices are placed inside, then the entire thing is barbecued. This bamboo cooking technique is one of the few traditions which remains of Manado's original food culture.

For simplicity, I braise the pork and replace the young cloves and nutmeg leaves with dried cloves and nutmeg.

Origin: Sulawesi

Preparation time: 10 minutes
Cooking time: 2 hours

Serves 4

* 2 tablespoons coconut oil
* 1 quantity Yellow Spice Paste (page 43)
* 1 kg/2 lb 4 oz pork shoulder, cut into 5-cm/2-inch cubes
* Juice of 1 lime

* Salt, to taste
* 4 makrut lime leaves, torn
* 3 spring onions (scallions), finely chopped
* 1 stalk lemongrass, crushed and tied into a knot

* 1 teaspoon ground cloves
* ½ teaspoon freshly grated nutmeg
* Handful of basil

Heat the oil in a medium saucepan over medium heat. Add the spice paste and cook for 3–4 minutes until fragrant. Season the pork with lime juice and ½ teaspoon salt. Add the pork to the pan and mix well.

Stir in the lime leaves, spring onions (scallions), lemongrass, cloves and nutmeg. Chop half of the basil and add to the pan. Pour in 500 ml/17 fl oz (2 cups) of water and bring to a boil. Reduce the heat to low, cover and simmer for 2 hours, or until the pork is tender.

Season to taste. Top with the remaining whole basil leaves and serve.

Crispy Pork Belly with Sambal
Babi Panggang dengan Sambal

Kalimantan-style roast pork – with its super crunchy crackling and sour, spicy and sweet flavour – is revered throughout Indonesia, especially when served alongside an umami-rich shrimp paste sambal.

I first sampled this great dish during a visit to Ambawang, a city in West Kalimantan. A suckling pig was seasoned with a five-spice dry rub and roasted for more than twelve hours. Then it was served with rice, sambal and sliced tomatoes and cucumber. You can use a store-bought five-spice powder or make your own version (page 41).

I've adapted the recipe by preparing a pork belly (side) in an oven in a fraction of the time. Use plenty of table salt to absorb all the moisture from the pork skin and make it super crispy.

Origin: Kalimantan

Preparation time: 30 minutes, plus 1 hour standing time
Cooking time: 2 hours

Serves 4–6

For the pork belly (side):
* 1 (800-g/1 lb 12 oz) pork belly (side)
* 200 g/7 oz (¾ cup) plus 1 teaspoon fine salt
* 1 tablespoon Chinese Five-Spice

For the sambal:
* 1 teaspoon shrimp paste
* 3 tablespoons coconut oil or sunflower oil
* 2 banana shallots, finely chopped
* 4 cloves garlic, finely chopped
* 2 large red chillies, coarsely chopped
* 2 red bird's eye chillies, coarsely chopped
* Juice of 2 calamansi or 1 lime
* 1 tablespoon sugar
* Salt, to taste

To serve:
* Steamed rice
* 1 cucumber, thinly sliced (optional)
* 2 tomatoes, cut into wedges (optional)

To prepare the pork belly (side), set it aside for 1 hour at room temperature.

Preheat the oven to 200°C/400°F/Gas Mark 6.

Pat-dry pork belly with paper towels. Place it, skin-side down, in a large roasting pan. Rub 1 teaspoon of salt and the Chinese five-spice over the meat, avoiding the skin. Turn the seasoned pork over, then carefully cover the skin with the remaining 200 g/7 oz of salt.

Carefully transfer the pork belly to a wire rack set in a roasting pan. Roast for 1 hour, until the salt has solidified into one piece and the edges are slightly golden.

Meanwhile, prepare the sambal. Dry-roast the shrimp paste in a frying pan over medium-high heat for 2–3 minutes. Transfer the shrimp paste to a small plate.

In the same frying pan, heat the oil over medium heat. Add the shallots and garlic and sauté for 3–4 minutes until softened. Add the chillies and cook for another 3–4 minutes, until softened. Stir in the shrimp paste and cook for a minute. Transfer the mixture to a blender and finely blend. Put the mixture into a bowl, then stir in the calamansi juice and sugar. Season to taste with salt. Set aside.

Remove the salt crust from the pork belly. Roast, skin-side up, for another 45–55 minutes until the skin turns very crispy. Remove the pork from the oven and set aside to rest for 8–10 minutes.

Serve with rice, sambal, cucumber and tomatoes.

Variation:
- **Flores-Style Roast Pork (Se'i Babi)**
  Omit the Chinese five-spice. Replace the shrimp paste sambal with Lemon and Chilli Sambal (page 48).

Spiced Beef Stew
Semur Daging

The sweetness in this beef stew is tempered by the spices, creating a comforting main course best served with steamed rice.

Semur daging is available around the region, with spices changing from region to region. And like most stews, a low and slow cooking time is a must for developing rich and intense flavours. Chopped tomatoes add a bit of vibrant colour. The traditional dish is like a thin stew, so I've thickened it with some flour to make it feel more substantial.

This famous dish of Idul Fitri often reminds me of the holiday with my Muslim friends in Jakarta.

Origin: Throughout Indonesia

Preparation time: 30 minutes
Cooking time: 1 hour 40 minutes

Serves 6–8

For the spice blend:
- 1 tablespoon coriander seeds
- 1 teaspoon ground cumin
- ½ teaspoon cloves

For the beef:
- 2–3 tablespoons sunflower oil
- 1 kg/2 lb 4 oz stewing beef or topside (top round), cut into 2.5-cm/1-inch pieces
- Salt and black pepper, to taste
- 2 tablespoons all-purpose (plain) flour, plus extra for dusting
- 3 banana shallots, finely chopped

- 3 cloves garlic, finely chopped
- 2 red bird's eye chillies, thinly sliced
- 1 (10-cm/4-inch) piece of fresh root ginger, finely grated
- 3 green cardamom pods, lightly crushed
- 1 teaspoon freshly grated nutmeg
- 1 teaspoon ground cinnamon
- 1 stalk lemongrass, crushed and tied into a knot
- 4 makrut lime leaves, torn
- 5 tablespoons Sweet Soy Sauce (page 38)

- 2 tablespoons dark soy sauce
- 300 g/10½ oz new potatoes with skins
- 2 carrots, unpeeled
- 2 tomatoes, chopped into ½-cm/¼-inch cubes
- Small handful of Chinese celery leaves or parsley
- 3–4 tablespoons Crispy Shallots (page 41, optional)
- Steamed rice, to serve (optional)

To make the spice blend, combine the coriander seeds, cumin and cloves in a frying pan and dry-roast for 5–6 minutes over medium-low heat until fragrant, stirring occasionally to prevent them from burning. Leave to cool. Finely grind using a pestle and mortar. Set aside.

Heat 2 tablespoons of oil in the same pan over medium-high heat. Season the beef with salt and pepper, then dust it with flour. Working in batches, add the beef to the pan and sear each side for 1–2 minutes. Transfer to a plate. Repeat until all the beef is cooked.

If needed, heat another tablespoon of oil in the same pan. Add the shallots and garlic and sauté for 2–3 minutes. Add the chillies and ginger and sauté for a minute. Add the beef and spice blend, mix well and sauté for 1–2 minutes. Sprinkle in the flour and sauté for 1–2 minutes until the flour turns brown.

Stir in the cardamom, nutmeg, cinnamon, lemongrass and lime leaves. Add the sweet and dark soy sauces and 1 litre/34 fl oz (4¼ cups) hot water. Mix well, then season with salt. Bring to a boil, then reduce the heat to medium-low. Cover and simmer for 1 hour.

Add the potatoes and carrots and cook for another 30 minutes. Add the tomatoes and half of the Chinese celery leaves. Mix well and cook for another 5 minutes.

Ladle the stew into soup bowls. Sprinkle with crispy shallots, if using, and the remaining Chinese celery. Serve with rice if you wish.

Variations:
- **Manado Pork Stew (Semur Babi)**
  Replace the spice blend with 1½ tablespoons Speculaas Spice Blend (page 41). Omit the cardamom and replace the beef with pork neck.
- **Vegetarian Stew (Semur Tempe dan Tahu)**
  Omit the potatoes. Replace the beef with 500 g/1 lb 2 oz firm tofu and 500 g/1 lb 2 oz tempeh, cut into 2.5-cm/1-inch chunks (do not sear). Add them to the pan with the soy sauce. Mix well and season with salt.

Beef with Black Nuts
Rawon Surabaya

Black nuts (*buah kluwak*) are uniquely Indonesian, adding rich mushroom flavours and a striking black colour to Indonesian stews. Here, tender beef shank is slow-cooked in a savoury broth, seasoned with black nuts, lemongrass, chillies, ginger, turmeric and makrut lime leaves. You can make it a day ahead to create greater depths of flavour.

If you don't have the black nuts, consider a black olive tapenade – interestingly, it has the same earthy character.

Origin: Java

Preparation time: 30 minutes
Cooking time: 1 hour 40 minutes

Serves 6

* 6 black (kluwak) nuts or 2 tablespoons black olive tapenade
* 4 tablespoons coconut oil or sunflower oil
* 1 kg/2 lb 4 oz sliced beef shank, cut into 2-cm/¾-inch cubes
* 1 teaspoon salt
* 1 teaspoon black pepper
* 1 quantity Yellow Spice Paste (page 43)
* 4 makrut lime leaves, torn
* 1 stalk lemongrass, crushed and tied into a knot
* 1 litre/34 fl oz (4¼ cups) beef stock or water
* 50 g/1¾ oz (1 cup) mung bean sprouts
* 2 spring onions (scallions), finely chopped
* 2 large red chillies, chopped
* 6–8 lime wedges

To serve:
* Boiled Sambal (page 53)
* Steamed rice (optional)

Clean and brush the black nuts. Steam for 1 hour to soften the shell or soak overnight. Crack the shell, remove the flesh and grind to a paste. Set aside.

Heat 3 tablespoons of oil in a large saucepan over medium-high heat. Season the beef with salt and pepper. Add a few pieces to the pan and sear for 1–2 minutes on each side, until browned. Transfer to a plate and repeat with the remaining meat.

Heat the remaining 1 tablespoon of oil in the same pan over medium heat. Add the spice paste mixture and sauté for 4–5 minutes. Add the lime leaves, lemongrass, black nuts and beef. Mix well.

Pour in the stock, season with salt and pepper and bring to a boil. Simmer for 1½ hours, or until the beef is very tender.

To serve, ladle into individual bowls. Top with mung bean sprouts, spring onions (scallions), chillies and lime wedges. Serve with boiled sambal and rice, if you wish.

Tamarind Beef
Asam Padeh

Asam padeh in Minangkabau means 'sour spicy' and, hence, reflects the flavours of this dish. It only requires a few ingredients to come together, most notably the *asam kandis,* also known as false mangosteen, which lends a distinct, sour note. It is not easy to find, so I've replaced it with tamarind paste and lime juice for an equally wonderful taste.

This dish reminds me of the feasts in Padang or Minangkabau restaurants, where tables would be laid out with a bounty of colourful and plentiful dishes.

Origin: Sumatra

Preparation time: 30 minutes
Cooking time: 1 hour 40 minutes

Serves 6–8

* 2 tablespoons coconut oil
* 1 quantity Red Spice Paste (page 43)
* 1 kg/2 lb 4 oz topside (top round) beef, cut into 2-cm/¾-inch pieces
* Salt and black pepper, to taste

* 4 makrut lime leaves, torn
* 1 stalk lemongrass, crushed and tied into a knot
* 2 tablespoons Tamarind Paste (page 44)
* Juice of 1 lime

To serve:
* Steamed rice
* Balado Sambal (page 51)

Heat the coconut oil in a large saucepan over medium heat. Add the red spice paste and cook for 3–4 minutes.

Season the beef with salt and pepper and mix well. Add the beef to the pan and sauté for 5 minutes until it is well coated in the paste.

Add the lime leaves, lemongrass and tamarind paste. Pour in 2 litres (2 quarts) of water and bring to a boil. Season with salt and pepper. Reduce the heat to low, cover and simmer for 1½ hours until the beef is tender and the sauce has reduced slightly and thickened. Add the lime juice, then season to taste.

Serve with steamed rice and balado sambal.

Variation:
- **Tamarind Fish (Asam Padeh Ikan)**
  Omit the beef. Add another crushed stalk of lemongrass and 2 finely chopped spring onions (scallions). Reduce the base by half, add 6 (150-g/5½-oz) fish fillets and cook for 6–8 minutes.

Rice and Other Staples

Beras dan Makanan Pokok

When I was growing up in Manado, we had a rice goddess known as *Lingkanbene*. As I grew older, I discovered that many regions around the archipelago held their own celebrations and rituals for the prized grain. In West Sumatra, locals celebrate the harvest by separating rice grains with their feet. In a particular Sundanese community in West Java, rice is cultivated according to constellation movements. When I travelled to Sumba Island, I was fortunate enough to witness a chant during the planting season, which ensured good rainfall and fertile soils. The most famous rice goddess is Dewi Sri of Java and Bali.

Rice has a special place at the Indonesian table. It can be simply steamed, stir-fried or compressed into cakes (*ketupat*) as part of everyday meals. And when special occasions call for more elaborate dishes, I cook rice in coconut milk infused with turmeric, lemongrass and lime leaves (page 201).

Sago, sweet potatoes, sweetcorn and sorghum were also prevalent in our home. These days, I prepare a delicious tri-coloured Sweetcorn Rice (page 201), which combines coarsely ground sweetcorn with white rice. I'm a fan of sorghum, with its quinoa-like flavour and texture. I love its hardiness, versatility and superfood qualities and prepare it as I would for steamed rice (page 210).

As a child, it was a dream to see the world. With time, I recognized that I grew up in one of the largest, most diverse countries in the world. And, more importantly, everything I could ever want to learn about my place in the world could be explored within the archipelago.

Compressed Rice
Lontong

Compressed rice often takes the place of steamed rice and is served with satay, *Gado-Gado* (page 86) or soto. Traditionally, banana leaves are made into 15-cm/6-inch logs, and each is filled about a third with rice. The leaves are boiled in water until the rice expands. Once cooled to room temperature, the rice cakes firm up.

It can be challenging to make, so I've simplified the process with this recipe (and added makrut lime leaves for fragrance).

Origin: Throughout Indonesia

Preparation time: 5 minutes, plus 3 hours chilling time
Cooking time: 35 minutes

Serves 4

- 200 g/7 oz (scant 1 cup) short-grain rice, well rinsed
- ½ teaspoon salt
- 3 makrut lime leaves, centre stem removed and thinly sliced (optional)
- 1 teaspoon sunflower oil, for greasing

Put the rice, salt and 600 ml/20 fl oz (2½ cups) of water into a medium saucepan. Bring to a boil, then reduce the heat to medium. Simmer, uncovered, for 20 minutes, until the water has evaporated. Mix well, then reduce the heat to low and cook for another 15 minutes. Using a wooden spoon, mash the rice until smooth. Stir in the lime leaves, if using, and mix well.

Grease a small baking dish. Add the mixture and press it into the dish. Set aside to cool, then cover and refrigerate for 3 hours to chill. Remove from the refrigerator, tip onto a chopping (cutting) board and cut into 2-cm/¾-inch cubes. Serve.

Ginger Coconut Rice
Nasi Jaha

This rice is traditionally combined with glutinous rice, wrapped in banana leaves and steamed in bamboo segments over an open fire. Served with spicy pork or chicken, it is an essential part of our Christmas festivities in North Sulawesi.

To enjoy the flavours from a modern kitchen, I cook the rice in water and coconut milk. Pair it with your favourite curry or stew and stir-fried vegetables.

Origin: Sulawesi

Preparation time: 15 minutes
Cooking time: 35 minutes

Serves 8

- 300 g/10½ oz (1½ cups) jasmine or Japanese rice, well rinsed
- 100 g/3½ oz (½ cup) glutinous rice

- 1 banana shallot, finely chopped or puréed
- 10 g/¼ oz fresh root ginger, finely grated
- 1 teaspoon salt
- 400 ml/14 fl oz (1⅔ cups) coconut milk
- 300 ml/10 fl oz (1¼ cups) coconut water

Combine all the ingredients in a large saucepan over medium heat. Cook, uncovered, for 15–17 minutes and stir occasionally until the coconut milk has evaporated. Cover, then reduce the heat to low and cook for 20 minutes.

Serve.

Variation:
- Ginger, Lemongrass and Coconut Rice (Nasi Uduk Betawi)
  This is a Jakartan breakfast dish. Add 1 stalk lemongrass, crushed and tied into a knot, to the rice. Remove the lemongrass before serving. Serve with Sambal Tempeh (page 155), Peanut Sambal (page 52), Indonesian Fried Chicken (page 182), omelette ribbons (page 219) and prawn crackers.

Mushroom and Tempeh Fried Rice
Nasi Goreng Jamur dan Tempe

A Jakartan dish of fried rice and goat meat, seasoned with spices and soy sauce, was the source of inspiration for this recipe. Here, a combination of herbs and spice transforms mushrooms and tempeh into a flavoursome vegan dish.

The spice blend is the equivalent of the Middle Eastern baharat but without the smoky paprika. (In fact, if you're short on time, you can use shop-bought baharat instead.)

Sweet soy sauce and chillies give it the recognizable taste of Indonesia. The tempeh and mushroom may be replaced with chicken, beef or lamb.

Origin: Java

Preparation time: 25 minutes
Cooking time: 10 minutes

Serves 4–6

For the fried rice:
* 1 tablespoon coriander seeds
* 1 teaspoon salt
* 250 g/9 oz tempeh, cut into 1-cm/½-inch cubes
* 3 tablespoons coconut oil
* 2 large cloves garlic, finely chopped
* 1 teaspoon cumin seeds
* 2 banana shallots, thinly sliced

* 2–3 red bird's eye chillies, thinly sliced, or 1–2 teaspoon chilli powder
* 2 green cardamom pods, lightly crushed
* 2 salam leaves or bay leaves
* 1 teaspoon ground cinnamon
* ½ teaspoon ground cloves
* 100 g/3½ oz assorted mushrooms, such as chestnut, oyster and shiitake

* 600 g/1 lb 5 oz (3½ cups) day-old cooked rice
* 3 tablespoons Sweet Soy Sauce (page 38)
* Black pepper, to taste

For the topping:
* 2 tablespoons Crispy Shallots (page 41)
* Small bunch of mint, leaves chopped

Heat a wok or frying pan over medium heat. Add the coriander seeds and dry-roast for 4–5 minutes until fragrant. Set aside to cool, then grind to a fine powder.

In a medium bowl, combine half the ground coriander, salt and 3½ tablespoons of water. Add the tempeh, mix well and marinate for 5 minutes.

Heat 2 tablespoons of oil in the same wok over medium heat. Add the tempeh and sauté for 2–3 minutes, turning the tempeh, to ensure an even golden colour on all sides. Transfer to a plate and set aside.

Add the remaining tablespoon of oil to the pan. Add the garlic and cumin and sauté for 1 minute. Add the shallots and sauté for another 3–4 minutes.

Add the chillies, cardamom, salam leaves, cinnamon, cloves and the remaining ground coriander and sauté for 1 minute. Add the mushrooms and sauté for 2 minutes.

Stir in the rice and sweet soy sauce, using a fork to separate the rice grains and break up any lumps. Season with salt and pepper. Mix in the tempeh and cook for another 3–4 minutes. Season to taste.

Transfer the rice to a large serving plate. Sprinkle with crispy shallots and mint leaves.

Turmeric Coconut Rice
Nasi Kuning

A delicious bowl of turmeric coconut rice, infused with lemongrass, lime leaves and coconut, always brings me to my grandmother's kitchen. A similar Javanese dish known as *tumpeng (see left)* has a rice cone surrounded by at least seven different vegetable, fish and meat dishes. The dish is often seen as a symbol of harmony between humans, nature and God. *Tumpeng* can also be served with steamed rice or ginger coconut rice *(nasi uduk)*.

Usually, spicy-sweet tuna, tomato sambal and potato sambal accompany this rice. A boiled egg, halved and wrapped in young palm leaves, is also served in Manado.

Origin: Throughout Indonesia

Preparation time: 10 minutes
Cooking time: 35 minutes

Serves 6

* 20 g/¾ oz fresh turmeric, peeled and grated, or 2 teaspoons ground turmeric
* 300 g/10½ oz (1¼ cups) short-grain or jasmine rice, well rinsed
* 200 ml/7 fl oz (generous ¾ cup) coconut milk
* 1 teaspoon salt
* 4–5 makrut lime leaves, torn
* 1 stalk lemongrass, crushed and tied into a knot
* 1 pandan leaf, tied into a knot

Place the fresh turmeric in 7 tablespoons of water. Mix well, then strain into a small bowl. (Alternatively, combine ground turmeric and water and mix well.) This is your turmeric extract. Set aside.

In a medium saucepan, combine all the ingredients. Pour in 200 ml/7 fl oz (generous ¾ cup) of water and bring to a boil over medium heat. Boil for 15 minutes and stir occasionally until the water has evaporated. Cover, reduce the heat to low and set aside for 20 minutes.

Remove the lemongrass, pandan and lime leaves before serving.

Variations:
- **Java Turmeric Coconut Rice (Nasi Kuning Jawa)**
  Omit the pandan leaves. In a small blender, create a paste with 1 banana shallot, 1 clove garlic, 1 tablespoon ground coriander, ½ teaspoon ground cumin and 2 candlenuts. Heat 2 tablespoons coconut oil in a medium saucepan, then add the paste and cook for 3–4 minutes until fragrant. Combine the paste with the rice ingredients and prepare as instructed.
- **Bali Turmeric Coconut Rice (Nasi Kuning Bali)**
  Omit the pandan leaves. In a small blender, create a paste with 10 g/¼ oz kencur, 1 banana shallot, 1 clove garlic and ¼ teaspoon white pepper. Heat 2 tablespoons coconut oil in a medium saucepan, then add the paste and cook for 3–4 minutes until fragrant. Combine the paste with the rice ingredients and prepare as instructed.

Sweetcorn Rice
Nasi Jagung

The combination of rice and cornmeal is common across Indonesia and I grew up with this rice dish. I use dried corn kernels in the recipe, grinding them myself with a spice or coffee grinder so that the texture is as coarse as couscous.

Origin: Throughout Indonesia

Preparation time: 10 minutes
Cooking time: 35–40 minutes

Serves 4

* 150 g/5 fl oz (⅔ cup) coarse cornmeal
* 200 g/7 fl oz (generous ¾ cup) jasmine rice
* 1 pandan leaf, tied into a knot (optional)

Soak the dry cornmeal in a bowl of water for 1 hour. Drain. Rinse the rice.

Put the rice and cornmeal in a large saucepan. Add 400 ml/14 fl oz (1 ⅔ cups) water and bring to a boil over medium heat. Boil for 16–18 minutes, until the water has evaporated, then reduce the heat to low and cover. Cook for 20–22 minutes. Serve.

Village Fried Rice
Nasi Goreng Kampung

Nasi goreng is at the heart of every village (*kampung*) in Indonesia. My Oma never let food go to waste, so this rice dish made a popular breakfast option at home. If we didn't have day-old rice to hand, she would cool down freshly cooked rice to room temperature.

I believe that a good nasi goreng must be light, colourful and fluffy with separated rice grains. The most affordable versions of this dish have a base of chillies, shallots, garlic and eggs. From this base, you can build flavour with additional protein such as chicken or prawns (shrimp). Or add a bounty of vegetables – such as grated carrots and peas – for a nutritiously well-balanced meal.

Generally, you serve a sambal alongside the dish, but I like to lace it with chillies for a fiery kick. I also serve nasi goreng with rice crackers for a boost of texture and flavour.

Origin: Throughout Indonesia

Preparation time: 15 minutes
Cooking time: 20 minutes

Serves 4

- 1 teaspoon shrimp paste or 2–3 tablespoons fish sauce
- 6 eggs
- Salt and black pepper, to taste
- 3 tablespoons coconut oil
- 2–3 red bird's eye chillies, finely chopped
- 2 large cloves garlic, finely chopped
- 1 large banana shallot, thinly sliced
- 800 g/1 lb 12 oz (4½ cups) day-old cooked rice, room temperature
- 4 tablespoons Sweet Soy Sauce (page 38)
- 2 tablespoons light soy sauce
- 2–4 pak choy, sliced (optional)
- 2 carrots, grated
- 100 g/3½ oz (⅔ cup) frozen peas
- Rice Crackers (page 42) or prawn crackers (optional)

Finely grind the shrimp paste with a pestle and mortar. Set aside.

Crack 2 eggs into a small bowl and season with salt and pepper.

Heat 1 tablespoon of oil in a wok or frying pan over medium heat. Add the eggs and scramble for 2–3 minutes, taking care not to over-cook. Transfer to a bowl and set aside.

Heat another tablespoon of oil in the same wok. Add the chillies, garlic and shallot and sauté for 4–5 minutes. Add the shrimp paste, mix well and cook for another 2 minutes. Stir in the rice and scrambled eggs.

Mix in the soy sauces and sauté for another 6–8 minutes, using a fork to separate the rice grains and break up any lumps.

Add the pak choy, if using, and half of the carrots and sauté for 2 minutes. If needed, add a tablespoon of water if the mixture looks dry. Season to taste. Reduce the heat to low. Stir in the peas.

Divide the fried rice between 4 serving plates and garnish with the remaining grated carrots.

Heat the remaining 1 tablespoon of oil in the wok over medium heat. Add the remaining 4 eggs and cook for 3–4 minutes for sunny-side up. Add an egg to each plate and finish with rice crackers. Serve immediately.

Variation:
- **Chicken and Prawn Fried Goreng (Nasi Goreng Ayam dan Udang)** Add 2 cooked chicken breasts, chopped, and 100 g/3½ oz cooked tiger prawns with the rice and eggs. Serve with Mixed Pickles (page 55) and Tomato, Chilli and Basil Sambal (page 53).

Manadonese Rice Porridge with Vegetables
Bubur Manado

In the good old days, farmers from the mountain region of Tomohon and Tondano would bring rice and sambal with them to work in the fields. When they got hungry, they made a simple porridge with rice, lemongrass and plenty of water in a pot over a wood fire, then topped it with the leafy vegetables and basil available in the field. They would then enjoy it with spicy sambal roa, made at home with dried smoked garfish.

This beautifully fragrant porridge is infused with lemongrass and basil.

Origin: Sulawesi

Preparation time: 15 minutes
Cooking time: 30 minutes

Serves 4

- 200 g/7 oz (scant 1 cup) short-grain rice, such as arborio, well rinsed
- 1 long stalk lemongrass, crushed and tied into a knot
- 1 teaspoon sea salt
- 700 g/1 lb 9 oz pumpkin, butternut squash or sweet potatoes, peeled and cut into 1-cm/½-inch cubes
- 2 cobs sweetcorn, kernels cut from the cob
- 100 g/3½ oz (3 cups) spinach
- Large handful of basil leaves
- Anchovy Sambal (page 51) or Miso Sambal (page 51), to serve

In a medium saucepan, combine the rice, lemongrass and salt. Add 700 ml/24 fl oz (generous 2¾ cups) hot water and bring to a boil. Reduce the heat to medium-low, cover and simmer for 10 minutes.

Add the pumpkin and cook for 15 minutes, until the pumpkin has softened and the rice is slightly over-cooked. Stir in the sweetcorn and cook for 4 minutes, until the rice has a risotto-like consistency. If necessary, add more hot water. Stir in the spinach and basil and cook for 2–3 minutes. Season to taste.

Serve the porridge with sambal.

Chicken Porridge with Turmeric and Chicken Broth
Bubur Ayam Kuah Kuning

This ubiquitous dish is served around the archipelago, from street food vendor to five-star establishments. It's a proper breakfast treat infused with a fortifying turmeric and chicken broth and finished with a medley of toppings. It can be easily made into a vegetarian dish by omitting the chicken.

Origin: Throughout Indonesia

Preparation time: 25 minutes
Cooking time: 1 hour

Serves 6–8

For the porridge:
- 200 g/3½ oz (scant 1 cup) short-grain rice, such as Japanese or arborio, rinsed
- 1 stalk lemongrass, crushed and tied into a knot
- 10 g/¼ oz fresh root ginger, finely grated
- 1 teaspoon salt

For the chicken stock:
- 3 cloves garlic, thinly sliced
- 1 banana shallot, thinly sliced
- 10 g/¼ oz fresh root ginger
- 10 g/¼ oz fresh turmeric
- 2 tablespoons coconut oil
- 4 bone-in chicken thighs, skinless
- 1 stalk lemongrass, crushed and tied into a knot
- 4 makrut lime leaves, torn
- 2 bay leaves
- 1 teaspoon salt

For the toppings:
- 12–18 small rice crackers (optional)
- 3–4 hard-boiled eggs
- 3 tablespoons finely chopped celery leaves or parsley
- 2 tablespoons Crispy Shallots (page 41)
- 2 tablespoons Sweet Soy Sauce (page 38)
- Boiled Sambal (page 53, optional)

To make the porridge, put the rice into a medium saucepan. Add the lemongrass, ginger and salt. Pour in 2 litres/64 fl oz (8½ cups) of hot water and bring to a boil. Reduce the heat to medium-low and simmer for 40 minutes, stirring occasionally, until soft and porridge-like. If it's too thick, add a little hot water.

To make the stock, combine the garlic, shallot, ginger and turmeric in a small blender and blend into a paste.

Heat the coconut oil in a medium saucepan. Add the paste and sauté for 3–4 minutes. Add the chicken and pan-fry for 2 minutes. Add the lemongrass, lime leaves, bay leaves and salt. Pour in 800 ml/27 fl oz (3½ cups) of water and bring to a boil. Simmer for 20 minutes over medium-high heat until the chicken is cooked through. Season with salt to taste.

Using a slotted spoon, transfer the chicken to a chopping (cutting) board. Using two forks, separate the meat from the bones. Set aside.

Arrange the porridge, stock, chicken and toppings on a table. Ladle porridge into each bowl, then add the stock and chicken. Have guests top the porridge with their favourite toppings. Serve hot.

Seafood and Sago Porridge in Turmeric Broth
Papeda dan Seafood Kuah Kuning

I first enjoyed sago porridge at a *warung* on the island of Ternate more than a decade ago. In 2019, I travelled to Papua and was reacquainted with this dish in the heart of a sago forest plantation.

Usually, the porridge features fish, but I find that seafood provides an extra dimension. Unlike other spice paste recipes, the ingredients for this bumbu only need to be sliced or grated. The fish broth has a fresh and clean taste and requires no addition of oil.

Origin: Papua

Preparation time: 30 minutes
Cooking time: 40 minutes

Serves 4

For the sago porridge:
* 100 g/3½ oz sago flour
* 1 teaspoon salt

For the stock and seafood:
* 2 red bird's eye chillies, finely sliced
* 2 makrut lime leaves, torn
* 1 large clove garlic, sliced
* 1 banana shallot, thinly sliced
* 1 stalk lemongrass, crushed and tied into a knot
* 10 g/¼ oz fresh turmeric, finely grated
* 1 teaspoon salt
* 2 limes
* 400 g/14 oz salmon fillets, cut into bite-size pieces
* 200 g/7 oz medium-sized prawns, shelled
* 100 g/3½ oz scallops
* 1 tomato, cut into ½-cm/ ¼-inch cubes
* Bunch of basil, chopped

To prepare the sago porridge, combine the sago flour and 250 ml/8 fl oz (1 cup) room-temperature water in a large bowl. Mix well, then set aside for 30 minutes.

Meanwhile, prepare the stock. Combine the chillies, lime leaves, garlic, shallot, lemongrass and turmeric in a large saucepan. Add 800 ml/27 fl oz (3½ cups) of water to the pan and bring to a boil. Reduce the heat to medium-low and simmer for 25 minutes. Add salt and the juice of 1 lime. Season to taste. Reduce the heat to low.

Drain as much water as possible from the sago. In a medium saucepan, combine the damp sago, salt and 400 ml/14 fl oz (generous 1⅔ cups) of water. Stir constantly over medium heat for 10 minutes, until sticky and translucent. Reduce the heat to low.

Meanwhile, add the salmon, prawns, scallops and tomato to the stock. Increase the heat to medium and cook for 2–3 minutes. Season to taste with salt and the juice of the remaining lime, if needed. Add the basil.

Ladle 4 tablespoons of sago porridge into 4 individual bowls, then add the seafood and stock. Serve.

Lace Bread
Roti Jala

This Sumatran bread is like a lacy pancake, rolled up and designed to mop up the savoury sauces of rich curry dishes. To create the netted effect, you will need a three-nozzle squeeze bottle (available online).

If you're looking for a bolder flavour, consider adding curry powder to impart subtle earthiness and warmth.

Origin: Sumatra

Preparation time: 30 minutes
Cooking time: 5–15 minutes

Serves 4–6

* 125 g/4¼ oz (scant 1 cup) plain (all-purpose) flour
* ½ teaspoon salt
* Pinch of sugar
* 5 tablespoons coconut milk
* 1 egg
* Vegetable oil, for greasing

In a medium bowl, combine the flour, salt and sugar. Mix well.

Add the coconut milk and egg and whisk gently. Slowly and gradually, whisk in 175 ml/6 fl oz (¾ cup) of water until the batter is smooth. Strain the batter through a fine-mesh sieve (strainer) and into a bowl. Set aside for 30 minutes.

Fill a three-nozzle squeeze bottle with the pancake mixture and put the cap back onto the bottle.

Heat a non-stick frying pan over medium heat and grease lightly. Working quickly, invert the water bottle and drizzle the batter into the pan with quick circular motions to form a net-like pattern. Cook for 1–2 minutes, untouched. If it looks like it's about to burn, reduce the heat to low.

Remove the lace bread from the pan. Carefully fold in the sides and roll up. Repeat with the remaining batter. Serve with your favourite curry.

Sorghum
Sorghum

Sorghum makes a healthy substitution in most rice dishes and can even be added to a salad. And if sorghum is not available, simply replace it with quinoa.

Origin: Nusa Tenggara

Preparation time: 5 minutes, plus overnight soaking time
Cooking time: 50 minutes

Serves 2–4

* 140 g/5 oz (1 cup) whole sorghum
* ½ teaspoon salt

Soak the sorghum in water overnight.

Drain, then rinse and put into a large saucepan. Add 750 ml/25 fl oz (3 cups) of water and bring to a boil. Reduce the heat to medium-low, cover and simmer for 40–45 minutes until the sorghum is tender.

Drain, then serve immediately. Alternatively, spread out the sorghum on a baking sheet and set aside to cool. Add to your favourite salad dishes.

Noodles

Mie

Noodles are a staple in Indonesia, and they are served everywhere from food carts to five-star restaurants. My aunt Juli loved her noodles, and she'd often take me out to the local restaurants in her quest to find the best dishes in Manado.

Indonesian noodles can be made with cassava, rice, mung beans, sago and, of course, flour. Some of my favourites include super thin rice vermicelli noodles (*bihun*), transparent glass noodles made with corn flour and mung beans (*soun*) and thick Sumatran noodles (*mie lidi*). We also have a noodle made grey with cassava and sweet potato flours known as 'ugly noodle' (*lethek*) and a tapioca noodle (*misua*).

While Classic Stir-Fried Noodles (*mie goreng*, page 219) is internationally renowned, every city around the archipelago boasts an eponymous noodle dish: Mie Jakarta, Mie Aceh (page 217), the list goes on. The main differences between the regional noodles are the local ingredients and the choice of spices. And all noodles are served with sambals and often melinjo or prawn crackers. And they come available pan-fried, with sauces, or even in clear broth.

It's always worth having packets of dried egg or rice noodles in the cupboard. They're such a useful flexible ingredient and perfect for when you want to prepare quick, healthy and delicious meals.

Jakartan Chicken Noodles
Mie Ayam Jakarta

Enjoyed any time of the day – breakfast, lunch or dinner – this iconic dish is served on every street corner of Jakarta (and hence its name). It's prepared on the spot by the food vendor, an individual experience for each customer and an enjoyable ritual. Egg noodles are seasoned with garlic oil, soy and white pepper, then combined with tender morsels of chicken and flavoured with a delightful infusion of sweet soy and herbs.

It tastes even better when the chicken mixture is prepared a day earlier. For added texture, consider a garnish of deep-fried wonton skins (pangsit goreng).

In Indonesian restaurants, this dish is known as bakmi Jakarta and is accompanied by a clear stock with sliced spring onions (scallions), Chinese celery leaves and meatballs on the side.

Origin: Java

Preparation time: 30 minutes
Cooking time: 35 minutes

Serves 4

For the garlic oil:
* 100 ml/3½ fl oz (scant ½ cup) vegetable oil
* 6 cloves garlic, finely chopped
* Salt, to taste

For the chicken and mushrooms:
* 3 tablespoons sunflower oil
* 2 large chicken breasts, cut into ½-cm/¼-inch cubes
* Salt and white pepper, to taste
* 1 banana shallot, thinly sliced
* 4 cloves garlic, finely chopped
* 100 g/3½ oz (1 cup) straw or button (white) mushrooms, quartered
* 3 makrut lime leaves, torn
* 2 salam leaves or bay leaves

* 1 stalk lemongrass, crushed and tied into a knot
* 10 g/¼ oz galangal, finely grated
* 100 ml/3½ fl oz (scant ½ cup) chicken stock
* 5 tablespoons Sweet Soy Sauce (page 38)
* 2 tablespoons light soy sauce

For the wonton crisps:
* 300 ml/10 fl oz (1¼ cups) sunflower oil
* 8 wonton skins, each cut into triangles

For the noodles:
* 400 g/14 oz fresh egg noodles or 300 g/10½ oz dried noodles

* 2 large pak choy, cut into 1-cm/½-inch-thick slices
* 4 teaspoons light soy sauce

To serve:
* 2 tablespoons finely chopped spring onions (scallions)
* Vinegar Sambal (page 53) (optional)

To make the garlic oil, combine the oil and garlic in a frying pan and sauté for 5 minutes over medium-low heat. Season with salt and let cool.

To prepare the chicken and mushrooms, heat 2 tablespoons of oil in a frying pan or wok over medium-high heat. Add the chicken, season with salt and sauté for 6–7 minutes until slightly golden. Transfer the chicken to a plate.

Heat the remaining oil in the same frying pan over medium heat. Add the shallot and garlic and sauté for 3–4 minutes. Add the mushrooms, lime leaves, salam leaves, lemongrass and galangal and sauté for 5 minutes or until the mushrooms have softened.

Return the chicken to the pan. Add the stock and both soy sauces and cook for another 10 minutes over low heat. Season with salt and pepper. Set aside. Remove the lemongrass and lime and salam leaves.

To make the wonton crisps, heat the oil in a small saucepan over medium heat. The oil is ready when a cube of bread dropped in sizzles on contact and turns golden in 10–15 seconds. (Alternatively, use a thermometer and heat to 180°C/350°F.)

Add the wonton skins and deep-fry for 1–2 minutes until golden brown. Using a slotted spoon, transfer the wonton skins to a plate lined with paper towels to drain.

To cook the noodles, bring a large saucepan of water to a boil. Add fresh noodles to the pan and cook for 1 minute. Drain, reserving the cooking water. (Alternatively, prepare the dried noodles according to the package directions.)

Cook the pak choy for 30 seconds in the reserved hot noodle water, then drain.

In a large bowl, combine the noodles, 4 teaspoons garlic oil and soy sauce and mix. Divide among the serving bowls. Top each with chicken, mushrooms and pak choy. Garnish with spring onions (scallions). Add 1–2 wonton crisps and serve with sambal, if you wish.

Acehnese Noodles
Mie Aceh

Aceh is a semi-autonomous province located on the northernmost point of Indonesia. Over the horizon to the northeast lies the Bay of Bengal, the west coasts of India and Sri Lanka, and the Middle East beyond this. Unsurprisingly, it's where the spread of Islam in Indonesia originated.

I tasted Aceh noodles for the first time during a visit to the capital city of Banda Aceh in 2014. It proved to be an explosion of taste – a unique curried dish, all at once sweet, spicy and tangy, that could be flavoured with prawn, crab or chicken. This dish does require time to come together, but the process will be worth it.

Bumbu is essential to the rich and smooth sauce used to coat the noodles (and give its distinctive flavour). A bounty of vegetables adds texture and colour, and thick egg noodles complete the dish.

You could easily replace the prawn stock with water and add tofu for a tasty vegan option. Or are you pressed for time? Replace the spice blend with 2 tablespoons shop-bought garam masala.

Origin: Sumatra

Preparation time: 20 minutes
Cooking time: 40 minutes

Serves 4–6

For the spice blend:
* 1 teaspoon fennel seeds
* 1 teaspoon cumin seeds
* 1 teaspoon coriander seeds
* 2 green cardamom pods, seeds only
* ½ teaspoon fenugreek
* 1 teaspoon black pepper

For the prawn broth:
* 20 medium king prawns
* 1 tablespoon vegetable oil

For the noodles:
* 400 g/14 oz fresh egg noodles or pack of dried noodles
* 2 tablespoons coconut oil or vegetable oil
* 4 cloves garlic, finely chopped
* 2 banana shallots, finely chopped
* 2–3 red bird's eye chillies, finely chopped
* 10 g/¼ oz fresh root ginger, finely grated
* 10 g/¼ oz fresh turmeric, finely grated, or ½ teaspoon ground turmeric

* 4 tablespoons Sweet Soy Sauce (page 38)
* 3 tablespoons light soy sauce
* 100 g/3½ oz (scant ½ cup) crab meat
* Salt, to taste

For the toppings and condiments:
* Crispy Shallots (page 41)
* 4–6 limes wedges
* Melinjo crackers (optional)
* Mixed Pickles (page 55)

To prepare the spice blend, heat a small frying pan over medium heat. Add all the ingredients and dry-roast for 4–6 minutes until fragrant. Set aside to cool, then transfer to a spice grinder and grind to a fine powder. (Alternatively, use a pestle and mortar.)

To prepare the prawn broth, peel the prawns, leaving the tails intact, and de-vein. Rinse thoroughly and reserve the prawns for later. Heat the oil in a saucepan over medium heat. Add the prawn heads and shells and cook for 3–4 minutes until the shells turn pink. Add 300 ml/10 fl oz (1¼ cups) of water and bring to a boil. Reduce the heat to medium-low and simmer for 20 minutes. Strain.

To prepare fresh noodles, bring a saucepan of water to a boil. Add the fresh noodles and cook for 1 minute. Drain. (Alternatively, to prepare the dried noodles, follow the package directions.)

In the same saucepan used for the noodles, heat the oil over medium heat. Add the garlic and shallots and sauté for 3–4 minutes, until softened and fragrant. Add the chillies, ginger and turmeric and cook for another 2–3 minutes. Stir in the spice blend and mix for a minute until fragrant. Add the soy sauces and prawn stock and bring to a boil. Season with salt to taste.

Add the reserved prawns and cook for 2 minutes. Stir in the crab meat and cook for another 2 minutes. Season to taste. Mix in the noodles and cook for another minute.

Divide the noodles among 4–6 plates or transfer them to a large serving plate. Top with crispy shallots, lime wedges and melinjo crackers. Serve hot with mixed pickles.

Glass Noodles in Chicken Soup
Sup Ayam dengan Soun

This delicious and comforting dish is made with wood ear mushrooms. You must soak the mushrooms first in hot water to soften them, then add the soaking liquid to the stock. Dried wood ear mushrooms are available in all Asian speciality food shops.

Origin: Throughout Indonesia

Preparation time: 30 minutes
Cooking time: 1 hour 20 minutes

Serves 6–8

* 1 (1.2 kg/2 lb 12-oz) whole chicken, skinned and cut into 8 pieces
* 50 g/1¾ oz dried wood ear mushrooms
* 2 large potatoes, cut into 1-cm/½-inch cubes
* 2 carrots, cut into 1-cm/½-inch slices
* 50 g/1¾ oz green beans, cut into 1-cm/½-inch lengths
* 2 spring onions (scallions), cut into 1-cm/½-inch lengths
* 100 g/3½ oz dried glass noodles
* Salt and white pepper, to taste
* Large handful of Chinese parsley or celery leaves, to garnish

In a large saucepan, combine the chicken and 500 ml/17 fl oz (generous 2 cups) of water. Bring to a boil and boil for 2 minutes. Drain, then put the chicken back into the pan and add 1.5 litres/ 50 fl oz (6¼ cups) of water. Bring to a boil, then reduce the heat to medium-low. Cover and simmer for 1 hour.

Meanwhile, soak the wood ear mushrooms for 25–30 minutes in 500 ml/17 fl oz (generous 2 cups) warm water. Drain, then set aside.

Add the potatoes and carrots to the chicken pan and cook for 15–17 minutes until softened.

Transfer the chicken to a chopping (cutting) board and de-bone the meat. Discard the bones and return the meat to the pan.

Add the green beans, mushrooms and spring onions (scallions) and cook for 10 minutes.

Put the glass noodles in a large bowl and add 1 litre/34 fl oz (4¼ cups) of hot water. Set aside to soak for 1–2 minutes. Drain, then add the noodles to the soup. Cook for 2 minutes or until soft. Season with salt and pepper, then garnish with Chinese parsley.

Javanese Stir-Fried Noodles with Chicken

Kwetiau Goreng Jawa

This stir-fried noodle dish is a close relative to the better-known *mie goreng* and similar to pad thai but without the fish sauce and coriander (cilantro) leaves. Available in Chinese-Indonesian restaurants around the archipelago, kwetiau noodles are often prepared just with oyster sauce and sesame oil. For a meat-free alternative, simply replace the chicken with tofu and tempeh.

Origin: Java

Preparation time: 15 minutes
Cooking time: 15 minutes

Serves 4

* 400 g/14 oz dried rice sticks or pad thai noodles
* 2 tablespoons sunflower oil
* 300 g/10½ oz chicken breast, sliced into ½-cm/¼-inch strips
* 4 tablespoons light soy sauce
* 1 teaspoon white pepper
* 3 cloves garlic, finely chopped
* 2 banana shallots, thinly sliced
* 2–3 red bird's eye chillies, thinly sliced
* 2 eggs, lightly beaten
* 4 tablespoons Sweet Soy Sauce (page 38)
* 2 spring onions (scallions), thinly sliced
* 6 tablespoons bean sprouts
* 2 tablespoons Dried Shrimp Powder (page 41)
* Salt, to taste
* 50 g/1¾ oz (scant ½ cup) roasted cashews, coarsely ground (optional)

Prepare the dried noodles according to the package directions.

Heat the oil in a wok or frying pan over medium heat. Season the chicken with 2 tablespoons of light soy sauce and the pepper. Add the garlic, shallots and chillies and sauté for 3–4 minutes or until fragrant. Add the chicken and cook for 5–6 minutes. Push the chicken to the side of the pan.

Add the eggs and scramble for 1–2 minutes. Mix the chicken with the eggs, sweet soy sauce and the remaining 2 tablespoons of light soy sauce. Mix well. Stir in the noodles, half of the spring onions (scallions) and bean sprouts and toss well.

Increase the heat to high and sauté for another 3–4 minutes. Add the dried shrimp powder and mix well. If the mixture is dry, add 2 tablespoons of water. Season with salt and pepper.

Transfer the mixture to a large serving plate and sprinkle with the remaining spring onions and the cashews. Serve.

Variations:
- Manadonese Fried Noodles (Mie Goreng Manado)
  Omit the bean sprouts, dried shrimp powder and cashews. Replace the chicken with smoked haddock or mackerel, cut into bite-size pieces. Cook for 2–3 minutes, then follow the rest of the recipe.
- Fried Vermicelli Noodles (Beehun Goreng)
  Omit the eggs, bean sprouts, dried shrimp powder and cashews. Replace the noodles with rice vermicelli and 2 large pak choy, cut into 2-cm/¾-inch slices. Add to the pan with the spring onions and cook for 2–3 minutes. Prepare a thin omelette, cut into thin strips and top the noodles.
- Pontianak-Style Rice Noodles (Kwetiau Goreng, Pontianak)
  Omit the bean sprouts, dried shrimp powder and cashews. Replace the chicken with pork tenderloin or bacon. Add 2 large pak choy, cut into 2-cm/¾-inch slices. Add 1–2 tablespoons oyster sauce and 2 tablespoons sesame oil to the final dish.
- Classic Stir-Fried Noodles (Mie Goreng)
  Omit the bean sprouts, dried shrimp and cashews. Add 2 large pak choy, cut into 2-cm/¾-inch slices, and use egg noodles instead.

Sweets

Makanan Penutup

I imagine many of my readers have enjoyed traditional Western desserts featuring Indonesia's world-famous spices (see more on page 25). Cloves, nutmeg, cinnamon and ginger have flavoured confections across the world.

I've always had a sweet tooth. When I was growing up, I'd happily indulge in desserts of all forms: European cakes, tarts and Thousand-Layer Cake (page 239). But my love affair with desserts doesn't stop there. One of my earliest memories was drinking the avocado juice that can be found in the largest cosmopolitan cities around the country. That flavour profile was the basis for the simple yet indulgent Avocado Mousse and Chocolate Ganache (page 225), which can be prepared in next to no time. It has the quintessential Indonesian dessert flavour found in the pairing of palm or coconut sugar with coconut milk.

I have also re-created classic European desserts with an Indonesian twist. My Apple Crumble with Speculaas (page 234) is prepared with a spice blend from my hometown Manado, and the Coconut and Strawberry Pavlova (page 233) makes a scrumptious tropical summertime confection. Pineapple Biscuits (page 235) and Cheese Sticks (page 236) – two of my favourite childhood treats – have even become ubiquitous additions at national celebrations such as Christmas, *Idul Fitri* and Chinese New Year.

I love how these food traditions have the power to bind us together and transcend race and creed.

Banana and Coconut Ice Cream

Kolak Pisang Es Krim

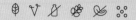

Kolak pisang is a delightful dessert of cooked banana with coconut and palm sugar, infused with pandan. It is a classic Indonesian dish and very popular during the fasting month; it is also the inspiration behind this recipe. I like the simplicity and wonderful banana ice cream with hints of caramel, coconut and cinnamon. It makes a superb vegan dessert.

Origin: Modern recipe

Preparation time: 10 minutes, plus churning and freezing time

Makes 1 litre/34 fl oz (4¼ cups)

- 800 g/1 b 12 oz ripe Cavendish bananas (about 6–8), peeled and sliced
- 650 ml/22 fl oz (2¾ cups) coconut milk
- 100 g/3½ oz grated palm sugar or coconut sugar
- 1–2 teaspoons ground cinnamon

In a blender, combine the bananas, coconut milk, palm sugar and cinnamon. Blend for 5–7 minutes until creamy. Transfer the mixture into an ice-cream maker and follow the manufacturer's instructions. Transfer to a freezer container and store in the freezer.

Set aside for 10–15 minutes at room temperature before serving.

Pineapple, Ginger and Chilli Sorbet

Es Serut Nanas, Jahe dan Cabe

This sorbet was inspired by an ice lolly (ice pop) my mother would create from papaya pickle, which was both spicy and sweet at the same time.

While you might expect a lot of heat from this sorbet, it's an unexpectedly refreshing and invigorating summertime treat, especially with the addition of ginger.

Origin: Modern recipe

Preparation time: 20 minutes, plus churning and freezing time

Cooking time: 10 minutes

Makes 500 ml/17 fl oz (2 cups)

* 1 (1.2-kg/2 lb 12-oz) pineapple, peeled, cored and chopped
* 20 g/¾ oz fresh root ginger, finely grated
* 1 teaspoon chilli powder
* 150 g/5½ oz (¾ cup) sugar
* Juice of 2–3 limes

In a blender, combine the pineapple, ginger and chilli powder and blend well. Place the pineapple mixture in a saucepan and add the sugar and lime. Cook over low heat for about 5 minutes, stirring constantly, until the sugar has dissolved. Turn off the heat and let it cool.

Transfer the mixture into a blender and blend well for 5 minutes to add more air into the mixture. Transfer into an ice-cream maker and follow the manufacturer's instructions. Transfer to a freezer container and store in the freezer.

Set aside for 10–15 minutes at room temperature before serving.

Variation:
- Papaya, Ginger and Chilli Sorbet (Es Serut Pepaya, Jahe dan Cabe)
  Replace the pineapple with ripe papaya (or mango) and adjust the amount of sugar to suit your taste.

Avocado Mousse and Chocolate Ganache
Alpukat dan Saus Coklat

I fondly recall the traditional concoction *jus alpukat*, made with avocado, condensed milk and a touch of coffee. This popular smoothie can be found in big cities, from street vendors to restaurants, and serves as the inspiration for this modern dessert.

The layered combination of silky avocado mousse, rich chocolate ganache and crunchy roasted cashews is a delight. You'll want to keep the ripe avocados in the refrigerator for 24 hours to ensure a cold dessert. The chocolate ganache is relatively quick to make, once you have roasted and cooled the cashews beforehand.

Origin: Modern recipe

Preparation time: 10 minutes, plus chilling time
Cooking time: 10 minutes

Serves 4

For the ganache:
* 200 ml/7 fl oz (generous ¾ cup) single (light) cream
* 100 g/3½ oz good-quality dark (bittersweet) chocolate, broken into small pieces
* 2 tablespoons salted butter
* 1 tablespoon sugar

For the avocado mousse:
* 4 large, perfectly ripe avocados
* 2 tablespoons sugar
* 50 g/1¾ oz (scant ½ cup) roasted cashews, chopped, for sprinkling

To prepare the ganache, combine all the ingredients in a heatproof bowl set over a pan of simmering water. (Ensure the bowl doesn't touch the water.) Stir for 8–10 minutes, until smooth. Set aside.

To prepare the avocado mousse, cut the avocados in half and remove the stones (pits). Scoop the flesh into a blender, add the sugar and blend for 2–3 minutes, until smooth and airy.

Divide the avocado mousse into four wide-rimmed glasses. Pour over the chocolate ganache, then refrigerate for 1–2 hours to chill.

Sprinkle with roasted cashews and serve.

Steamed Plantain with Strawberry Granita and Coconut Custard

Es Pallu Butung

I've served this winning dessert at many events across Asia and Europe. It has a true taste of the tropics with its refreshing strawberry granita and compote and creamy coconut sauce. (There are six varieties of strawberries cultivated in the Indonesian highlands, which offer the most suitable temperate growing conditions.)

Traditionally, we use the local king banana (*pisang raja*) which is wonderfully fragrant, slightly tangy and, of course, deliciously sweet. It's not easily found outside Indonesia, so a plantain or Cavendish variety is acceptable.

Origin: Sulawesi

Preparation time: 30 minutes, plus freezing time
Cooking time: 1 hour

Serves 4–6

For the strawberry granita:
* 500 g/1 lb 2 oz (generous 4 cups) strawberries, hulled and halved
* 100 g/3½ oz (½ cup) sugar
* 2 tablespoons lime juice

For the steamed plantain:
* 1 ripe plantain or 2–3 ripe Cavendish bananas

For the strawberry compote:
* 600 g/1 lb 5 oz (5 cups) strawberries
* 4 tablespoons sugar
* 1 tablespoon vanilla extract
* Juice of 1 lime

For the coconut custard:
* 1 pandan leaf, tied into a knot
* 1 tablespoon sugar
* Pinch of salt

* 400 ml/14 fl oz (1⅔ cups) coconut milk
* 2 tablespoons rice flour

To serve (optional):
* 2–3 tablespoons condensed milk
* Small bunch of mint leaves, to garnish

To make the strawberry granita, combine all the ingredients in a food processor and purée. Pour into a 500-ml/17-fl oz container and cover. Freeze for 2 hours. Using a large fork, stir the contents. Cover and leave overnight in the freezer. Set aside for 10–15 minutes at room temperature before serving.

To prepare the steamed plantain, place the plantain in a steamer basket. (If necessary, cut it in half so that it fits.) Steam for 30 minutes until the plantain is softened. Leave to cool.

To make the strawberry compote, put half of the strawberries into a blender and purée. Cut the remaining strawberries into quarters and place them in a saucepan. Add the strawberry purée and remaining ingredients. Pour in 100 ml/3½ fl oz (scant ½ cup) of water and bring to a boil. Reduce the heat to medium-low and simmer for 20 minutes until syrupy. Leave to cool.

To make the coconut custard, combine the pandan leaf, sugar, salt and coconut milk in a saucepan. In a small cup, combine the rice flour and 3½ tablespoons of water and mix well. Strain the mixture through a fine-mesh sieve (strainer) and into the pan. Bring the mixture to a boil, then reduce the heat to medium. Gently simmer for 6–8 minutes and stir until thickened. Discard the pandan leaf, then let cool. Transfer into a bowl and chill in the refrigerator for at least 1 hour.

In individual glasses or bowls, add 2 tablespoons of granita and 4 slices of plantain. Top with 4 tablespoons of coconut custard, a drizzle of strawberry compote and 2 more tablespoons of granita. Drizzle with condensed milk and garnish with mint leaves, if using, and serve.

Coconut Pudding with Palm Sugar Syrup and Roasted Cashews

Bubur Sumsum

In Indonesian, *bubur* means 'porridge' and *sumsum* means 'bone marrow', used metaphorically to describe the smoothness and colour, rather than taste, of this recipe.

This pudding is like a light and silky panna cotta made with creamy coconut milk and caramelized palm sugar – perfect for those who prefer to avoid dairy and gluten.

Don't be alarmed by the salt in the recipe; its savoury flavour is designed to balance the sweetness of the palm sugar. It's a unique and modern interpretation of a classic pudding, especially with the roasted cashew nuts, to add flavour, colour and contrasting crunch.

Origin: Java

Preparation time: 20 minutes, plus 1 hour chilling time
Cooking time: 25 minutes

Serves 10

* 100 g/3½ oz (¾ cup) cashews
* 90 g/3¼ oz (½ cup) rice flour
* 1 long pandan leaf, tied into a knot
* 1 teaspoon salt
* 400 ml/14 fl oz (1⅔ cups) coconut milk

* 1 quantity Palm Sugar Syrup (page 39)

Preheat the oven to 180°C/350°F/Gas Mark 4.

Place the cashews on a baking sheet and roast for 14–16 minutes, shaking the pan every 5 minutes, until golden brown. Leave to cool.

In a small bowl, combine the rice flour and 100 ml/3½ fl oz (scant ½ cup) of water and mix well. Set aside.

In a medium saucepan, combine the pandan leaf, salt and coconut milk. Add 500 ml/17 fl oz (generous 2 cups) of water and bring to a boil over medium heat. Strain the rice flour mixture through a fine-mesh sieve (strainer) and into the pan. Whisk over medium-high heat until thick and smooth. Remove the pandan leaf.

Pour the mixture into 10 dessert glasses or ramekins. Set aside to cool. Chill in the refrigerator for at least 1 hour or overnight to set.

Remove the chilled pudding from the refrigerator, then drizzle 2 tablespoons of palm sugar syrup into each glass. Sprinkle with roasted cashews and serve.

Variations:
- Coconut Pudding with Caramelized Banana (Bubur Sumsum dengan Pisang Karamel)
  Chop 2 bananas into 1-cm/½-inch cubes and place in a small saucepan. Add 3½ tablespoons palm sugar and 4 tablespoons of water and bring to a boil. Simmer for 3–4 minutes, until the banana is caramelized and the water has reduced by half. Leave to cool. Top pudding with the banana, palm sugar syrup and roasted cashews.
- Pandan Coconut Pudding (Bubur Sumsum Pandan)
  Prepare the Pandan Extract (page 39). Top up (top off) the liquid with water to yield 600 ml/20 fl oz (2½ cups). Replace all water within the recipe with this pandan water.

Grilled Pineapple with Palm Sugar and Coconut Milk

Kolak Nanas Panggang

During the Islamic fasting month, a light *kolak* is a gentle finish to the daily fast. Traditionally, the dish is made with sweet potatoes or bananas and simmered in sweetened pandan-infused coconut milk and palm sugar with comforting notes of vanilla. This popular dish is always a hit at parties – guests just love the distinctive combination of palm sugar and coconut, and it is a taste of home.

Origin: Throughout Indonesia

Preparation time: 20 minutes
Cooking time: 20 minutes

Serves 8

* 1 (1.2-kg/2 lb 12-oz) ripe pineapple, peeled and cored
* 1 teaspoon salt
* 1 tablespoon Speculaas Spice Blend (page 41)
* 1 pandan leaf, coarsely chopped
* 150 g/5½ oz chopped palm sugar or coconut sugar
* 400 ml/14 fl oz (1⅔ cups) coconut milk
* 4 tablespoons coarsely ground roasted cashews

Preheat the grill (broiler). Rub the salt and spice mix over the pineapple. Place the pineapple on a baking sheet and grill for 20 minutes, turning every 3–4 minutes, until the outside is charred and the pineapple is softened. Set aside to cool.

In a medium saucepan, combine the pandan leaf, palm sugar, a pinch of salt and the coconut milk. Add 3½ tablespoons of water and bring to a boil. Reduce the heat to medium-low and simmer until the sauce is thick and syrupy. Leave to cool, then pour into a jug (pitcher).

Carve the pineapple into 8 discs and slice each in half. Serve 1–2 slices with the sauce and roasted cashews.

Variation:
- **Grilled Banana with Palm Sugar and Coconut Sauce (Kolak Nanas Panggang)**
Replace the pineapple with 8 ripe bananas. Peel, then place the bananas on a baking sheet. Brush the bananas with 2 tablespoons of coconut oil. Sprinkle with the speculaas (omit the salt) and grill for 10 minutes, turning halfway through, until the banana is charred and caramelized. Serve with Kolak Sauce (page 39) and coarsely chopped cashews.

Coconut and Strawberry Pavlova
Kelapa dan Strawberi Pavlova

This dessert, inspired by a popular slush iced drink (es puter), is enjoyed by the young and old on warm, sunny days. Coconut milk, young coconut flesh and strawberry cordial give it a baby pink colour. Back in the day, the cordial was made with strawberry essence. Today, we make it with the locally grown strawberries.

It's an ideal dessert for when fresh strawberries are abundant and packed with flavour. Pavlova lovers will enjoy the sweetness of this dish, especially when served with strawberry coulis and a pandan-infused coconut sauce – keeping this dish dairy- and gluten-free.

Origin: Modern recipe

Preparation time: 45 minutes, plus 8 hours cooling time
Cooking time: 1 hour and 30 minutes

Serves 8–10

For the pavlova:
* 4 free-range egg whites, room temperature
* 250 g/9 oz (1¼ cups) caster (superfine) sugar
* 3 tablespoons unsweetened desiccated coconut
* 2 teaspoons cornflour (cornstarch)
* 1 teaspoon white wine or apple cider vinegar
* 1 teaspoon vanilla extract

For the coconut custard:
* 1 pandan leaf, tied into a knot
* 1 tablespoon sugar
* Pinch of salt
* 400 ml/14 fl oz (1⅔ cups) coconut milk
* 2 tablespoons rice flour

For the strawberry coulis:
* 300 g/10½ oz (scant 3 cups) strawberries, hulled and quartered

* 2 tablespoons icing (confectioners') sugar
* 1 tablespoon lemon juice

For the topping:
* 500 g/1 lb 2 oz (generous 4 cups) strawberries, hulled and quartered
* 200 g/7 oz (1¼ cups) raspberries
* Small bunch of mint leaves, to garnish

To make the pavlova, preheat the oven to 150°C/300°F/Gas Mark 2.

Using a dinner plate, about 22 cm/8½ inches in diameter, mark out a circle on baking (parchment) paper. Turn the paper over and place it on a baking sheet.

In a clean bowl, whisk the egg whites for 3–4 minutes, until soft peaks form and they do not slide when the bowl is tipped. Whisk in a tablespoon of sugar at a time until smooth and glossy. Add the coconut, cornflour (cornstarch), vinegar and vanilla and whisk for 30 seconds.

Spoon the mixture onto the baking paper and spread out to the circle's edge, creating a small crater in the centre. Bake the meringue for 1½ hours, until the pavlova is golden and slightly cracked on the surface. Turn off the oven and leave the pavlova inside the oven, without opening the door, to cool completely for 8 hours.

To make the coconut custard, combine the pandan leaf, sugar, salt and coconut milk in a saucepan. In a small cup, combine the rice flour and 3½ tablespoons of water. Strain through a fine-mesh sieve (strainer) into the pan. Bring to a boil, then reduce the heat to medium and gently simmer for 6–8 minutes, stirring occasionally, until thickened and fragrant. Discard the pandan leaf, then pour the mixture into a bowl and set aside. Chill the mixture in the refrigerator for at least 1 hour.

To make the strawberry coulis, combine all the ingredients in a saucepan. Cook over medium heat for 8–10 minutes until the strawberries are completely softened. Using an immersion blender, blend the strawberries into a smooth sauce. Leave to cool, then pour into a jug (pitcher).

Assemble the pavlova just before serving. Place the pavlova on a large serving plate and top with half of the berries. Pour over the coconut custard, then add the remaining berries. Garnish with mint and drizzle over the strawberry coulis. Slice and serve.

Apple Crumble with Speculaas
Apel Remah Panggang dengan Spekulas

Apples grow well on Java, particularly in the city of Malang, which is known for its mild highland climate, and the closest British variety to our local Indonesian apples is the Bramley.

This British dessert, infused with Indonesian flavours, is loosely inspired by my mother-in-law's recipe and a firm family favourite. Whereas the Dutch speculaas often includes cardamom, star anise, mace and white pepper, the Manadonese spice blend combines nutmeg, cloves, ginger and cinnamon, adding deliciously warm, earthy notes of the archipelago to the apple filling.

When attending our eldest son's high school graduation ceremony at the British School in Jakarta, we received two surprises. The first was when the deputy headmistress handed him an award, and the second was when she mentioned that my apple crumble was well known around the school!

Origin: Modern recipe

Preparation time: 15 minutes
Cooking time: 55–60 minutes

Serves 6–8

* 1.4 kg/3 lb 2 oz cooking or Bramley apples, peeled, cored and thinly sliced
* 150 g/5½ oz (¾ cup) sugar
* 1½ tablespoons Speculaas Spice Blend (page 41) or 2 tablespoons ground cinnamon

* 200 g/7 oz (1¼ cups) plain (all-purpose) flour
* 140 g/5 oz (1¼ sticks) cold salted butter, cut into small cubes
* Double (heavy) cream or Coconut Custard (page 226), to serve (optional)

Preheat the oven to 200°C/400°F/Gas Mark 6.

In a large bowl, combine the apple, 4 tablespoons sugar and spice mix and mix well. Place in a 25 x 17 cm/10 x 7-inch baking dish, flattening the mixture with your hands to a depth of 5 cm/2 inches.

In a medium bowl, combine the flour and remaining 100 g/3½ oz (½ cup) sugar and mix well. With your fingertips, rub the butter into the flour for 3–4 minutes until pea-size lumps form.

Pour the crumble over the apples and use your hand to even it out. Gently press down on the surface with the palm of your hand. Bake for 55–60 minutes until the crumble is golden and a caramel forms around the edges of the baking dish.

Serve with cream or coconut custard, if you wish.

Pineapple Biscuits
Kue Nastar

I'm proud to say that we have the most delicious pineapples around the archipelago, and pineapple biscuits (cookies) are a favourite among Indonesians, often enjoyed as an afternoon treat with tea or coffee and at most celebrations around the year. Filled with a spice-infused pineapple jam, they have been part of my family's Christmas tradition since I can remember. We prepare them as two shapes in Manado: either round and topped with a single clove or an oval leaf. Any left-over pineapple jam can be used for toast or as a sponge cake filling.

Origin: Throughout Indonesia

Preparation time: 20 minutes, plus 25 minutes chilling time
Cooking time: 45 minutes

Makes about 24

For the pineapple jam:
- 1 (1.2-kg/2 lb 12-oz) pineapple, peeled, cored and chopped
- 120 g/4¼ oz (generous ½ cup) sugar
- 2 (5-cm/2-inch) cinnamon sticks
- 30 whole cloves
- ½ teaspoon salt

For the dough:
- 250 g/9 oz (scant 1⅔ cups) all-purpose (plain) flour, plus extra for dusting
- 50 g/1¾ oz (scant ½ cup) cornflour (cornstarch)
- 50 g/1¾ oz (¼ cup) sugar
- 200 g/7 oz (1¾ sticks) butter, room temperature
- Pinch of salt
- 2 eggs, beaten, plus 2 beaten yolks for glazing

To make the pineapple jam, transfer the pineapple to a blender and purée for 1–2 minutes. Transfer the purée into a saucepan, then add the sugar, cinnamon and 6 cloves. Simmer over medium heat for 25 minutes, or until the liquid has evaporated. Increase the heat to high and boil for 4–5 minutes until the mixture is sticky and dark amber. Set aside to cool.

Meanwhile, make the dough. Combine all the ingredients into a food processor and process for 3 minutes until smooth. Transfer the dough into a bowl and shape it into a log, about 6 cm/2½ inches in diameter.

Line a baking sheet with baking (parchment) paper. Cut the log into ½-cm/¼-inch slices and flatten one in your palm. Put a generous teaspoon of jam in the centre of the dough. Fold the dough towards the centre, covering the jam and creating a disc. Place on the prepared baking sheet. Repeat with the remaining biscuits (cookies), evenly spacing them apart. Chill in the refrigerator for 25 minutes.

Preheat the oven to 180°C/350°F/Gas Mark 4. Set aside the biscuits at room temperature for 5 minutes.

Brush egg yolk over each biscuit. Add a clove to the centre and gently push it in. Bake for 20 minutes, or until golden. Set the baking sheet aside for 1–2 minutes, then transfer to a wire rack to cool. Serve.

Cheese Sticks
Kastengel

While these cheese sticks may not be a sweet dessert, I truly enjoy them after a meal, especially with a cup of coffee or tea.

Kastengel derives from the Dutch words *kaas* (meaning 'cheese') and *stengels* (meaning 'sticks'). In fact, these are better described as cookies and are much enjoyed during Christmas gatherings. They are also associated with the end of Ramadan, or *Idul Fitri,* as it is known in Indonesia.

When fresh cheese was hard to come by, my grandmother and mother relied on processed cheese. These days local cheesemakers, especially in Java and Bali, are creating more artisanal options. A harder cheese keeps the cookies crunchy, so I use a combination of Parmesan and extra-mature Cheddar. I often freeze a big batch of dough so I can enjoy the cheese sticks on a whim.

Origin: Throughout Indonesia

Preparation time: 20 minutes, plus 1 hour chilling time
Cooking time: 25–30 minutes

Makes 80

* 300 g/10½ oz salted butter, room temperature
* 4 egg yolks
* 350 g/12 oz (scant 2¼ cups) plain (all-purpose) flour, plus extra for dusting
* 6 tablespoons cornflour (cornstarch)
  200 g/7 oz (6¼ cups) grated Parmesan, plus extra for sprinkling
* 100 g/3½ oz (scant 1 cup) grated extra-mature Cheddar

In a stand mixer fitted with a paddle attachment, beat the butter for 2–3 minutes. Add 2 egg yolks and mix. Add the flour, cornflour (cornstarch) and both cheeses and mix for another 1–2 minutes at low speed until combined. Do not overmix.

Transfer the dough to a chopping (cutting) board and shape it into a log, about 5 cm/2 inches in diameter. Chill in the refrigerator for 2–3 hours.

Preheat the oven to 170°C/338°F/Gas Mark 3. Line 2 baking sheets with baking (parchment) paper. Remove the dough from the refrigerator and cut into 3-cm/1¼-inch-thick slices. On a clean work counter lightly dusted with flour, roll each piece of dough with your hands into a 2-cm/¾-inch diameter. Flatten the top of the dough and cut it into 7-cm/2¾-inch lengths.

Arrange the cookies on the prepared baking sheet. Put the remaining 2 egg yolks in a small bowl and beat. Brush the egg wash over the cookies, then sprinkle with Parmesan cheese. Bake for 25–30 minutes until golden brown.

Leave to cool for 5 minutes on the baking sheet, then transfer the cheese sticks to a cooling rack and cool down completely. They can be stored in an airtight container for 4 weeks.

Thousand-Layer Cake
Kue Lapis Legit

This Indonesian signature cake is an essential part of annual celebrations at Christmas, *Idul Fitri* and Chinese New Year across the archipelago. When I grew up in Manado in the 1970s, making this cake was always an effort as we didn't have access to electricity and modern cooking equipment. My sisters and I would help our mother, taking turns to beat the mixture by hand until it turned light and fluffy.

Even today, this dessert is an exercise in patience as you'll need to build up the cake, layer by layer, with 12 in total (better than 1,000!). It also requires nearly two dozen eggs, so while it's a spectacularly enjoyable cake, I recommend serving it in small slices with coffee or tea.

Here are a few tips to ensure a perfect cake:

- Use a square or rectangular baking sheet, as it'll be easier to slice the cake.
- For uniform layers, each layer should weigh 190 g/6¾ oz or equivalent to a 4 tablespoon mixture for a 20-cm/8-inch square baking dish.
- Once the oven has been preheated, switch it to the grill (broil) setting during the baking process, as you'll need to direct heat from the top of the oven onto each layer of the cake.
- As you start to bake the initial layers of the cake, keep the pan on the middle shelf of the oven. Once you've built 4–5 layers, re-position the pan to the bottom shelf to avoid drying out the cake.
- Use a flat spoon or the back of a large spoon to gently flatten each layer once it's been cooked, as it helps to maintain an even density throughout.

Origin: Throughout Indonesia

Preparation time: 45 minutes
Cooking time: 2 hours

Serves 8–10

- 350 g/12 oz (3 sticks) butter, room temperature, plus extra for greasing
- 2 tablespoons condensed milk
- 22 egg yolks (425 g/15 oz)

- 175 g/6 oz (1⅓ cups) icing (confectioners') sugar
- 2 tablespoons vanilla extract
- 3 tablespoons plain (all-purpose) flour
- 4 tablespoons milk powder

- 1 tablespoon Dutch-process cocoa powder
- 2 tablespoons Speculaas Spice Blend (page 41)

Grease a square 20-cm/8-inch baking pan, at least 7 cm/2¾ inches deep. Line it with baking (parchment) paper.

In a stand mixer fitted with the whisk attachment, beat the butter on medium speed for 3 minutes until light and fluffy. Add the condensed milk and beat for 2 minutes. Transfer the mixture to a large bowl.

Preheat the oven to 170°C/338°F/Gas Mark 3.

In a clean stand mixer fitted with the whisk attachment, beat the egg yolks until thick and doubled in volume. Gradually add the icing (confectioners') sugar and vanilla. Whisk for 2 minutes.

Add the butter mixture, little by little, and mix on low speed until smooth. Add the flour and milk powder and mix gently with a rubber spatula until mixed. Do not overmix. Separate the batter into two bowls. Stir the cocoa powder into one of the bowls.

Spread 4 tablespoons of the plain mixture evenly across the baking dish. Put in the oven and bake for 5–7 minutes. Remove the pan, then transfer to a chopping (cutting) board. Leave to cool for 2 minutes. Using the back of a large spoon, gently press the cake layer flat. This ensures that the surface is prepared for the next layer.

Preheat the oven to grill (broiler) setting to 140°C/275°F/Gas Mark 1.

Spread 4 tablespoons of the chocolate batter to create the next layer. Bake for 5–6 minutes, then remove the pan. Leave to cool for 1–2 minutes and flatten. You must keep an eye on the temperature of your oven. As you increase the layers, the baking time is reduced to 30 seconds or 1 minute. (Baked too long and the cake will turn golden when it should be off-white.) Repeat with the next layer. At the 6th layer, move the oven rack to the lowest shelf to prevent the subsequent layers from burning. Continue until you have 12 layers in total.

Increase the oven temperature to 170°C/338°F/Gas Mark 3 and return to a normal setting. Cover the cake with aluminium foil and bake for another 5–7 minutes. Remove the baking dish from the oven and place it on a cooling rack. Set aside.

Gently remove the cake from the pan. Trim off the edges to make the cake very neat. (Someone will be lucky enough to enjoy them!) Slice and serve.

Drinks

Minuman

The subject of beverages in Indonesia is as extensive as the food itself. An excellent place to start is fresh coconut water. The refreshing *es kelapa muda* combines coconut water, young coconut flesh, a touch of palm sugar and lime (page 243).

Beyond the coconut plantations and rice fields, there are abundant coffee and tea plantations, especially in the highlands where many varieties are cultivated in Sumatra, Java, Sulawesi or by small coffee producers in Bajawa, Flores. Wherever you travel around Indonesia, it's very easy to find a good variety of teas and coffee at small local eateries (*warung*).

I grew up with *air goraka*, a ginger tea with local almond (page 245) and I adore *wedang uwuh*, Java tea with ginger, lemongrass and dried leaves of Indonesian classic spices – cloves, nutmeg and cinnamon (page 243). These teas are known for their medicinal properties – and we believe ginger tea is the best remedy for a cold.

The selection of tropical fruit juices is outstanding, with shaved ice, ice cream-based beverages, and traditional health-giving tonics combined with herbs and spices. One of my favourite beverages is the natural herbal drink known as *jamu*, and a wonderful subject to explore further in its own right. Java is the home of jamu, which is an abbreviation of the Javanese words *jampi usodo*, meaning 'prayer for good health always', a powerful and holistic message on the importance of preventing illness through a good healthy diet. Jamu is more than a drink – it includes wisdom on exercise, the use of regular massage, the application of ointments and the consumption of the right foods. This ancient tradition is closely connected to the spa culture and balanced diets of contemporary life. I have chosen to introduce readers to several easily made Indonesian drinks; elixirs designed to boost overall health and mood.

Carrot, Pineapple and Ginger Juice
Jus Wortel, Nanas dan Jahe

Ginger is the star of this refreshing tonic. I love any juice with ginger – Manado has a smaller variety of red ginger that's slightly stronger.

Origin: Modern recipe

Preparation time: 10 minutes

Serves 2

* 4 Granny Smith apples, coarsely chopped
* 2 carrots, coarsely chopped
* 1 small pineapple, peeled and coarsely chopped
* 40 g (1½ oz) fresh root ginger

Put all the ingredients through a juicer. Add a few ice cubes, if you like, and serve.

Variation:
- Mixed Juice (Jus Buah dan Sayur)
  Add 4 more Granny Smith apples, 4 beetroots (beets), a head of celery and an additional 12 g/¼ oz fresh root ginger. Serves 4.

Mixed Fruits, Coconut Milk and Crushed Ice
Es Teller

Teller means 'drunk' in Indonesian, but you won't trace any alcohol in this drink. As the story goes, a Javanese fruit seller from central Java made a drink with local fruit, coconut milk, condensed milk and shaved iced. He was so proud of his invention, declaring that he was drunk from its deliciousness.

This drink continues to be popular with everyone, young and old. These days you can find *es teller* with ripe jackfruit, avocados, young coconut flesh, melon or apple. I have tweaked this classic recipe by adding strawberry and strawberry coulis for flavour, sweetness and colour. Easy to make, it must be assembled at the last minute.

Origin: Java

Preparation time: 10 minutes

Serves 6

* 2 young coconuts or 1 (425-g/15-oz) can young coconut in syrup, cut into bite-size pieces
* 2 avocados, pitted and cut into 1-cm/½-inch cubes

* 200 g/7 oz ripe jackfruit flesh or 1 (565-g/1 lb 4-oz) can ripe jackfruit, drained and cut into 1-cm/½-inch cubes
* 100 g/3½ oz strawberries, cut into 1-cm/½-inch cubes
* 600 ml/20 fl oz (2½ cups) coconut milk

* 600 ml/20 fl oz (2½ cups) crushed ice or 6–7 small ice cubes
* 6 tablespoons condensed milk

If using fresh whole young coconut, simply crack the coconut and reserve the water. Using a spoon, scoop the young coconut flesh into a bowl. Set aside. If using canned young coconut, drain and reserve the syrup for later use.

Divide all the fruits into 6 dessert glasses. Add 100 ml/3½ fl oz (scant ½ cup) coconut milk to each and fill with crushed ice. Drizzle with condensed milk. Serve.

Young Coconut with Palm Sugar and Lime Juice

Es Kelapa Muda, Gula Aren dan Jeruk Nipis

Whole young coconuts are ubiquitous around the archipelago, sold at traditional markets and by street food vendors. You can enjoy the coconut water on its own with its natural sweetness, but a touch of palm sugar syrup and lime juice are commonly added.

Origin: Throughout Indonesia

Preparation time: 10 minutes, plus 1–2 hours chilling time

Serves 1–2

* 1 young coconut or 500 ml/ 17 fl oz (generous 2 cups) coconut water
* 2–4 tablespoons Palm Sugar Syrup (page 39)
* Juice of 1 lime
* Plenty of ice cubes

Using a spoon, scrape out the young flesh from the coconut and put it into a glass container. Pour the coconut water into a separate container. Chill for 1–2 hours in the refrigerator.

To serve, add 1–2 tablespoons each of palm sugar syrup and lime juice into each glass. Fill with ice cubes. Slowly pour in the coconut water to create the colour contrast.

Spiced Tea

Wedang Uwuh

Many decades ago, the leaves of nutmeg, cloves and cinnamon were prized for making teas. While tastes have changed, I couldn't resist the opportunity to show off this classic Java tea, which combines these traditional leaves with lemongrass and ginger.

The challenge was creating a tea with these hard-to-find leaves. Instead, I've replaced them with the fragrant spices of cloves, cinnamon and nutmeg.

Traditionally, sappan bark is added for its reddish-orange hue, but you could replace this with dried hibiscus, which will give it a beautiful colour and a tart note.

Origin: Java

Preparation time: 5 minutes
Cooking time: 10 minutes

Serves 2

* 4 whole cloves
* 2–3 sappan barks or 2 dried hibiscus flowers
* 1 (2-cm/¾-inch) cinnamon stick
* 1 stalk lemongrass, crushed and tied into a knot

* 30 g/1 oz fresh root ginger, unpeeled and thinly sliced
* 1 whole nutmeg, coarsely crushed with a pestle and mortar
* Honey (optional)

Combine all the ingredients, except the honey, in a medium saucepan. Add 600 ml/20 fl oz (2½ cups) of water and bring to a boil. Reduce the heat to medium-low and simmer for 10–12 minutes. Strain, then sweeten to taste with honey, if you like. Serve hot.

Spiced Tea with Almond Flakes
Air Goraka

Air goraka (literally meaning 'ginger water') is the popular name for a delicious, much-consumed tea in Manado and parts of Eastern Indonesia and Maluku and is frequently served with banana fritters. It is made with red ginger, the comparatively smaller yet spicier, red-skinned cousin of regular ginger, and can be sweetened with coconut or palm sugar. Locals will serve it with a regional almond called pili nuts or *kacang kanari*.

If you like the flavouring, you may want to try the variation with pandan and lemongrass.

Origin: Maluku Islands

Preparation time: 5 minutes
Cooking time: 10 minutes

Makes 500 ml/17 fl oz
(generous 2 cups)

* 50 g/1¾ oz fresh root ginger, crushed
* 4 tablespoons toasted almond flakes
* 2–3 tablespoons coconut sugar (optional)

In a medium saucepan, combine the ginger and 500 ml/17 fl oz (generous 2 cups) of water. Bring to a boil, then reduce the heat to low. Simmer for 10–15 minutes until the flavours are fully infused.

Strain the tea into a teapot. Sweeten with coconut sugar, if using.

Variation:
- Java Ginger Tea (Wedang Jahe)
  Omit the almonds. Add 1 crushed lemongrass stalk and ½ pandan leaf.

Iced Coffee with Palm Sugar
Es Kopi dengan Gula Aren

Indonesia offers a wonderful range of delightful coffees with regional varieties reflecting the different soils and growing conditions. There are numerous ways to enjoy Indonesian coffee. One way is as a traditional *kopi tubruk*, where finely ground coffee is combined with hot water and optional sweetness, but only after the sediment settles to the bottom.

Some people like to sweeten their coffee with condensed milk. You can flavour coffee with spices, such as nutmeg and cinnamon, fermented fruits, or even egg yolk to create *kopi talua* (as they do in West Sumatra). In Java, they add a small lump of charcoal (*kopi joss*) for smokiness. One of my favourite ways is to simply enjoy it chilled.

Origin: Throughout Indonesia

Preparation time: 5 minutes

Makes 2 tall glasses

* 4–6 tablespoons Palm Sugar Syrup (page 39)
* Ice cubes
* 200 ml/7 fl oz (generous ¾ cup) espresso coffee
* 300 ml/10 fl oz (1¼ cups) cold milk or oat milk

Divide the palm sugar syrup between the 2 glasses. Add the ice cubes. Fill each with coffee, then slowly pour in the milk to create coloured layers. Mix before drinking.

Sour Turmeric
Kunyit Asam

A purifying tonic when you need a mental and physical boost, *kunyit asam* is just one of many different *jamu* beverages that would be sold door-to-door in Jakarta by ladies in beautiful batik sarongs. Although *mbok jamu* are a rarer sight these days, jamu culture remains alive in many cool jamu cafés around this city – a reassuring reminder that people still appreciate the value of this healthy and natural remedy.

Sour turmeric gives an instant jolt of energy when the temperature drops.

Origin: Java

Preparation time: 15 minutes
Cooking time: 25 minutes

Makes 1¾ litres/1¾ quarts
(7 cups)

* 70 g/2½ oz fresh turmeric
* 50 g/1¾ oz fresh root ginger
* 5 makrut lime leaves
* 1 stalk lemongrass, crushed and tied into a knot
* 1 pandan leaf, tied into a knot
* 180 g/6 oz palm sugar, coarsely chopped, or coconut sugar
* 120 g/4¼ oz tamarind pulp, pulled apart into small pieces
* 1 teaspoon salt
* Juice of 2 limes (optional)

Put the turmeric and ginger into a small blender and blend well. Transfer to a large saucepan and add the remaining ingredients, except the limes. Pour in 2 litres/2 quarts of water. Bring to a boil, then reduce the heat to medium. Simmer for 25 minutes, stirring occasionally.

Strain, then add the lime juice, if using, to give it sourness. Serve hot or at room temperature. It can be refrigerated for 1 week.

Variation:
- **Sour Turmeric Shot (Kunyit Asam Murni)**
As more and more home cooks are discovering the benefits of turning waste into taste, this superb way of preparing a concentrated jamu with optimal nutrients has practically no waste. Combine 10% of all the ingredients into a blender and adjust the amount of water to 100 ml/3½ fl oz (scant ½ cup). Blend until smooth. Add another 100 ml/3½ fl oz (scant ½ cup) of water and blend. No need to strain.

Cinnamon Coffee
Kopi Talua

There are many ways to enjoy coffee around the archipelago. I was in Bukit Tinggi, a beautiful city surrounded by mountains and a two-hour drive from the capital, Padang city of West Sumatra, where I savoured *talua* coffee for the first time. This unique beverage features one to two egg yolks in each glass, whisked until frothy. Freshly brewed hot coffee is added, along with a dash of cinnamon and condensed milk. Here, I have replaced the condensed milk with single (light) cream. You'll need a long, yet small, whisk.

Origin: Sumatra

Preparation time: 10 minutes

Serves 2

* 3 tablespoons medium-coarse ground coffee
* 1–2 tablespoons sugar (optional)
* 1 teaspoon ground cinnamon, plus extra for dusting
* 2 egg yolks
* 2–4 tablespoons single (light) cream

Add the coffee, sugar, if using, and cinnamon to a cafetiere and fill with 400 ml/14 fl oz (1 ⅔ cups) hot water. Set aside for 6–8 minutes to brew.

Add an egg yolk to each glass. Whisk gently with a beater until frothy. Add 1–2 tablespoons of cream to each glass. Pour in the coffee along one side of the glass until the egg yolk reaches the top. Dust with cinnamon and serve.

Phaidon Press Limited
2 Cooperage Yard
London E15 2QR

Phaidon Press Inc.
65 Bleecker Street
New York, NY 10012
phaidon.com

First published 2023
© 2023 Phaidon Press Limited
ISBN 978 1 83866 628 6

Commissioning Editor:
Emilia Terragni

Project Editor:
Michelle Meade

Production Controller:
Gif Jittiwutikarn

Design:
Hans Stofregen

Layouts:
Cantina

Photography:
Yuki Sugiura

Printed in China

Author's Acknowledgements
Thank you to the entire Phaidon team, especially Emilia Terragni,
Ellie Smith and Michelle Meade for their guidance. Thank you to
my brilliant photographer Yuki Sugiura for capturing the vibrancy
of Indonesian food traditions in a contemporary manner and food
stylist Hanna Miller for her tireless enthusiasm.

Little of this would have been possible without the support of
many dear friends and family: Rachel Malik, Janice Gabriel, Judy
Joo, Amanda Rackham, Josien Chalmers, Rene Viner, Petra Wright,
Ati Kisjanto Aglionby, Helianti Hilman, Janet De Kneef, Ayu Kresna,
Priscilla Partana, Arimbi Nimpuno, Chynthia Wirawan, Jerry Winata,
Sari Kusumaningrum, Reno Andamsari, Jed Doble, Viana Igah,
Margie Gunawan, NIHI Sumba, Engel Tanzil and many others. (You
know who you are.)

To my siblings, especially my sister Esty who is always there to
support me. To my husband Nick and my two sons, Jeremy and
Chris, thank you for sharing my dream and encouraging me to do
what I love. Thank you Mami for all your prayers and encouragement.

This book is for all Indonesians at home or abroad, so we can
carry our heritage wherever we go and remember we have the
most powerful asset, namely our unity in diversity that embraces
different cultures, languages and religions.

Publisher's Acknowledgements
Phaidon would like to thank James Brown, Iva Cheung, Julia
Hasting, João Mota, Ellie Smith, Tracey Smith, Sally Somers, Phoebe
Stephenson, Ana Teodoro and Michael Wallace.

Recipe Notes

Unless otherwise specified:
- Butter should always be unsalted.
- Spices are freshly ground.
- Eggs and individual vegetables and fruits, such as carrots and apples, are assumed to be medium.
- Sugar is white caster (superfine) sugar and brown sugar is cane or demerara (turbinado).
- Cream is 36–40% fat heavy whipping cream.
- Milk is full-fat (whole) at 3% fat, homogenized and lightly pasteurized.
- Salt is kosher salt.
- Parsley is flat-leaf (Italian).
- Breadcrumbs are always dried.
- Fresh roots spices, such as ginger, turmeric and galangal, are left unpeeled, but you should trim off any old parts.
- Fish assumed cleaned and gutted.

Cooking times are for guidance only, as individual ovens vary.
If using a conventional oven, follow the manufacturer's instructions
concerning oven temperatures.

Exercise a high level of caution when following recipes involving
any potentially hazardous activity, including the use of high
temperatures, open flames and when deep-frying. In particular,
when deep-frying, add food carefully to avoid splashing, wear long
sleeves, and never leave the pan unattended.

Some recipes include raw or very lightly cooked eggs, meat,
or fish, and fermented products. These should be avoided by
the elderly, infants, pregnant people, convalescents, and anyone
with an impaired immune system.

As some species of mushrooms have been known to cause allergic
reaction and illness, do take extra care when cooking and eating
mushrooms and do seek immediate medical help if you experience
a reaction after preparing or eating them.

Exercise caution when making fermented products, ensuring all
equipment is clean, and seek expert advice if in any doubt.

When no quantity is specified, for example of oils, and sugars used
for finishing dishes or for deep frying, quantities are discretionary
and flexible.

Both metric and imperial measures are used in this book. Follow
one set of measurements throughout, not a mixture, as they are
not interchangeable.

All spoon and cup measurements are level. 1 teaspoon = 5 ml;
1 tablespoon = 15 ml.

Australian standard tablespoons are 20 ml, so Australian readers are
advised to use 3 teaspoons in place of 1 tablespoon when measuring
small quantities.